What People Are Saying about
Boosting Your Baby's Brain Power ...

When it comes to parenting during your baby's crucial first year, *Boosting Your Baby's Brain Power* is the perfect combination of learning and loving!
~Patty Hansen, co-author, *Chicken Soup for the Child's Soul*

As founder of the Active Parenting program, I am a strong advocate of parent education. *Boosting Your Baby's Brain Power* is an important tool for teaching expectant and new parents about their baby's intellectual development. It is enjoyable to read and brimming with practical information.
~Michael H. Popkin, Ph.D., author, *Active Parenting Now* and
Taming the Spirited Child

Inside that sweet-smelling baby head is the most complex structure on earth— the human brain. *Boosting Your Baby's Brain Power* shows parents how to interact with their baby in such a way as to encourage optimal brain development. A must-read for anyone caring for a new baby!
~Diana Hoppe, M.D., OB/GYN, founder,
The Pacific Coast Research Center for Women's Health

Most new parents wonder at one time or another whether their baby is "normal." *Boosting Your Baby's Brain Power* removes the worry by showing parents how they can help their baby reach his full potential when it comes to hearing, walking, talking, seeing, and more.
~Bettie Youngs, Ph.D., Ed.D., author, *The House that Love Built:*
The Story of Linda and Millard Fuller, Founders of Habitat
for Humanity and the Fuller Center for Housing

During first-year development, the brain is still young and impressionable. Early experiences cause physical changes to the brain that will have a huge impact on your child's later success in life. *Boosting Your Baby's Brain Power* provides parents with concise answers to the question, "How can I help my baby reach her full potential?"
~Dr. Lisa Love, author, *Beyond the Secret: Spiritual Power and the*
Law of Attraction

Babies' brains undergo tremendous development in the first year of life, and there is much that parents can do to stimulate this growth from the very first days of life. *Boosting Your Baby's Brain Power* is essential reading for all parents interested in nurturing their baby's intellect.

~Jennifer Youngs, author, *The Moments & Milestones Pregnancy Journal: A Week by Week Companion*, and co-author, *Oh, Baby! 7 Ways a Baby Will Change Your Life the First Year*

Boosting Your Baby's Brain Power is a must-have for all new parents wanting to do all they can to help their child succeed in life!

~Francinne Lawrence, MRE, MSW, LICSW, author, *Cooking with a Baby on Your Hip*

The authors have a gift for untangling the mysteries of newborn and early childhood development, both neurological and behavioral, with an elegance rooted in its simplicity. I hope you enjoy this work as much as I have.

~Kenneth Adams, M.D., F.A.C.O.G.

As a mother of four, I marvel at how each child is different. This book explores fascinating and important elements of that first year in a totally different way from anything I've ever read. I wish I'd had this when I was expecting. I am sure it will be part of every new parent's "must-read" list.

~Erica Orloff, mother of four, novelist

When we parents have a new life to look after, there's so much to know, to learn, so many questions to ask: Are we doing it right? What does that mean? Is this normal? How best can I help? *Boosting Your Baby's Brain Power* is a wonderful and empowering tool to help new parents relieve the anxieties and answer questions. It's a book whose time has come.

~Leon Scott Baxter, author, *A Labor with Love: A Dad's-to-Be Guide to Romance during Pregnancy*

Boosting Your Baby's Brain Power

Other Books by the Authors

By Holly Engel-Smothers

The Read and Respond Series:
Ancient Egypt, Colonial America,
Native American, Frontier American

The Real World Series:
Math, Science, Reading

By Susan M. Heim

Chicken Soup for the Soul:
Twins and More

It's Twins! Parent-to-Parent Advice
from Infancy through Adolescence

Oh, Baby! 7 Ways a Baby
Will Change Your Life the First Year

Twice the Love: Stories of Inspiration for Families
with Twins, Multiples, and Singletons

Boosting Your Baby's Brain Power

Holly Engel-Smothers
and
Susan M. Heim

Great Potential Press™

Boosting Your Baby's Brain Power

Cover design: Huchinson-Frey
Interior design: The Printed Page
Copy Editor: Jennifer Ault

Published by Great Potential Press, Inc.
P.O. Box 5057
Scottsdale, AZ 85261

Printed on recycled paper.

10 09 08 07 06   5 4 3 2 1

Library of Congress Cataloging-in-Publication Data
Engel-Smothers, Holly, 1969–
  Boosting your baby's brain power / Holly Engel-Smothers, Susan M. Heim.
    p. cm.
  Includes bibliographical references and index.
  ISBN-13: 978-0-910707-90-9
  ISBN-10: 0-910707-90-1
1. Infants—Development. 2. Parent and infant. 3. Parenting. I. Heim, Susan
M. II. Title.
  HQ774.E54 2008
  649'.122—dc22
                        2008033817

For Bailee, Rilee, and Jaynee—I love you more than all the tiger stripes, all the kitty cat whiskers, and all the butterflies in the world.

~ Holly

To the four boys I brought into this world—Dylan, Taylor, Austen, and Caleb—whose brilliant minds and loving hearts continually fascinate, inspire, and challenge me.

~ Susan

Acknowledgments

From Holly:

I'm so grateful to my pediatrician, Dr. Cindy Kirby-Diaz, for sharing her thoughts with me about optimizing the parent/doctor relationship. Her information and expertise were invaluable to this book. Dr. Kirby-Diaz will be as great of a mom to her soon-to-be-born twins as she is a pediatrician.

I'd also like to thank Dr. Kenneth Adams for sharing his vast knowledge of pre- and postnatal care of mothers and their babies. Dr. Adams literally saved my life and those of my twins during their birth, and it is an honor to have his enthusiastic review and support for this book.

In addition, I owe thanks to Paul Lichtenauer, who added so much to my understanding of attachment disorders. He is a patient teacher with a big heart.

Finally, a big thank-you goes out to my husband, Dan, who must be crazy for sticking around our daughters and me while I constantly work on my "little hobby." He always gives me more incentive to achieve great things!

From Susan:

I'm extremely grateful to all of the wise and wonderful people who endorsed this book: Dr. Michael Popkin, Patty Hansen, Dr. Diana Hoppe, Dr. Bettie B. Youngs, Dr. Lisa Love, Jennifer Youngs, Francinne Lawrence, Dr. Kenneth Adams, Erica Orloff, and Leon Scott Baxter.

Thank you to my husband, Mike, for his ever-present support for my decision to be a work-at-home mom. Without his enthusiasm and encouragement, I never would have had the opportunity to write books and pursue a career I love. Thanks, too, to my parents, who always encouraged their "bookworm" daughter's love of reading and writing.

And finally, I'm always amazed at how God continues to open "windows of opportunity" in my life. He makes the roads smoother, the seas calmer, and the days brighter. Thank you, Father.

From Holly and Susan:

We extend enormous gratitude to everyone at Great Potential Press, including Dr. James Webb, Janet Gore, Kristina Grant, Anne Morales, and Alicia Markham, who have been so enthusiastic about this project, as well as wonderful to work with. We couldn't have asked for better publishing partners! We'd also like to thank our amazing copyeditor, Jennifer Ault, who gave our manuscript just the right polish and provided valuable feedback. In addition, we greatly appreciate Lisa Liddy, our layout editor, who put all of our words in just the right place for maximum appeal.

And last but not least, if you're a parent reading this book, we'd like to thank you for allowing us to share our ideas and experiences with you. Know that we applaud your efforts to bond more fully with your baby and your desire to be more involved in "boosting your baby's brain power"!

Contents

Introduction to *Boosting Your Baby's Brain Power*

If you're like most parents, you've undoubtedly wondered at one point or another whether your baby's development is "normal." You've asked yourself questions like, *Shouldn't she be talking by now? When will he roll over? Why isn't she progressing as quickly as her older brother did?* Sure, there are plenty of lists available that tell when your baby should be walking and talking, but very little has been written about how parents and caregivers can play an important part in helping babies reach these critical milestones.

Of course, you can talk to your pediatrician about your concerns—and we encourage you to do so—but these visits are frequently not conducive to getting all of the answers you need. At your 10- to 15-minute appointment, nurses and doctors often work in a tag-team fashion to get patients in and out on time, leaving very little leeway for in-depth discussions. So where can you turn to find out what you really want to know?

Getting this information is not just a matter of calming your fears—although that certainly helps. It really goes beyond determining whether your baby's development is on track. In fact, not educating yourself about these crucial developmental milestones could affect your child's entire future! You see, first-year developments must be met before any more progress and learning is possible in later years. These developments are the building blocks for life. And any problems relating to development must be addressed while the brain is still young and malleable in order for early intervention to be optimally effective.

The fact is that the first year of life is an extremely vital period of time that lays the foundation for whether your little one will be able to walk, talk, smile, dress herself, draw a picture...even get into college! It is an astonishing year that demands great respect from sleep-deprived parents like yourself.

Baby development is not simply a list of "to-dos" or "have dones" to check off. It is a long-term building event, with each day being important in how your baby develops the next day, and each event being important in how your baby develops for the next event. Nourishing food, comfort, face-to-face interaction, tummy time, music, and even the lilt of your voice are all brain developers. It is not a random happening when a milestone is reached. Just as an athlete has to practice his sport in a certain order to build up to the main event, so do infants have to take "baby steps" toward optimal brain development, which is created and driven by experiences with Mommy, Daddy, and caregivers. You and others close to baby play a critical role in your baby's life, because milestones need personal experiences to be reached.

Of course, we all want the best for our baby. We want him to be "normal." But beyond that, we want him to reach his full potential. We want to know how we can help that incredibly complex little brain make all of the right connections for a full and fruitful life. This book will show you how to do just that. Each chapter of *Boosting Your Baby's Brain Power* features one of your baby's key areas of development—such as vision, hearing, language, motor skills, and temperament—and shows you how you can help your baby's brain to grow so that he will excel in these areas. Here's a sampling of what you'll find in this book:

Chapter 1. Baby's Got Brains: Jumping through Vital "Windows of Opportunity"

This chapter provides an overview of your baby's phenomenal brain, which was born with more than 100 billion neurons that, if laid end to end, would stretch for 62,000 miles! But the majority of the connections between neurons must be established within the first eight months of life so that the foundations for lifelong learning are set in place. Parents are not helpless players in this complicated process. They are *vital* players by creating an optimal environment for brain growth in the womb, as well as early, positive, and rich experiences during critical "windows of opportunity" after birth. Without these personal experiences and interactions, your baby would not be able to do much more than when first born.

Chapter 2. Attachment and Baby Brains: Spoiled Rotten Is a Good Thing

In a safe, secure environment in which your baby's needs are met, you and your little one "attach." This attachment is vital for future learning and a feeling of security in the world. Baby brains grow rapidly, with secure attachments from which all developments, milestones, and achievements will come. You can never spoil a newborn. Here's how to interpret your baby's cries and form a loving bond in the first few months.

Chapter 3. Language: Getting Baby Ready to Read

Waiting for your baby to call you "Mama" or "Dada" often turns into a lesson in endurance. But your baby communicates in other ways, too. You might be surprised to learn that literacy development is important for language development even before your baby is born! This chapter will demonstrate the importance of reading to your baby from birth, and it will also explain how this helps your baby move from coos and babbling to speaking in sentences during this critical opportunity for brain growth.

Chapter 4. Vision: Seeing Is Believing—and Bonding

The eyes are the window to the soul—and a very critical component for learning. Discover how your baby sees from birth to one year and what you can do to take advantage of critical periods in vision development. We include problems or "red flags" to look for.

Chapter 5. Hearing: Little Ears Do Big Things

Your baby must be able to hear well in order to talk and learn normally. During this "window of opportunity," your baby learns to hear at various distances and angles with help and input from Mommy and Daddy. Preventing ear infections and other ways to help your baby hear better are included in this chapter, as well as a simple hearing test that you can do in your home.

Chapter 6. Motor Skills: From Crawling to Walking to... Watch Out!

When the "window of opportunity" opens for developing certain motor skills, it's time to baby-proof the house! Your baby's slow and steady steps quickly turn into the pitter-patter of little feet that will run from the first possible moment—and won't stop running until puberty! There is a wide range of "normal" when it comes to developing motor skills, but you and others play a crucial role in their development.

Chapter 7. Temperament: Is Your Child a Shrinking Violet or a Thorny Rose?

Your child's temperament is present at birth. Whether your baby is feisty or laid back, the signs are evident even in the first day of life. Knowing your baby's style of behavior and teaching her how to handle it in life will help her in dealing with feelings, following rules, and even future classroom education. We offer tips for assessing your baby's temperament and suggestions for accommodating them.

Chapter 8. Going to the Doctor: Why the Doctor/Patient Relationship Is So Vital

This chapter will teach you how to effectively be a part of each visit to the pediatrician, which should never be a one-way experience in which the doctor simply pours instructions into your head. Learn how to give the right information to receive the right information, as well as how to ask questions to make sure that you understand all of the charts and examinations. We developed this chapter after a firsthand consultation with a pediatrician who told us what you can do to make the doctor visit most effective for your child's growing brain and body.

So are you ready to get started? We hope you are, because the earlier you start engaging in activities that help your baby's brain, the better for your baby's development and future progress. Even if your baby is no longer a newborn, it's never too late to begin helping him to reach critical milestones.

We'd venture to say that being a parent is the most important job you will ever do. You are the most influential person in your child's life, and that begins even before your baby's birth. Just as importantly, engaging in play with your baby will build a stronger bond between the two of you—one that gets your baby off to a great start and a lifetime of memories for both of you.

I no longer believe babies are pure and simple.
They are miraculous not because they're blank slates,
but because they're just as complex as we are—
only with smaller fingers and toes, and smaller vocabularies.
~Shoshana Marchand

Chapter 1

Baby's Got Brains: Jumping through Vital "Windows of Opportunity"

*Giving birth and realizing that the new life has come from you
and the father is incredibly inspiring, but it's also incredibly challenging
to think that…what he or she becomes has a lot to do
with what [his or her] life is like growing up.*
~Elizabeth Colton

In the beginning, there was hope. There were dreams. There were expectations. There were nine months of parties, decorating, doctor's appointments, bathroom breaks, sonograms, and blood tests. You even had a schedule going on in utero—hiccups at 7 PM, exercise (in the form of karate kicks, somersaults, and elbow jabs) at various increments during the day, equally interspersed with restful naps. After all of these preparations and your growing girth, you'd think the baby would be born fully grown and functioning, with her personality completely formed and understood by you. Heck, you halfway anticipated a walking, talking mini-you!

But after labor and delivery, baby doesn't look anything like a "Hollywood baby" with big eyes, chubby legs, and shiny pink skin. This baby is slimy and bloody and bluish grey. She is covered with cream-cheesy glop when you first see her. Her eyes squint at the bright lights, and she's curled up in a little ball. But take heart! The strange alien-like features you first see are very temporary, so take tons of pictures. This creature is the baby you've been growing inside of you all this time!

The first time you hold your baby, you check out every inch of her little self. You count her 10 fingers and toes, which will soon outrun and out-explore her mommy and daddy. Her two eyes will soon see the hundreds of dust bunnies under the couch. The little mouth will soon be making cute little coos, followed by babbles, then talking, and finally, back-talking. Her mouth, with its sucking reflex, triggers her to forcibly suck on an object put into her mouth (including those dust bunnies she pulled out from under the couch). Her two ears will listen to you sing (not even minding if you're out of tune), but someday, they'll not hear a word you say. Her little nose will soon smell McDonald's a mile away, and her tiny tummy will be forever hungry for junk food.

You can hardly wait for this child to call you Mama or Daddy and kiss your cheeks with peanut-butter kisses. Your baby has a grasp reflex that she uses to tightly close her little hand when pressure is applied to the inside of her palm. You are blown away when her whole hand wraps around your little finger. She has a "startle (Moro) reflex" that causes her to throw her arms out to the sides and then quickly bring them back in to the chest when startled by a loud noise, sudden movement, or even a strong smell (like hospital food).

Your baby's head may be a strange shape for a very short time from squeezing through the birth canal. A newborn's head is made up of several separate bones, like a puzzle. These pieces will eventually fuse together, but for the process of birth, the skull bones shift and overlap, making her head look stretched and elongated at birth. Don't worry. Within a few days, the bones will move into a more rounded configuration.

And the most important thing: your baby's got brains! Under that downy, soft, melon head is the most complex structure on earth. Built for survival, it is the most important part of your baby. If we could peek inside your baby's little head, the brain wouldn't look much different from a reddish brown bowl of Jell-O. This brain tissue functions to provide your baby the potential for thinking, talking, feeling, and becoming a fully formed human in just a few short years. In fact, her experiences in the first five years of life will dominate the direction of this primitive ball of Jell-O, bringing your baby into childhood and on through adulthood. Amazing!

The Brain 101

Everything you do or say is absorbed by your child's brain.
This happens whether you want it to or not,
so welcome to your second role as parent, that of teacher.
~Sandra Hardin Gookin & Dan Gookin, *Parenting for Dummies*

Let's take an even closer look at your complex new bundle of joy. The brain that you have been growing in your womb is the most complicated organ in the world. It is more complex than any machine ever made. At birth, your baby can already do some very simple things—breathe, hear, suck, startle—because the amazing brain has been working in utero. The brain cells responsible for those sweet newborn reflexes are already set and connected. The next set of milestones in baby's life need special patterns of connections that, in turn, need the right kind of stimulation to develop.

Brain function is almost like a structure made of Legos—pieces that fit together are attracted to each other and hook up. But instead of Lego pieces, our brains have building blocks called *neurons*. Thousands of neuron cells make more connections than stars in the universe. If you were to compare a piece of brain tissue to a sand grain at the beach, that tiny space would occupy about 100,000 neurons. Your newborn baby has more than

Glossary

Axon: the part of a neuron that transmits electrical signals away from the cell body

Cell body: the nucleus and surrounding cytoplasm of a nerve cell, excluding the axons and dendrites

Dendrite: the branching process of a nerve cell that conducts electrical impulses from adjacent cells inward toward the cell body

Moro reflex: "startle reflex"; when infants' limb and neck muscles contract if they're startled by a sudden noise or if they feel as if they're falling

Myelin: a fatty, whitish substance that forms a sheath around nerve fibers, insulating the nerves and allowing the rapid transmission of nerve impulses

Neuron: the functional unit of the nervous system; a specialized cell consisting of the cell body and its processes, the axon and dendrites, that conducts nerve impulses

Synapse: the closely adjacent space between two nerve cells across which nerve impulses travel

100 billion neurons—all of the brain cells that he will ever need for his whole life, and then some extras that will be pruned away if not used.[1]

A neuron looks kind of like an octopus—a round cell body with several long arms—or a tree with many branches. The branches are called *axons* and *dendrites*. Neurons work by sending information throughout the body in the form of electrical signals connecting axons to dendrites. Axons send out messages, and dendrites receive them. Information is sent through one neuron and passed on to the next by jumping through a minute space called a *synapse*. The signals go on and on even when we sleep. It is like a big forest with overlapping tree branches, sending electrical signals to each other that make the mind and body function.

The *cell body* is the control center of the neuron. Information is collected from the dendrites, and then the decision is made whether to send that information on to other cells. If the information coming into the dendrites is strong enough, the cell body opens the gate and lets the electrical information flow out across the synapse to the next neuron.

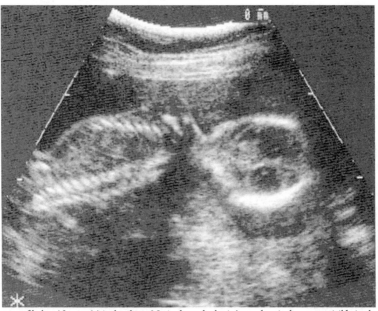

Sonogram of baby: 13 oz., 11 inches long. Notice how the brain's two hemispheres are visible in the right side of the photo.

Neurons must connect with other trillions of neurons to work so that our bodies and minds function the way we want. The total length of "wiring" between neurons is estimated at 62,000 miles! And the majority of these connections between neurons will be established within the first eight months. So the foundations for lifelong learning begin with early, positive, and rich experiences.

These experiences come from you, the environment, activity, sounds, and songs. You play an important role in creating a healthy environment for your baby. Everything from the food and substances you consumed while pregnant to feeding, holding, touching, talking, and singing to your baby are important in creating a healthy environment for your baby's brain. These early experiences cause physical changes to his brain (the making and breaking of neuron connections) that will have a huge impact on his success later in life.

Factors that Influence Brain Growth in the Womb

The brain is a monstrous, beautiful mess. Its billions of nerve cells— called neurons—lie in a tangled web that displays cognitive powers far exceeding any of the silicon machines we have built to mimic it.
~William F. Allman, *Apprentices of Wonder*

By now, you've certainly gotten the picture that the human brain is incredibly complex. Researcher Jerome M. Sattler notes in his book, *Assessment of Children: Cognitive Foundations*: "The human brain is the most complex computational system known. Although desktop computers can be much faster than the brain, the brain is unequaled in the complexity of its operations."[2] That's why it's so important that conditions be optimized in the womb for good brain development.

Scientists still don't know all of the factors that influence a baby's intrauterine growth and development, especially when it comes to the complicated brain. Some studies have shown that prenatal consumption of an essential nutrient called choline may cause positive changes in those parts of the brain that are responsible for learning and memory.[3] When the diets of pregnant rats were supplemented with choline, their offspring displayed better memory skills. Choline can be found in egg yolks, nuts, liver, milk, and other meats, although pregnant women are cautioned to check with their doctor before supplementing their diets with choline-rich foods because too much choline can have harmful effects.

A study reported in the *American Journal of Clinical Nutrition* found that when pregnant women consumed a type of omega-3 fatty acid called docosahexaenoic acid (DHA), their infants performed better on problem-solving tasks.[4] Foods with DHA include certain fish and seafood, nuts and seeds, and canola and soybean oils. However, seafood may also be contaminated with methyl mercury, PCBs, and dioxins, so medical advice should be sought before adding it to your diet.

According to Sattler, other factors in addition to a prenatal diet may affect a baby's developing brain, especially on the negative side. They include:

- *Illnesses and infections experienced by the mother.* Infections such as syphilis, rubella, and cytomegalovirus can cause mental retardation. If the mother contracts Lyme disease, malaria, meningitis, HIV, or encephalitis, these infectious diseases can also interfere with fetal brain development.

- *Exposure to alcohol and drugs.* The use of alcohol, heroin, cocaine, and marijuana by a pregnant woman can negatively affect her baby's intellectual development.

- *Environmental toxins.* Chemical pollutants found in pesticides, cosmetics, plastics, and even seafood may cause problems for the fetal brain. According to Sattler, "prenatal exposure to inorganic lead, organophosphate pesticides, or cigarette smoke increases the risk of a child's developing attention-deficit/hyperactivity disorder."[5]

- *Birth complications.* If the mother is diabetic, has anemia or high blood pressure, or experiences hemorrhaging at the time of birth, this could affect her baby's cognitive development. Babies born with digestive or respiratory difficulties may also experience cognitive effects. Severe prematurity may also be harmful to the brain. Says Sattler, "Surviving infants who weigh less than 3.3 pounds are at increased risk for several cognitive and physical developmental disabilities."[6]

Although this is certainly a scary list of items that can negatively affect your baby's growing brain, the good news is that they are usually rare, and many of them are preventable. By practicing good prenatal habits, such as taking multivitamins (speak with your doctor about recommended vitamins), avoiding drugs and alcohol, and following a nutritious diet, you'll be making great headway in ensuring that your baby's brain has a favorable environment in which to grow.

Fattening Up the Brain

Baby Jaynee lay in her mother's womb in a strange, twisted position—hardly the classic fetal position. For months after she was born, Baby Jaynee twisted herself in the crib into this safe, cozy position: legs crossed daintily at the ankles, hips twisted outward, tiny fists under the chin, and her sleepy head bent back almost as if she was trying to make a backward circle with her body. The neural pathway for Jaynee's favorite position had been repeated over and over in the womb. And in her prenatal brain, connections were being made through this repetition. The more Jaynee lay like this, and the more she now curls and twists happily in her crib, the stronger the brain connections involved become.

But repetition and creating the right environment and early experiences aren't the only factors that contribute to neurons "talking" to each other. No, your baby's brain needs to get fat! (This is probably why

Growing a Healthy Brain in the Womb

Studies show that you can start encouraging optimal brain growth even before your baby is born! Here are some suggestions during pregnancy:

- Eat a well-balanced diet, and talk to your doctor about taking a vitamin supplement. The absence of certain essential nutrients can impair neurological development.

- Don't smoke or use alcohol or drugs. All can harm your baby.

- Make sure you gain enough weight to help your baby grow. Talk to your doctor about your recommended weight gain.

- Exercise. (Again, ask your doctor what exercises you can do during pregnancy.) A healthier body is more likely to produce a healthier baby.

- Practice good hygiene to avoid picking up infections that can be passed on to the baby.

you instinctively craved those hot fudge sundaes when you were pregnant!) Yes, now that your baby has arrived, fatten him up with breast milk or pediatrician-recommended formula. The fat from these life-sustaining foods does so much more than just fill his tummy. This fat is used to create *myelin*. The neurons need a fatty layer so that the electrical signals do not "jump the track" while traveling. Imagine, in that dendrite forest, squirrels jumping from branch to branch. If the neurons and dendrites (trees and branches) are not lined with fatty tissue, the squirrel falls off the branch and the message doesn't get through.

Like insulation on an electrical cord, myelin makes it possible for nerve pathways to be used. Myelin keeps the electrical signals issued by neurons from leaking out. As we touched on with reflexes and baby's favorite position to lie, only a small portion of neurons have already been myelinated at birth. Myelination begins before birth, but it takes many, many years to complete; some studies suggest into a person's twenties.

Windows of Opportunity

A window of opportunity won't open itself.
~Dave Weinbaum

From late pregnancy through age three, baby's brain grows at an accelerated rate. It adds 70% of its mass after birth and grows to 90% of its adult size in the first three years of life! Imagine that! This critical period uses higher amounts of energy than any other stage in life.

Now, like all things in nature, our bodies and our brains have a plan all prepared for us to follow. There is a time and a place for everything in the world, and the same is true of each person's growth. Many years of studying brain autopsies have given scientists some knowledge of the brain. But modern PET, EEG, and MRI scans have given us much additional information, such as what part of the brain is stimulated by what action; how activities, noises, and images affect the brain; and even the effects of neglect and various kinds of abuse on the brain.

In this relatively new area of brain study, scientists have found that there are critical periods for learning. These times are called "windows of opportunity." When nature's timeline deems it ready, a "window opens" in the brain, and almost all of the learning for baby milestones are done during this nature-specified time. Specific input and experiences are necessary for optimal brain development—for baby's lifetime of learning. When the corresponding window is open, baby learns to kick, coo, babble, blow raspberries, walk, talk, and every other thing that we can do. When the critical period is over, the window nearly completely closes.

Judith A. Willis, M.D., M.Ed., in *Building Better Brains*, refers to this as the "use-it-or-lose-it phenomenon." She explains, "The more that certain neural pathways are stimulated, the stronger and more efficient they become."[7] So most of what is learned is accomplished when a particular window is wide open, just long enough for a great wind gust of learning to pass through. When the window begins to close, specific therapies may be necessary to build those skills that were not developed when the window was wide open. Even after critical periods are over, practicing still makes newer and stronger connections between brain cells—but it takes more time and repetition.

One example that we will expand on later involves the "vision window." If a baby has cataracts during the time when the vision window is open, the eye will not learn to see. Even if the cataracts are later removed and every part of the eye is working properly, the eye will still not see because the brain did not receive the right stimulation during the critical period. The neural circuits were not connected that must be present for the brain to process the information that comes in through the eyes. The neurons will not wire properly. The result is blindness. The eyes may be perfect in their physical formation, but without the brain circuits for processing visual information, normal vision is impossible.

Love Is NOT All Your Baby Needs

From the day they bring their newborn home,
the proud parents' ears are cocked for baby's first word....
The father who first hears his infant son pronounce the word
"Daddy" as clear as day has disrupted more than one christening.
~Stan & Jan Berenstain, *The Berenstains' Baby Book*

As we noted in the introduction to this book, what follows in the subsequent chapters is not merely a list of milestones. It is knowledge about *how* the brain works in order to reach those milestones. Why does the baby have such urgency when learning to kick? Why does your baby seem to use all of her energy when trying to sit up? And why do parents get such a variance of timetables as to when baby should meet

---

Is My Baby Gifted?

Most parents don't officially find out that they have a "brainy baby" until their child enters school, but many of us begin to suspect that our child has that "extra something" in the brain department long before she starts school. In fact, some experts say that above-average intelligence can be identified even in infancy.

Researcher Jerome M. Sattler notes that gifted children often "show unusual alertness in infancy."[8] In an article for iParenting.com, Wendy Skinner, author of *Infinity & Zebra Stripes: Life with Gifted Children,*[9] noted that intelligence in infants might be shown first through "social smarts," including a strong emotional attachment to parents. In that same article,[10] Dr. Deborah L. Ruf, author of *Losing Our Minds: Gifted Children Left Behind,*[11] noted these characteristics of gifted children at around one year of age:

- Insists on doing things for him- or herself
- Long attention span
- Interest in letters, numbers, books, talking
- Good eye-hand coordination, such as shape sorting
- Loves toys and puzzles geared to older children
- Doesn't chew on or damage books
- Wants to please others; gets feelings easily hurt

---

certain milestones? Should you panic if your baby isn't reaching the milestones on the given list? Is something wrong with your baby?

Together, we will explore the windows of opportunity—the critical periods of learning—and how to best take advantage of them. We'll discuss what makes your baby move on to other milestones, the timing of milestones, and most importantly, how to take advantage of these periods to grow the best baby brain.

Love isn't all a baby needs. It is an excellent start—as we'll see in the next chapter—but there's so much more you can give your baby. By using the information in this book, you will be growing a brain, a personality, a character, a lover, a thinker, a learner—your child!

Chapter 2
Attachment and Baby Brains: Spoiled Rotten Is a Good Thing

It's impossible to spoil your baby during the first four months of life.
~Harvey Karp, M.D., *The Happiest Baby on the Block*

"Put that baby down before you spoil it!" groan grandmas and great-grandmas across the country. "Your baby needs to learn that you are not at its every beck and call!" Well, that myth has been busted. The truth is, Grandma, you can't spoil a young infant. You need to teach her that you *are* at her every beck and call. That is *exactly* what you have to communicate to your baby's brain.

Attachment to your newborn baby is the first and most important influence on brain growth. It is a personal and complex experience that takes time. Nature has an "attachment gene" built into your baby's brain to ensure her survival and socialization. It makes parents want to shower their baby with love and affection, protect their baby, and nourish their little one—even in the middle of another long night.

The window of opportunity for this bonding is during the first three years. In this chapter, we will cover the first three months of your baby's life. This is the time when you are getting to know her, and "play time" is gentle and involves few toys. Bonding is extremely vital during this new time in your family's life. But before you start thinking that you'll have to jump up and run over every time your child calls you for the rest of her life, later chapters will cover more ideas for bonding with your baby as she grows older and is ready for baby games and toys.

Needs change as your baby grows, but attachment is key to brain development throughout babyhood, toddlerhood, and into the preschool years. In "Your Child's Growing Brain," child-development educator Stephen Santos Rico, M.A. noted, "The brain is use-dependent, so the more that it's experiencing something, the stronger it makes the connection. In the absence of some of those experiences, connections are not made."[1] In other words, playing, simple pleasures, and loving grow a baby's brain. Without these experiences, critical neural connections will not be made, and baby's brain will likely fail to thrive and meet milestones. Most parents do not realize just how influential they are to their child's growing brain. Feeling an early, strong attachment to their parents gives children a secure view of the world, fosters positive self-esteem, and provides a model for other intimate relationships. Thus, the need for immediate response to needs, especially in the difficult first three months, is crucial.

When your baby cries, she is communicating her needs to you. Newborns cannot survive on their own, and all needs must be met through a tight bond with a caregiver. So in a way, it is good that your baby is crying and letting you know that she needs something. However, the distressed baby brain must be comforted immediately for at least the first three to six months. Letting your baby cry without attention for prolonged periods of time can be damaging. Let's look at some examples of what can happen when attachment fails to occur.

The Chilling Effects of Lack of Attachment

Babies who are held more cry less often.
~Sandra Hardin Gookin & Dan Gookin, *Parenting for Dummies*

Do you remember the heart-breaking footage of orphanages in Romania from the 1990s? When the Iron Curtain fell, the Western world was shocked at the appalling sights coming from orphanages. Families had been required by the dictatorship government to produce many children, which they could not afford. However, the government thought they had that problem covered by providing orphanages where babies could be brought up. Children in these orphanages were prisoners of their cribs. Humanitarian agencies encouraged nurses and attendants in the newly discovered orphanages to hold the babies and children and give them attention, but they were often unsuccessful. Even after intervention, Romanian orphans still received only five to six *minutes* of attention a day. Instead, the attendants hung out in hallways, smoking and drinking coffee, while the little ones rocked themselves endlessly in their cribs.[2]

In other stories and video footage, we saw orphan children banging their heads against the sides of their cribs, squalid conditions, babies swaddled in rags, and bottles propped in their mouths with no bonding, contact, or holding. Children in crib-cages were listless, with vacant looks on their faces. They huddled in cold, cramped, filthy dormitories, painfully thin. And what became of these thousands and thousands of children? Few were adopted, and many ended up on the streets, in prison, living in sewers, or dead. Those who were fortunate enough to be adopted frequently suffered from "attachment disorders," unable to bond with their new families and form healthy, loving relationships.

Also in the 1990s, we had report after report of Chinese "orphanages" over-whelmed with baby girls who were deemed of little value and referred to as "maggots in rice." The Chinese government had passed laws allowing only one child per family due to overpopulation. "Population control officials" killed babies as soon as they were born or forced abortions, even as late as the eighth or ninth month of pregnancy. Chinese cultural beliefs are such that boys carry on the family line and take care of their parents in old age. In their view, girls are not as valuable since they simply go along with their husband to take care of the

> ## Glossary
>
> *Attachment disorder:* a child's inability to trust and bond to other human beings, usually caused by a lack of affection, stimulation, and comfort during the first three years of life
>
> *Bonding:* attachment between parent and child; when a child trusts that his parents will protect and care for him
>
> *Colic:* inconsolable crying in infants less than three months old which cannot be traced to a specific cause and lasts for hours at a time for at least three weeks
>
> *Cortisol:* a hormone released by the adrenal cortex, often during periods of stress, which influences the immune system and the body's metabolism
>
> *Oxytocin:* a hormone released by the pituitary gland that aids in contracting the uterus during labor and releasing milk for breastfeeding
>
> *Swaddling:* an ancient technique used by parents to wrap a baby snugly and securely in a blanket

husband's family. In a country without Social Security, 401ks, and other retirement accounts, boys are invaluable for this purpose, which is why many girls were given away so that families had opportunities to try to produce a son.

In a 1996 article in *The Atlantic Monthly,* Anne F. Thurston reported that visitors to an orphanage on the outskirts of a Chinese city were convinced that what appeared as retardation in roomfuls of young children was often simply the result of very little love and attention. Two or three untrained staff members were assigned to care for about 48 babies. They tossed bottles into cribs for babies to figure out how to feed themselves; many, of course, were too young to do so.

> **Authors' Note:** This information is not meant to discourage couples from adopting, but to make parents aware that they may need to more thoroughly explore the issues involved in attachment if their baby is not adopted shortly after birth.

Lessons Learned

A baby is born with a need to be loved—and never outgrows it.
~Frank A. Clark

We learned a lot from this suffering that we witnessed in Romanian and Chinese orphanages—mainly, the need for love, for stimulation, for bonding, medical attention, cuddling, laughter, and bright and beautiful colors. In a word, *humanity.* But lest we in the United States think we've mastered the concept of bonding, there's still plenty of room for improvement. Author Rae Pica writes in the article "Skinship: Better Bonding with Baby," "Where infants are concerned, America is considered a 'low-touch' society. In many other cultures, babies are held for hours, stroked when in need of soothing, and carried close to the bodies of their mothers. In ours, babies spend lengthy periods alone in cribs; we fear that unless they're allowed to 'self-soothe,' they'll be spoiled and grow up dependent; and, though we may carry our infants, they're more likely to be 'containerezied' than carried body to body."[3]

It's plain to see from the orphanage experiences, extreme though they may be, that your baby needs you. And your baby's brain needs your *immediate attention* for up to six months of age. This means no "crying it out" at bedtime. This means feeding on demand. This means keeping your baby close to your body. For extended periods of time, many parents find it less demanding on their arms to use slings or front or back packs. Your baby is *not* trying to manipulate you at this age. He is trying to make you aware of his needs.

Be cognizant of sounds or sights that may alarm your baby. Hug him, pat his back, and hold him. Build up the trust that will last a lifetime. Teach your spouse, the grandparents, and other caregivers this vital information. Tell them that this is what you expect. No one is going to care for and love your baby like you. You must be an advocate—the best and loudest voice—for your child. No one else understands your baby better. Rely on that "mother's instinct" and be that "mama bear" that you feel inside when your baby cries. He cries for you to fix things. And in your sensitivity to your baby, you are teaching him how to regulate his physical and emotional state.

What Is Reactive Attachment Disorder (RAD)?

According to the RAD Consultancy (www.RADConsultancy.com), children with Reactive Attachment Disorder (RAD) acquire it "from insufficient early bonding with their mothers." These children may display impaired social development and sociopathic behaviors, as well as defiance, violence, and disrespect. A similar condition resulting from insufficient bonding is called Oppositional Defiant Disorder (ODD), which is defined as "failure to complete the 'terrible twos.' …Most children with RAD suffer from ODD as well."

Children with RAD may be classified as "inhibited" or "disinhibited."[4] "Inhibited" children do not seek out or respond to comfort. They tend to be emotionally withdrawn, relying only on themselves for survival. "Disinhibited" children, on the other hand, may seek out comfort and affection from almost anybody, even adults who are unknown to them.

Of course, not all children who experience insufficient bonding as babies will develop RAD. "The fact that there are many children who face adverse circumstances without necessarily developing RAD is most likely due to individuality. Not everyone will react in the same way to a given situation."[5] In other words, a child's inborn temperament may affect the degree to which she develops RAD. Read more about assessing temperament in Chapter 7 of this book.

Find a Daycare Provider Who Supports Your Goals to Boost Your Baby's Brain Power

If you work outside of the home and your baby will have another caretaker during a substantial part of the day, it's important that he be cared for by someone who shares your goals to do all you can to stimulate his brain growth. As we discuss in this book, children's intellectual development can be stunted when they are placed in non-stimulating environments. Here are some factors to consider when deciding who will care for your baby while you're at work:

- Visit several potential daycare centers. Leave your baby at home so that you can focus on observing the teachers. Do they interact with the children? Do they play with them? Are there lots of hugs and laughter? Do they appear to love children and enjoy their work?

- Ask about the daily schedule. Does it involve a variety of activities with the children? Are there structured exercises designed to promote babies' growth and development?

- Are teachers trained or do they have the educational background to evaluate babies' progress and alert parents about delays?

- Check out the environment. Are there lots of books? Are there plenty of toys and stimulating artwork on the walls? Is the place clean enough to encourage floor play?

- Observe the children in the center. Are there enough staff members to attend to their needs? Do the children appear to be happy and involved?

- If you are considering childcare in a private home, observe and look for the same signs of a brain-friendly environment as with the daycare centers above. In addition, speak with the daycare owner about your parenting philosophies. Be alert to signs that you share the same parenting style.

Ideally, your baby's daycare environment should be as conducive to brain growth as your home. Although cost and location are important, your most important criteria in selecting a daycare provider should be whether they share your views about raising children. Evaluate as many places as necessary until you find the perfect one!

Babies and Stress

Babies suffer from stress, just like all of us do. Baby stress includes emotions such as fear, anxiety, sadness, and short separation from Mom, all along the spectrum to fear related to abuse or neglect. New situations also cause your baby to be upset. She needs to know that Mom is there and available.

In stressful situations, resources that are usually dedicated to brain growth are redirected to basic survival. This retards potential growth. When babies and children are stressed out, overscheduled, or overstimulated, their brains produce a hormone called cortisol, known as the "stress hormone." Brain researchers have found an overabundance of cortisol in the brains of neglected children. Too much cortisol can cause impaired cognitive function, blood sugar imbalances, decreased bone density, decrease in muscle tissue, lowered immunity, and inflammatory responses in the body.[6]

Dr. Megan Gunnar studies the relationship between attachment security and reactions to stress in human infants and toddlers. Some of her studies point out that chronic stress is known to disturb parts of the brain involved in fearfulness, focusing, learning, and memory. She suggests that secure attachments buffer these effects, while an insecure attachment

Do You Have Postpartum Depression?

Babies aren't the only ones who can feel stressed. Certainly, parents are going to feel stressed out when they're sleep-deprived and trying to meet the many needs of their new baby. However, there's a difference between the normal stress that parents feel and postpartum depression, which is usually influenced by a mother's shifting hormones. Symptoms include:

- Feeling restless, irritable, sad, hopeless, worthless, guilty, or overwhelmed.
- Excessive crying.
- Lack of energy or motivation.
- Eating and/or sleeping too much or too little.
- Problems with focus, memory, or decision making.
- Lack of pleasure or interest in activities or in the baby.
- Distancing oneself from family and friends.
- Headaches, chest pains, heart palpitations, hyperventilating.
- Fear of hurting oneself or the baby.

If you experience any of these signs of postpartum depression, please see your doctor right away. According to the U.S. Department of Health and Human Services, "Postpartum depression can affect a mother's ability to parent. She may lack energy, have trouble concentrating, be irritable, and not be able to meet her child's needs for love and affection.... Researchers believe that postpartum depression can affect the infant by causing delays in language development, problems with emotional bonding to others, behavioral problems, lower activity levels, sleep problems, and distress."[7] Very effective treatments that may include medication and/or talk therapy are available.

leaves the brain open to problems that result in a lifetime of anxiety, timidity, and learning difficulties.[8]

Your job is to "love on your baby"—something not hard to do. According to Pica, "In Japan, the closeness between mother and child is so much a part of the culture that there's a word for it: *skinship*."[9] Isn't that a great term? So practice "skinship" with your baby. Snuggle her on your chest and under your chin. Trace her little face with your finger. Kiss her fingers and gently stroke her cheek. Better than apple pie or cherry pie, love your little cutie pie.

Cry, Baby, Cry

Despite your best efforts to soothe him, your baby will cry. It may start out as an "eeek" and might gradually become a shriek. You may be relieved when you first hear your baby cry at birth—a sound that many parents associate with the first sign of their baby's life. But your baby will continue to cry—probably more often than you expect. Let's take a look at the four types of crying that you may encounter with your baby.

The newborn cry

The first kind of crying that you will experience is the "newborn cry." Right after birth, your baby is going through huge changes emotionally, physically, and mentally. He has lived his whole life in an environment designed only for him. No matter how hard you try to soothe him, some babies are simply very sensitive to the immense changes. He is learning just like you. He doesn't understand his communication system any better than you do for the first few weeks. But you and your baby will learn to relate to each other together. Your baby will refine his communication skills, and you will understand him better with time and attention.

> *Baby Benjamin, at a few days old, exasperated his parents by crying seemingly non-stop. He cried night and day, when he was held or put down, hungry or full, clean or dirty. It got to the point at which Mom and Dad were nervous wrecks and thought that their baby was sick or in pain. Every grandma and experienced mom on the block had an idea for a solution, but to no avail. But*

when Baby Benjamin passed the 10-day mark, he was able to be soothed. He had simply been "out of his element," so to speak. He wasn't in his mama's quiet, dark, warm womb. He couldn't get comfortable. The lights were too bright, and the temperature was all wrong. Sounds and movement were everywhere, and he was overstimulated by being passed from adoring relative to adoring friend.

The needy cry

The second and easiest type of crying to "fix" in your baby is the cry for needs to be met. A hungry, sleepy, dirty baby will let you know right away that he wants something fixed, and then he will be your happy little baby again. You will get to know this cry, as well as your baby's own internal clock or routine. Notice times when he is hungry—how many hours has it been since his last feeding? Does he usually have a dirty diaper after feeding or naps? The more information you record in a journal or baby book, the more in control you will feel because you'll be better able to predict your baby's needs and respond to them.

The stressed-out cry

The third type of crying that you will probably experience during the early bonding period is when your baby is releasing tension. As overwhelmed as this may make you feel, you don't have to stop your baby from this type of crying. Believe it or not, your baby may just need to release some tension that has built up from the day—kind of like you do when you watch TV for a while after work. Take note of when your baby's fussy periods occur. They will most likely be around

---

Helpful Hints to Stop the Crying

- Change the scenery. Go for a walk in the stroller or a ride in the car.

- Play soothing music or sing to your baby.

- Distract your baby with a toy or game of pat-a-cake.

- Offer a bottle or breast if it's feeding time; try a pacifier if baby's been fed.

- Rock your baby in the rocking chair or try a baby swing.

- Change your baby's diaper or clothing. Something may be bothering her.

- Burp your baby. She may have gas.

- Hold your baby. She may just want your love!

the same time of day, usually in the evening, maybe for 45 minutes or so. Your duty is to stay calm and hold your baby. Sit in a comfortable spot. You can even have the TV on quietly. Pat your baby gently. Rock him easily. Whisper to him and stroke his head or forehead softly. Lay him on your lap and rub his belly. It is okay for your baby to cry in these common instances *if* you are being attentive and responsive.

After the crying episode, the baby stops and falls asleep,
by which time the parents are crying themselves.
~Melissa M. Burnham, Ph.D., & Jennifer Lawler, Ph.D.,
The Complete Idiot's Guide to Sleep Training Your Child

The colicky cry

Then there is the issue of colic, the fourth type of crying that you may experience. Colic is defined by the rule of threes: the crying begins within the first three weeks of life, lasts about three hours a day, and continues for at least three weeks, and perhaps longer, in an otherwise healthy baby. When you're going through it, this seems like an immense amount of time and is very disruptive.

Some good news: colic does not mean that you are doing anything wrong or that there is necessarily something wrong with the baby. Colic is not contagious. It doesn't have any lasting effects on the child or the mother later in life. And the light at the end of the tunnel is that colic will pass at around the three-month mark. Yes, it seems like a long tunnel when you're passing through it, but comforting your baby and asking for help when you need it will help maintain your well-being and, in turn, your baby's.

With colic, your baby's crying is loud, and he may cry so hard that his face gets red. He draws in his limbs and clenches

Breastfeeding and Brain Power

Studies have shown that children who were breastfed as babies have IQ scores seven to 10 points higher than babies fed only formula. Keep in mind that this is just an average and does not necessarily reflect each individual child, but it does say that we could be raising a generation of smarter kids as breastfeeding is used more and more. Children who were breastfed also earn higher grades, and their intellectual advantage is increased in proportion to how long they were breastfed. Scientists believe that this is due to the nutrients found in breast milk.[10]

his fists like he's very angry. He cries inconsolably, excessively, and constantly. His belly may look enlarged or tight because he is crying so hard for so long.

The onset of colic will frighten you. Even seasoned mothers are caught off guard by the intensity of the situation. Call your pediatrician whenever your baby cries for an unreasonable amount of time. You will feel much better after having your baby checked out and realizing that it's nothing more than colic.

To deal with colic, first remember to respond consistently to your baby's cries. He is not manipulating you. Rock your baby, play music, and dance with him. Take him for a walk in the stroller. (This helps alleviate some of your stress, too.) Don't smoke or allow anyone to smoke around your baby. Run "white noise" machines, or simply run a vacuum, hair dryer, or clothes dryer while your baby is in an infant seat. "Shushing" your baby with your voice may help, too, as these methods simulate the whooshing sound that he heard constantly while in utero. A car ride may help. You can also try baby massage (more on this later).

If you are still apprehensive, discuss your concerns with your pediatrician again. The doctor may want to see your baby just to rule out any medical reason for the crying. Chances are, however, that your baby will become used to his new world, attached to you, and happy before the pain of delivery is a distant memory. While bonding with your baby, you'll soon get to know him, enjoy him, and fall in love with him.

Breastfeeding, continued

Breastfed babies' brains have higher levels of DHA (docasa-hexaenoic acid), a fat that's extremely important for developing brain tissues. Mothers can increase the DHA in their diets by eating fish, especially tuna and salmon. Breast milk also contains plenty of cholesterol, which is important for growing nerve tissue in the brain. In addition, breast milk contains a sugar called lactose, which the body breaks down into glucose and galactose. The latter, too, is critical for brain tissue growth.

Finally, breastfed babies' brains benefit from the closeness with Mommy that is necessary for breastfeeding. It is a bonding experience, which is always great for brain growth. If you are unable to breastfeed for medical reasons, ask your doctor to recommend a formula that most closely resembles mother's milk, and make sure your baby gets lots of hugging and snuggling!

For new babies, loud shhhing is the "sound of silence," the anti-cry.
~Harvey Karp, M.D., *The Happiest Baby on the Block*

How to Bond with Your Newborn

When you anticipate what your baby needs, you are able to read her signals and respond appropriately. Keep your baby's environment calm and pleasant. Keep lights low, as your new baby's eyes are still getting used to the light. Play quiet songs or even read the paper out loud so that she hears your comforting voice. Provide quiet times when she seems overstimulated (acting fussy or bored and looking away). You are teaching her that you and her new life are a secure and safe anchor. And in such a place, your baby's brain will grow.

Personal interaction with your newborn is the best toy ever. Show your happiness when handling your baby, and smile at her. Look deep into her eyes and watch how she stares back. Soon baby will stop crying if held and comforted, and she will smile when she sees you after the first few weeks of life. What a treat! Let's take a look at more specific ideas for encouraging your baby's attachment to you—and growing her brain.

Face-to-face contact

As a newborn, your baby will gaze at faces, especially at the eyes and mouth. In fact, she will gaze at faces longer than at anything else. She can see clearly eight to 12 inches away, about the space between her face and yours while feeding. Human faces, after all, are full of motion and sound. Stick out your tongue, and your baby just might stick hers out, too! Position yourself close enough when singing or talking to your baby. She'll get to know your face very quickly. It will seem like she is examining every part of your face—every nook and cranny. And that is exactly what she is doing. Repetition will make baby remember who Mommy is and that she is the sure thing in her life. (Most infants prefer female faces more than those of males due to this "mommy connection."[11]) This security enables her to soon move on, in baby steps, to the next milestones. It is also an early intellectual development—college, here she comes! Imagine her studying a chemistry book as deeply as she is studying your face!

Sucking

This natural reflex provides your baby with great comfort and satisfaction. Her sucking will become better and voluntary a few weeks after she is born. Allow her to use her thumb, fist, or pacifier to meet the natural need for sucking. You can even help her put her fist or thumb in her mouth. Remember that repetition makes strong neural pathways that make baby's brain grow.

> *Baby Heather was born with blisters on her thumbs from sucking them while in the womb. As soon as she was born, her thumb went straight back into her mouth, as if birth had only temporarily disrupted her. Her mother did not have to help baby Heather find her thumb for the next five years!*

Babies are born naturally knowing how to get nutrition through the sucking reflex. At first, this is an involuntary action. Soon, however, your baby will make the connection that sucking is pleasurable and provides feelings of security. Experts disagree on thumb-sucking as the baby gets older. Some point out that thumb-sucking in toddlers and preschoolers can interfere with the alignment of teeth and can influence the shape of the child's palate and facial development. Other experts feel that an older child will be too busy playing and running to remember to suck her thumb, and therefore the habit of thumb-sucking will die out on its own. Work with your pediatrician on this issue as your child grows into toddlerhood and preschool. But in the first year, thumb-sucking, pacifiers, and fist-sucking are calming and positive experiences for the brain.

Swaddling and SIDS

Babies should be put to sleep on their backs to reduce the risk of Sudden Infant Death Syndrome (SIDS). However, studies have shown that up to 30% of parents abandon the practice of putting babies on their backs to sleep within weeks or months because the baby doesn't sleep well on his back. This is especially disturbing since two to four months is the peak risk period for SIDS.[12]

Babies who are swaddled, though, often sleep better on their backs because they're not startled awake by the Moro reflex. Since swaddled babies are more likely to be placed on their backs to sleep, it decreases their chances for SIDS. Ask the nurses at the hospital to show you how to swaddle properly for maximum benefit and safety. Special swaddling blankets are also available.

Tummy time

This is important for strengthening your baby's upper body, and it's another way to teach your baby that her world and you are safe and secure. Lay your baby on her tummy on a soft blanket. Put one or two colorful toys in front of her or around her in a circle. Allow her to practice movements for very short periods of time at first. One minute of tummy time three times a day is a good goal for a newborn. She will work hard to hold up her head and look around. She may drop her head in exhaustion, bonking her little nose in the process. Pick her up and don't let her get frustrated. Make tummy time just part of play. As weeks pass, you'll pick up on her cues that tummy time can last longer. Never leave your baby by herself while she's on her tummy (to avoid the risk of suffocation). Rub her back, talk to her about what she can see, rattle a toy. You can even lie on your back and have baby lay on your belly, looking at your face. Chances are that your baby will keep her head up longer if she sees your face and hears your voice. If she's not a big fan of tummy time, it may help to put a firm pillow or Boppy under her chest with her arms out in front of her so that she can see what's going on.

Massage

Babies need to be touched, caressed and held just as much as they need to eat and sleep. Baby massage is another great way to really feel connected to your baby. Loving touches nourish your baby's emotional development and improve her sensory awareness. They stimulate the production of her growth and digestive hormones. Skin-to-skin contact is also soothing and comforting. It reduces stress and helps your baby to sleep.

Your baby's emotional needs are not the only ones met during a baby massage. When you massage your baby, it stimulates the release of oxytocin in your own body, which facilitates attachment and bonding. Oxytocin is a hormone that causes your uterus to contract during labor, promotes the "let-down reflex" during breastfeeding, and relaxes you for nursing.

Simply touching your baby in your day-to-day interactions (such as when you change her diaper or clothes) does not stimulate your baby's brain as much as *intentional* touching and caressing. Your baby picks up nonverbal messages from you and discovers what it means to trust. These strong feelings of trust for their moms carry over to other people who are nurturing, loving, and warm. When you massage your fussy baby, you show her how to relax with your soothing touch and voice.

There are many avenues to learn about baby massage. Ask the nurses at the hospital if there are any baby massage classes available during your stay. Check with your pediatrician for classes. Local daycare centers or parent education programs may sponsor classes. There are also numerous books and websites to educate yourself, your spouse, or even the grandparents. Simply rubbing down your baby with aromatic lotion in a loving, mild manner will work wonders. Soothing lights, a warm room, and music make a wonderful memory for you and make neural connections in your baby. And your baby will *love* it.

You can massage your baby a few times a day. Work it into your routine, maybe after her morning bath or before a nap and in the evening just before bedtime. Big sister or brother can help massage the baby's feet, choose the music, and pick out the lotion and blanket for the baby to lie on. Massage can be a family affair as well as one-on-one time.

Baby massage is about learning to communicate
your love for your baby through touch.
~Jill Vyse

Singing

Another way to play and bond with your baby is singing. Babies love to be rocked and sung to. Nursery rhymes are fun for baby, too, even at a young age. Find songs that you like from a bookstore, off the Internet, in nursery rhyme books, and in hymnals. Choose five to 10 and make copies of the lyrics. Keep these by the rocking chair, couch, and kitchen to sing to your baby at various times during the day. At play time, sing in a silly, happy voice with lots of laughter and tickling of toes. At sleepy time, hold your swaddled baby gently in your arms while you feed her. Sing in a soft, sweet voice, and look deep into her eyes. You can feel the love for your baby swell inside you as you do this time after time.

Swaddling

You may notice that the nurses have your baby tightly wrapped up like a little burrito for nearly her whole hospital stay. There is a reason for this. It is soothing, warm, and calming. Swaddling also helps confine your baby's limbs, keeping the Moro reflex at bay, which causes your baby to startle and throw her limbs out, often waking her up. Let's face it, once your baby is asleep, you want her to stay that way for a while! Swaddling also mimics the tight, very cozy feeling of being in the womb and reduces the symptoms of colic. Some babies like their little hands or arms free from swaddling, so watch for your baby's cues on what she prefers. Also, be aware of overheating in warm weather. Use all of those darling blankets that you received at your baby showers. Learn how to swaddle your baby from the pros at the hospital.

Holding baby close

A sling allows your baby to fold up as she were in utero. This feels good to your baby for several weeks after birth. Wearing a sling or front pack with your baby will increase the bond that you and she feel toward each other. She will get to know your smell, voice, and movements. She will feel your hand patting or rubbing her. You can pick up on her cues more quickly, too, if you and your baby are so close. (And imagine how much faster you'll sense a dirty diaper if your baby is next to you rather than across the room or in a stroller!)

By engaging in these activities, your baby's brain will learn when it is bedtime, play time, or talking time. Not only will she get closer to you, but she will learn about communication, in both verbal and physical ways. Start these activities on the very first day of your baby's life—you can't start too soon! Neurons in her brain are connecting every time you repeat these activities with your baby, making the transition to the next baby milestones sooner and easier.

There is one last thing that will help you bond with your baby which may sound contradictory to our previous advice but truly isn't: get some rest. An overtired, recovering mom isn't what you want to be. Motherhood is hard; it requires a lot of thinking and energy. To handle both of these things adequately, you need sleep. Ask for help! Grandmas, aunts, cousins, and friends will love playing with or holding your baby while you take a nap or rest.

> *Baby Trevor's mom knew that she was too tired and was beginning to feel frantic as night fell. She dreaded another all-nighter. She began to cry and feel like her life was going to be endless days followed by endless nights of crying, feeding, and diaper changes. Luckily, her next-door neighbor was home and had volunteered previously to take care of the baby. At 10:30 that night, Mom handed off her baby, along with a loaded diaper bag and a bottle of breast milk, to a well-rested, well-trusted friend. She then slept deeply for five to six hours and woke up ready for another day with her baby. She was happy and refreshed—the best kind of mom to be!*

Conclusion

Your nightgown or sweat suits might be the only things you wear over these hectic first few months. You may only be able to take a shower a few times a week. You may subsist on graham crackers and coffee (although we suggest that you eat as healthy as possible, especially if you're breastfeeding). Dust bunnies will float across the room, and you may feel cut off from the rest of the world. But when you ask anyone who's been through the experience, they'll share that your baby will grow out of this stage before you know it. He will be wearing the next-size diaper and the bigger clothes from his full closet. He'll be holding his head steady and eating more. And you'll be so deeply in love, head over heels, starry-eyed, and crazier about your baby than you ever thought possible. You'll be the image of Mommy that you always thought you'd be—only better.

Chapter 3

Language: Getting Baby Ready to Read

Books are the bees which carry the quickening pollen
from one to another mind.
~James Russell Lowell

Amazingly, while your baby is growing in the womb, he is already learning communication, language, and comprehension skills. Since his conception, he has been listening to and lulled by the sound of the blood swooshing through your body and the tick-tock of your heart. These sounds have created messages of comfort, security, and happiness.

Starting at around seven months' gestation, your baby is able to hear noises made *outside* of the womb. He actually lets you know that he is aware of outside stimuli and sounds through his movement in response to an external belly jiggle, his kicks and elbow jabs when music is playing, and his rolling when he is read to. When having a sonogram, try wiggling your belly a bit. Your baby will probably respond by doing a roll or limb extensions.

Researchers have been able to test the unborn baby's heart rate in relation to these external sounds.[1] A baby's heartbeat decreases in utero when hearing his mother's voice, perhaps because the soft, underwater voice is soothing to him. Even in the first moments after birth, your baby will recognize your voice and others he heard often while in the womb.

Baby's small but very complicated brain provides the knowledge and skills needed for him to mirror, copy, and mimic facial expressions and movements. If you stick out your tongue, pucker your lips, or even blink your eyes dramatically, you will be surprised to see your baby try to imitate these expressions! He is looking for meaning and ways to communicate right after birth. He communicates both verbally and physically.

From birth, your baby is intrinsically drawn to faces. Within his field of vision (eight to 12 inches from his face), he studies your face as he nurses, peers at Dad's face as he reads to him, stares at Grandma's face as she sings to him, and notices Grandpa's face as he reads the newspaper to him. The more real-life language experiences that the baby has, the more readily he will learn language. Intentionally interacting with your baby by speaking, singing, and reading to him creates opportunities for him to practice language. His best toy and learning tool is *you*.

> *As soon as Samantha found out she was pregnant, she started talking to her baby. She would tell her little boy about her day and how much she was looking forward to welcoming him into the world. Her husband Mike thought it was kind of silly, but he played along with Samantha, especially when he'd tell their future son, "You'd better be a Cowboys fan!" But Mike didn't realize that talking to his son wasn't just cute; he was already help-ing him to develop language skills! Little did he know that his baby would soon respond to his voice after birth, a voice that already sounded very familiar and comforting to him, thanks to their "in-womb" conversations!*

Language Development in the First Three Months

During the first days of her life, when your baby is alert, she may stop all activity when she hears your voice. She may turn unsteadily toward you, and she may even have a look on her face as if she is saying to herself, "Hey, I recognize this sound! It reminds me of safety and security." Your baby may slow her breathing and movement in response to your voice. She may even be still when she hears a hair dryer, music, or stories that she heard while in the womb. It is amazing to see her experiencing a pleasant memory!

A very strange phenomenon occurs when one is talking to a baby. Using a kind of voice called *parentese*, people often speak to a baby using a high-pitched, sing-song voice, elongated words, and short, simple sentences.[2] Your baby's brain is wired at birth to recognize this particular tone. Mother Nature has built in the ability to distinguish this sound so that your baby can attend to the speaker when spoken to but filter out the rest of the noise. Her brain sends a message, "Someone is talking to you." A room may be full of people, and your baby can tune out all of that "adult" noise. When someone gets close to her and begins speaking parentese, however, she will become alert and seem to know that this noise is especially for her. There is nothing like a baby to bring an adult down to a blubbering, silly-talking, nonsensical being!

This response from your baby tells us that she is learning every moment. Interact with her by narrating your day, your routines, and your actions. "I am cleaning up the dishes." "Let's go for a walk." "Do you want to listen to some music?" Tell her what you are seeing: "I see a bird." "Look, there's a pretty flower!" Talk about what you are doing while caring for your little one: "You need a bath." "Let's change your diaper." "Here's your blanket. Let's wrap you up." Talk to your baby about the people in her life: "Daddy is home!" "Grandma wants to hold you." "The kitty wants to see you." As your baby hears these common words over and over again, her brain makes connections between objects and words, between people and words, and between emotions and words.

At first, you probably won't notice much of a response. Perhaps your baby will quiet her breathing and movement. She will look at

> ## Glossary
>
> *Babbling:* an early form of talking in which a baby imitates the sounds that she hears in her environment
>
> *Expressive vocabulary:* words that your baby can speak, even if imperfectly
>
> *Fine motor skills:* small, precise movements made by the fingers, hands, and wrists
>
> *Gross motor skills:* activities such as jumping, running, and walking
>
> *Otitis media:* an inflammation of the middle ear; also known as an "ear infection" when it's classified as "acute"
>
> *Parent Report Card:* getting "feedback" in the form of gurgling, smiling, cooing, and so on from your baby when you speak to her
>
> *Parentese:* an exaggerated, high-pitched, sing-song way of speaking to babies by adults
>
> *Passive vocabulary:* words that your baby can understand but cannot speak; also known as "listening vocabulary"

you, and she may possibly look for an object that's mentioned. But gradually, you will notice your baby really listening intently. Around three months of age, she will begin gurgling or cooing in response. Be sure to answer back when she utters a sound. Even though she cannot make correct speech, she is learning the give and take of a conversation: you say something, I respond; I say something, you respond.

According to a new Power of Talk study, children between birth and age 3 need to hear 30,000 words every day from their parents and caregivers to ensure optimal language development and academic success.
~*MomSense* magazine, May/June 2008

Simply playing a CD or DVD does not grow the communication part of your baby's brain. Since we are social creatures, babies must learn through real experiences with people, not a cartoon on TV or a song on the stereo. Your baby needs to see your mouth move while talking. She needs to see your lips go up and down, your tongue stick out or hit the roof of your mouth. She cannot see this while watching TV. If your baby is watching a show, don't leave her in isolation. Interact with her while she watches, repeating important words or singing to your baby with the video.

Half of communication is listening, and your baby is working every minute to create a "passive vocabulary." This is made up of the words that your baby understands but may be unable to physically imitate or utter yet. Eventually, she will understand words like "milk," "dog," and "mama" long before she is able to manipulate her tongue, lips, and teeth in order to respond to you. Your baby learns language while you speak to her and to others. The more you talk to her, the sooner she may begin to talk herself.

Reading Promotes Language Development

It's a huge advantage to have parents who read to you.
And it's an advantage that lasts a lifetime.
~Former First Lady Laura Bush

A great way to encourage the growth of language skills and promote later literacy is to read to your baby. When it comes to building literacy, experts agree that you can never start too early. Begin reading to your baby when he's a newborn…yes, a newborn! You may think that he is too young to be read to, but he's not. Reading to your baby boosts language development. According to Caroline J. Blakemore and Barbara Weston Ramirez in their book *Baby Read-Aloud Basics*, reading to little ones helps them understand the meanings of words and learn uncommon ones. "Compared with ordinary talk between a child and parent, children's books have three times more rare words." In fact, by age four, children who are read to are exposed to 32 million more words than children who haven't been read books.[3]

Even in the first few weeks of life, your baby's little brain is making connections in understanding the rhythm of language, the particular sounds of your native language, and the meaning of voice tones when you read. Reading improves listening skills, memory, and attention span. Each time your baby hears a particular word or song, memory is built up in the brain. Eventually, these memories, or "connections," become strong enough to create a skill or move the baby forward to achieving a language milestone. An added benefit of reading aloud to your baby is that it promotes parent/child bonding, an important concept that we addressed in the previous chapter. Soon, your baby will associate book time with "lovey" time, cozy time, and happy time.[4]

How to Read to Your Baby

Kids who are read to (and who read) are associated with higher IQs, better vocabularies, and increased language skills.
~Sandra Hardin Gookin & Dan Gookin, *Parenting for Dummies*

Keep reading time with your little ones short but frequent. Aim for five times a day for about five minutes each. You can change the reading time as you pick up on your baby's cues. Fussing and looking away are indicators that reading time is over. Calm breathing, focusing on the reader's face, and quietness are signs that reading time can continue. Allow your baby to decide how much time to spend together reading. Of course, as a young infant, your baby is simply listening to your voice with relaxed joy and satisfaction. As he becomes able to hold up his head and sit in a bouncy seat or on your lap, he is able to show that he is bored by fussing or turning away. And when he becomes mobile, he will tell you that reading time is over by scootching, crawling, or rolling away. At this age, he will probably be more interested in moving around than sitting and listening to a story, but don't let this stop you from reading. You just need to do more things to capture his attention. Use funny voices for different characters. Use sound effects for animals, machines, and trains. Exaggerate your facial expressions. (See "Language- and Literacy-Building Activities" at the end of this chapter for more ideas on getting your baby excited about reading.) Your baby is listening, watching, and absorbing all that you say and do.

Children and Television

The American Academy of Pediatrics urges parents to avoid television viewing for children younger than age two.[5] Research on early brain development shows that babies and toddlers have a critical need to interact directly with parents and others for healthy brain growth and to develop appropriate social, emotional, and cognitive skills. Even background TV can be disruptive. Children from heavy-television households:

- read less than other children.

- are less able to read than other children.

- have shorter attention spans.

- engage in less frequent parent-child interactions.

Pictures are important to share with your baby, as they provide visual stimulation, as well as more opportunities to comprehend and build vocabulary. It is not true that babies can only see in black and white. They see contrasts in vivid colors, such as a green frog on a light blue background or a brown cat on a yellow background. Keep this in mind when choosing books.

As noted previously, newborn babies can clearly see faces and items that are eight to 12 inches from their faces. Nature has this built in as the distance between your face and your baby's during feeding, which allows for another way to bond. So take your cue from nature and hold the book slightly away from your baby's face when showing him the pictures. However, it is not always necessary at this early stage to show the pictures. In fact, your baby will stare more at your face while you read animatedly.

Remember, sharing books with your baby should be fun, not homework. Reading time should be a happy time, with tickling of toes during play time, a snuggly blanket during quiet time, and happiness from you at all times. Create a routine that includes snuggles, smiles, and serenity. Turn off the music and TV so that your baby can really focus on the lilt of your voice, the joy that you express while reading, and the sounds and rhythms made in your particular language. Turn off the phone as well. Before starting, change diapers and wrap up your baby in a warm blanket or set him in the bouncy seat. Sit close to him as you read.

What Books Should You Read?

Just as they are fascinated by the spoken word,
children are fascinated by the written word.
The conscientious parent introduces the youngster
to books as soon as possible.
~Stan & Jan Berenstain, *The Berenstains' Baby Book*

When visiting the library, ask for help in finding the board book section. Since your young baby is simply listening and not manipulating or chewing the book, the library is a great way to get to know what kinds of books are available before you purchase ones that will eventually get chewed up, banged on, and slept with.

Although you may have heart connections to a few certain books, especially those that were favorites when you were growing up (see box "Popular Books for Babies"), there are plenty of board books available. These books are "stiff as a board and light as a feather." While feeding your baby, simply lay the book beside you and read. The pages are easy to turn and are actually made so that when you read one page, the next page pops up slightly to ensure that little ones can grasp and turn it with their little fingers.

Popular Books for Babies

- *Baby Faces,* by DK Publishing
- *Bunny My Honey,* by Anita Jeram
- *Counting Kisses,* by Karen Katz
- *Eyes, Nose, Fingers, and Toes,* by Judy Hindley
- *Goodnight, Moon,* by Margaret Wise Brown
- *Guess How Much I Love You,* by Sam McBratney
- *Hop on Pop,* or any of Dr. Seuss' early rhyming books
- *Moo Baa La La La,* by Sandra Boynton
- *Pat the Bunny,* by Dorothy Kunhardt
- *The Runaway Bunny,* by Margaret Wise Brown
- *Ten Little Fingers,* by Annie Kubler
- *The Very Hungry Caterpillar,* and other books by Eric Carle
- *Where Is Baby's Belly Button?* by Karen Katz
- *Where the Sidewalk Ends,* or other rhyming books by Shel Silverstein

---

Gather some Mother Goose or nursery rhyme books. The sing-song, rhyme structure is another way to "turn on" your baby's brain. The more language your baby hears in diverse ways, the better. Tickle songs and lullabies all develop early literacy because these are all ways that your baby hears and comprehends language.

There is no need to rush to build your own army of books. Request bookstore gift certificates, books, or nursery rhyme CDs as gifts. When buying books, pick out ones that you like, because as your baby grows, she will want her favorite books read over and over again.

Baby's on a Roll! (4-6 Months)

A house without books is like a room without windows.
~Heinrich Mann

Seemingly in the blink of an eye, your little one is no longer a newborn. She will surprise you with the speed in which she reaches developmental milestones. You will begin to notice her developing more personality characteristics, sleeping habits, and a preference for that extra-special "lovey." These milestones make parents and grandparents jump and cheer, make long-distance phone calls, and take tons of video and still pictures. Let's examine how the milestones from four to six months will add to the ways in which you "book play" with your baby.

During this time, your baby will be gaining strength. She will hold her head more steadily. When placed on her tummy, she will do a "mini push-up" using her arms for support. As she continues to do these push-ups, she will develop the upper body strength that is necessary for rolling over and sitting up. During this tummy time, prop up books for your baby to see as she examines her world. Everything looks different to your baby now that she can hold her head steady. There's a lot to take in!

As your baby masters flipping and rolling over, she will realize that her newfound skill enables her to get books and toys that are slightly out of reach. Lie on your belly and encourage your baby to roll toward a book. You can help her roll with a gentle push or achieve a reach by moving the book closer. After just a few tries, your baby will be rolling and flipping across the floor. (Time for baby gates!)

For your four- to six-month-old, choose a board book with simple, bright pictures. She will especially enjoy a book with faces. Stand the book up just a little bit away from your baby, or hold it up and point to the pictures and name them. Your baby is learning to focus at a longer range, and the bright pictures will encourage this.

Don't worry about boring your baby. Your voice and enthusiasm will make her happy. Watch for signs of a favorite picture: kicking legs, smiles, babbling, and giggles. If you are borrowing this book from the library, it may be one to add to your personal library.

Reading is to the mind what exercise is to the body.
~Richard Steele

The babbling that your baby has begun to do is the result of imitating the sounds that she has heard in the environment and from hearing books. Babies pick up and remember the sounds that they hear, and they lose sounds not needed in their own language. This is what we like to call "Parent Report Card Time," as you are getting feedback from your baby—kind of like a grade on a test. The more you read, speak, and sing to your baby, the more she will babble back.

Effects of Recurrent Ear Infections on Language Development

Most children will have at least one ear infection, also called *otitis media*, before their first birthday. Between 10-20% will have three or more infections. Fluid in the ear may last an average of a month per occurrence and is especially common in children under age two. This can cause mild hearing loss, which is of greatest concern when children are developing language skills. According to the U.S. Department of Education, a child with mild hearing loss "may not hear or may hear very faintly the soft sounds at the beginnings and ends of words, such as the 's' in 'sun' and the 't' in 'cat,' and words spoken quickly such as 'and.'" A child with moderate hearing loss will "have trouble hearing most speech sounds," making it difficult for him to emulate them.[6] Because the signs of hearing loss may be subtle in a baby's first year, parents should be especially conscientious about having their baby's hearing checked if he has repeated ear infections so that language development is unaffected. Learn more about ear infections in Chapter 5.

At this age, look for books that have textured pictures: fuzzy kittens, scaly fish, and smooth egg shells. Babies learn through all of their senses. Holding your baby in your lap, take her hand and run it over the "touchable" pictures. She will be enchanted. And again, a new experience will help her baby brain to connect and grow, which enables her to reach the next milestone with ease.

When your baby reaches about six months of age, you may want to begin buying her favorite books (as opposed to borrowing them from the library). This is the beginning of a very oral time for babies—drooling, putting everything in their mouths, and blowing raspberries. Being exposed to germs from library books is something your baby does not need (nor do you want to be fined if you return the books damaged).

Some books are to be tasted, others to be swallowed,
and some few to be chewed and digested.
~Francis Bacon

Repeat, Repeat, Repeat! (7-8 Months)

Beginning around seven months, your baby will want to repeat a play-time activity again and again—singing a song, carrying around the same truck, playing pat-a-cake. There is a method to this madness. Your baby's brain gets stronger and smarter every time an action is repeated. So when you are asked for the umpteenth time to read the same story, do it. Your little one's brain is connecting somewhat like a spider's web. Each time you repeat any activity, the web becomes stronger and, in this way, makes baby's mind grow.

If you have not established a bedtime ritual that includes reading, between the ages of seven to eight months is a prime time. Even if your baby doesn't look at each picture or is on his back kicking or rolling around in his bed, keep reading about three to four short books (one to two words per page). After you have read a story, stack it neatly in a corner of the crib or between the mattress and the crib bars. Soon, books will become part of the secure feeling at sleep time. And when he wakes up in the morning, what is he going to do? "Read" the books from the previous night! Then, you can wake up slowly to the babble of your baby "reading" and talking with happiness. After all, happiness is a warm book!

Many parents become dismayed if their babies will not sit still to listen to a book or look at the pictures. Don't worry about it. Just keep reading! The important thing is that your baby is hearing the language. He will learn proper "book etiquette" soon enough. For now, let him roll on the floor, chase the cat, or look out the window as you read.

Building Vocabulary (9-12 Months)

I would be most content if my children grew up to be
the kind of people who think decorating consists
mostly of building enough bookshelves.
~Anna Quindlen

By the time your baby is a year old, he will have developed quite an extensive "listening vocabulary." He understands many things that you say regarding pet names, preferred toys, food and drink, family members, familiar pictures, and animal sounds. Your baby's vocabulary is being expanded at an incredible rate right now. In a notebook or baby book, write the date and list the words that your growing baby uses. Also, write the words that your little one understands, even if he cannot say them. It is fun to go back and review these lists even a few weeks later to see how much progress your baby has made in language development.

Your baby's mind has made many connections between words and the objects that they represent. It is exciting when your little one can identify a dog in a story, but for him to translate that into a real life dog is a huge milestone. Point out things from your stories when you come across them in your day-to-day routines. A walk, a trip to the zoo, or a visit to Grandma's house allows for occasions to verbalize pieces from favorite stories and words that he is learning.

Starting at around nine to 10 months, to increase both expressive and listening vocabulary, create opportunities for your little cutie to interact with stories when you read to him. Asking *where* questions is a good start. "Where is the pig?" "Where is the girl?" To take comprehension and verbalization to the next level, turn the question around a bit. Ask *what* questions, like "What is this?" while pointing to a picture. This allows for your child to express vocabulary and build upon it. Another way for your child to actively engage in the story is to ask *who* questions. "Who is Johnny?" "Who is at the zoo?" Ask questions that have simple, one-word answers. Even though your baby may understand much, his little mouth, tongue, and teeth (or lack of) limit the ability to answer. But just as you see him progressing in his ability to walk, run (usually away from you!), climb steps, and pull a toy, his mouth muscles are also getting stronger with each speaking effort and verbal performance.

Do not expect your baby to articulate perfectly. He is not physically able to do it. When your baby says a word like "hay" for "happy," accept this word without reprimand. However, do repeat it correctly in a small sentence: "You are happy?" This reinforces his attempt in a positive way, models the correct enunciation, and adds to his vocabulary. Likewise, when he makes a wide generalization, like calling anything round a "ball," model the word accurately. Pumpkins, rocks, ornaments, and wheels can all be referred to as a ball. Simply adjust to the correct word in a short sentence: "The pumpkin is big."

Language- and Literacy-Building Activities

A book that is shut is but a block.
~Thomas Fuller

When you deem that your baby is ready to participate, choose some of these fun games and giggles-and-grins activities to make books—and your baby's world—come alive:

- Create voices for the story characters, such as a low, "growly" voice for a wolf, crocodile, or fox; a high-pitched voice for a fairy; a squeaky voice for a mouse.

- Pretend to pick a favorite food from a picture of a picnic or breakfast table. Name the food and pretend to eat it with gusto: "Yum! I love red strawberries!" Ask your baby what food she wants. She may attempt the word or simply point. Respond with a short, simple sentence that includes the word: "Here is your glass of milk. Drink it up!"

- Imitate animal actions. Make a little inchworm with your finger. Make him crawl to your baby, up her leg, and to her neck or belly with a tickle. Flap your arms for a bird. Pant for a dog. Jump for a bunny.

- Get into the characters. For a giant, stomp your feet. For a chick or bird, clap your pointer finger and thumb together to imitate a beak. Hop for a frog.

- Imitate machines: "toot-toot" for a train, "buzz" for an airplane, a grumble for construction vehicle engines.

- Vary your pitch to signal opposites: high, low. Up, down. Off, on. In, out.

- Allow your baby to turn pages or even hold the book. She may not let you finish reading a page, but that's okay. Just tell the story that you remember, or make it up for a story that is new.

- Make the story come alive. When reading action words, get into the show! Jump, clap, bite (pretending), stomp, and kick your legs out. Stick your thumb in a pretend pie and pull it out dramatically. Tip your hat, brush your hair.

- While reading number books, show the numbers with your fingers. Try to manipulate your baby's fingers to show the numbers, too.

- Some books have puppets available to go along with the story. These are a wonderful investment that you and your baby will use for years. Also, look for bath mitts that may go along with a favorite story or song.

- Explore poetry. The rhyme, cadence, and sing-song tone are interesting for your baby to listen to.

- Don't forget tickle time. Laughter is the first step in developing a sense of humor. Watch for silly stories or pictures, and add a tickle for emphasis.

- Weave books into your everyday activities. Pack some books in the diaper bag to have on errands. Read a book about doctors before an appointment. Tie a cloth book onto the grocery cart. There are even waterproof books for the pool, beach, or tub.

- Learn some sign language for common pictures and actions. Consistently demonstrate while reading. Soon your baby will begin to imitate you, eventually making the sign even before you do.

- Exaggerate. Elongate and dramatize recurring phrases like "hippity-hop" or "round and round." Cover your mouth with your hand when the character does something naughty. Cheer when someone wins a race.

- Read things in your baby's environment, such as traffic signs, food labels, and menu items. Let your child see that the world is made up of words!

Raising a Future Writer—and Computer User

Language is the blood of the soul into which thoughts run
and out of which they grow.
~Oliver Wendell Holmes

Your baby may be a few years away from writing his name, but babies older than six months can get an early start on building their fine motor skills and eye-hand coordination, which will help them make the transition to writing that much easier. It will also make them better prepared to work on computers and manipulate a mouse.

These fun activities will help your baby with his future writing, typing, and mouse-moving:

- Introduce your baby to blocks. Playing with blocks provides many wonderful teaching opportunities about spatial relationships (figuring out how objects fit in space), as well as cause and effect. When your baby picks up blocks, he is developing strong fingers. Ask your baby to hand blocks to you. Build a structure, and let him knock it down. Such squeals of laughter will ensue!

The Long-Term Benefits of Promoting Literacy from Birth

According to researchers at the Bernard van Leer Foundation in the Netherlands, "Studies demonstrate that reading to pre-school children, books in the home and children's own direct experience with print are all facilitative precursors for language development, reading and success in school."[7]

Reading is the major foundational skill for all school-based learning. After all, one has to read in order to learn science, math, philosophy, social studies, and so on. Reading and writing skills continue to develop our whole lives, but the period from birth to age eight is the most critical for literacy development.

Many early literacy skills need to be learned by the time a child enters kindergarten and actually learns to read. These conventions of print include an understanding that print goes from left to right and top to bottom, knowing where the story begins and ends, realizing that books tell stories, understanding that a picture goes with the story, alphabet knowledge, and phonological awareness. All of these skills are built on one another. Take tiny steps with your baby and books. A journey of a thousand miles begins with the first step, or in this instance, the first page!

- Establish a low kitchen cabinet or drawer with non-breakable bowls, pots, measuring cups and spoons, and wooden spoons. The act of taking objects out of the cabinet will strengthen fingers.

- Read board books with lift-the-flaps. These books are of the simple peek-a-boo type with large flaps so that your baby can lift them up for story surprises like lions, bunnies, or dogs. Allow your baby to turn the pages.

- Buy construction or colored paper. Set out some during play time, and teach your baby to tear and crumple. Have a basket, bucket, or bag ready to fill. Discuss colors when the moment is right. ("Mommy is tearing a blue sheet. Here is a green piece for you.") You may even see your baby transfer objects from one hand to the other. He may also show a preference for a certain color by choosing it over and over.

- In the bathtub or kiddie pool, provide cups, sprinkling cans, and various measuring cups for your baby to hold and pour. For more play, encourage your baby to wash a doll's hair. Scrubbing and pouring water on the doll's hair allows for hand strengthening.

- When your baby is old enough to eat finger foods, place small pieces of food, like Cheerios or raisins, on his high-chair tray, and let him pick them up by himself. Hopefully, he will find his mouth, but be prepared when he also practices his throwing skills!

- Under close supervision, set up an area for coloring. One of the best ways to do this is to get a paper (blank or from a coloring book) and tape it onto the highchair tray. Give your baby only two (washable!) crayons, and demonstrate coloring on the paper. You may need to put a crayon in a little hand and, while holding baby's hand, make a mark on the paper. After a few of these lessons, your baby will catch on quickly. Don't forget to "ooh" and "ahh" over his first masterpieces. (You might want to date them and put them in a baby book.)

Caution: Your baby cannot help putting crayons in his mouth. Mouthing objects is another way that babies get information to their brains—as a sort of 3-D picture. Don't take away the coloring time, but make it short and under close supervision. When necessary, take the crayon from your baby's mouth and say, "Color. Pretty. You do it."

Conclusion

As with all baby milestones, start small. Each day's developments build on the next. Let your baby's interests guide your play time, but continue offering finger-strengthening activities. Remember, all of the flowers of tomorrow are in the seeds of today.

When Mike noticed that they received several board books as baby shower gifts, he rolled his eyes at first, expecting that they'd sit in storage until his son was a toddler. But Samantha soon taught him what she'd learned—that children should be read to from the very first months of life. The other night, Samantha peeked into little Jared's room to see Mike giving a spirited reading of Hop on Pop *to his son. It warmed Samantha's heart to see that Mike shared her hopes of raising a reader!*

Chapter 4
Vision: Seeing Is Believing—and Bonding

Babies can see inside your soul.
~Bill Engel

Before she is born, your baby is preparing for the "real world," particularly through development of her five senses. Due to its complexity, vision is the last sense to develop in the womb. Your baby's thin eyelids remain fused shut until about the 26th week, allowing the retina to fully develop. While watching a sonogram after week 26, you may see your baby's eyes open and even blink!

From that time until her birth at approximately 40 weeks, there are plenty of opportunities for her to look around, listen, and stretch her muscles. Surprisingly, the womb is not completely dark. As early as 18 weeks, with the eyes still closed, a baby's retina can detect a small amount of light filtering through her mother's tissue. If you shine a flashlight on your growing girth, your baby may move away because her eyes are sensitive. She may even see light filtering through on a sunny day. At 37 weeks, researchers have found that shining a bright light on your belly shows the baby's heart rate speeding up in response to the stimulus, or she will even turn toward the light as if she is curious about this new phenomenon. Don't have too much fun with this! Bright lights can damage a fetus's or newborn's eyes (especially if she's premature).

After birth, your baby begins to learn about her world immediately with all five of her senses, even though they're still quite immature. Just like in the womb, vision is the least developed sense; your baby is not born with a fully functioning pair of eyes.[1] She can detect light, shapes, and movement as a newborn, but it can take years

49

for her to develop the visual skills to equal adult levels. However, playing games and having toys that stimulate eyesight can help. If babies do not get enough visual stimulation, it may actually affect the quality of their future vision, or their vision may develop very slowly. Babies who are stimulated to develop good early vision will enjoy enhanced curiosity, concentration, attentiveness, and—especially important—a stronger parent/child bond.

When babies look beyond you and giggle, maybe they're seeing angels.
~Eileen Elias Freeman, *The Angels' Little Instruction Book*

Crossed Eyes Are Common (0-2 Months)

At birth, you may notice your baby's eyes "wandering" apart from each other or becoming "cross-eyed." This is very normal, and there is no need for immediate alarm. This condition is called *strabismus*, and it occurs when the muscles of one eye pull more than the muscles of the other eye. Tell your pediatrician if this happens with your baby, but most likely, he or she will announce that even though your baby's eyes are not moving in tandem or are moving in random ways, by the time he is one to two months old, his eye muscles will strengthen and begin to work together.

Ensure that your baby's vision, as well as the rest of his development, is on track by monthly visits to the pediatrician. According to the American Optometric Association, baby's eyes should be examined every six months. You may wonder how the doctor tests a baby's eyes when baby can't even speak, but there are many ways to test for astigmatism, impaired eye movement, farsightedness, nearsightedness, and other eye health problems. Although these problems are uncommon, if they do occur, they can be more easily corrected with early detection and before they affect your baby's learning ability and total development.

As mentioned in Chapter 3, a newborn baby is only able to see objects from eight to 12 inches in front of his face. His eye muscles aren't able to consistently focus. Baby's peripheral vision is also very underdeveloped at birth but develops rapidly in the first few weeks of life. Your baby's eyes see about 40 times worse than an adult with good vision. As your baby receives more visual stimulation from you and the world around him, his vision-related nerve cells will start to connect with other nerve cells, allowing him to see better.

So with his minimal vision, what does baby like to look at? Studies have shown that by a few days after birth, babies already prefer looking at designs that resemble faces.[2] They are fascinated by the soft contours of a face, with its dark eyebrows, hairline, lip color, and eye color. A beard or mustache is especially intriguing. Babies will also look longer at their own mother's face than those of strangers. He may recognize you by your hairstyle or the contour of your chin. Baby will study your face and eyes so much that it feels like he can see your soul and spirit! He will also see objects in black and white better, as he can only detect large contrasts between dark and light. He is physically unable to distinguish between similar colors, like orange and red. Busy patterns at this early age are too complicated.

You might be surprised to read that vision is a *learned* skill. Your baby is born with a complete visual system but must

Glossary

Amblyopia: "lazy eye"; causes reduced vision in one eye if not treated early

Cataracts: clouding of the eye's lens

Hyperopia: farsightedness; inability to focus on things up close

Melanin: naturally occurring pigments responsible for the dark color of skin, hair, and eyes

Myopia: nearsightedness; inability to focus on things at a distance

Object permanence: the understanding that things continue to exist even if they're out of sight

Pterygium: abnormal mass of tissue over the cornea of the eye that obstructs vision

Spatial awareness: being aware of oneself in space and in relation to objects around one

Strabismus: "crossed eyes"; when both eyes cannot be directed at the same object at the same time

Stranger anxiety: distress experienced by children when exposed to unfamiliar people

Tracking: observing or monitoring the course of something in motion

learn to see. If your baby's vision is working well, it guides him in nearly all that he does, from seeing bright, contrasting colors to noticing faces, toys, or the family pet. If vision problems are not detected and treated in the first three years of his development, vision impairment may last a lifetime.

Introduce vision-stimulating activities when baby is alert and playful. Remember, babies are just little humans with likes and dislikes, periods of alertness and times of boredom. If you see your baby showing disinterest, save game time for later. Frustration and boredom shut down the intelligent part of the baby's mind, kind of like when you have a busy day and can't find your car keys. Play time will increase every day, so keep on your toes anticipating what to play next.

Following are some "games" that you can play with your newborn to help his eyesight develop:

- One activity that helps baby's eyes gain strength is called "tracking." Hold a simple rattle or toy about eight inches away from your baby's face. Rattle it a bit to take his attention away from your face and refocus it on the toy. Move the toy from side to side a short distance and watch how he tracks it. Tracking also helps to build up neck muscles.

- In another variation on tracking, lock eyes with your baby and slowly move your head from side to side. Because your baby is enthralled with faces, his little eyes will follow your slow, simple movements. By the end of two months, both of your baby's eyes will begin moving together.

- Get some black and white infant visual stimulation flashcards from the Internet (such as at GeniusBabies.com) or from baby stores (or make your own by drawing bold shapes on white paper with a thick black marker). Tape or safety pin one of the flashcards to the back of the seat where your baby can see it while in the car. Or place the cards in areas that have little contrast and can be boring to your baby, such as on the ceiling or the walls around him. You can even attach

Protect Baby's Eyes from the Sun

Sun protection is a must to protect your little one's eyes. Exposure to the sun in the first 10 years of life is linked to the development of cataracts, cancer of the surface of the eye, and *pterygium*—a thin film that covers the surface of the eye and obstructs vision. Purchase sunglasses with both UVA and UVB protection that will keep sun out of your baby's eyes. Special baby sunglasses are designed to stay on baby's head. Also make sure that your baby wears a hat with a three-inch brim outside. (A baseball cap is good.) This will help block indirect sun, which can enter the eyes around the edges of sunglasses.

them to his mobile. Change the contrast cards often to kindle some excitement. As with all things, easy does it. Just a few cards will do.

- As noted in the previous chapter, it's never too early to read to your baby. Purchase or borrow some special books with contrasting colors especially designed to stimulate baby's early vision.

Continue playing these games with your newborn for brief periods about five times a day. Start with baby steps, and soon your baby will be seeing everything, including the spilled cat food or a bug on the grass.

Baby Henry's parents began to notice that he always looked like he was crying, even when he was happy. He'd often have tears in his eyes, and he'd wake up with them crusted shut and oozing pus. Alarmed, his parents took him to the pediatrician, who diagnosed a blocked tear duct, a common condition that affects as many as one-third of all infants. Henry's parents were instructed to massage the area between his eye and nose several times a day and to apply warm compresses. They were told that if the condition continued by the time Henry was six to eight months old, he might require surgery to probe the tear duct. Fortunately, the massage and warmth cleared up Henry's condition within three months.

The World Comes into Focus (3-4 Months)

Between three and four months, the colors in your baby's life become more distinguishable. She is also increasing her ability to perceive depth. This allows her to see how far away a toy, the dog, or a sibling is from her. She is also gaining better control of her arms. These two simultaneous developments create a wardrobe hazard—dangling earrings, hair, necklaces, blouses with big buttons, and the dog's collar tags will definitely be noticed by your curious little one, leading to plenty of pulls and tugs. At this age, your baby may notice the mobile above her bed and try to bat at it.

Find toys like little "gym sets" that baby can lie under and practice batting. You can even make a simple batting toy by tying a string onto a favorite brightly colored toy. Hold it over her and encourage her to bat at it. Demonstrate a gentle swipe with your hand. Then take her hand and bat at the toy. Do this a few times each day, keeping an eye out for signs of boredom. (Be sure to keep the toy out of baby's reach when you're not in the immediate vicinity.)

Visual stimulation created by a loving parent creates opportunities for your baby's curiosity, concentration, and attentiveness to develop. Don't forget to talk during this play time. Baby is growing quickly, so use every available minute to advance her mind in all possible ways.

"Look, Ma, I've Got Hands!" (5-6 Months)

*One of the most wonderful things in nature is a glance of the eye;
it transcends speech; it is the bodily symbol of identity.*
~Ralph Waldo Emerson

Toward the end of five months and moving into the sixth month, your baby can see as far as 15 feet away. His depth perception is improving, and he can distinguish colors even better. He will also discover his hands. ("Wow! Look at those! I can make them move or shake a toy!") You will be thrilled to hear your baby vocalize his excitement through coos, raspberries, vowel sounds, and laughter, as if he is holding a secret dialogue with his new discoveries. Be sure to respond—he is trying to carry on a primitive conversation with you, too!

Your baby is also learning the idea of "object permanence." He understands that even though he may not see something (like Mommy's face behind her hands) or only part of something (like the corner of a book sticking out from under a blanket), the item is still there. At this age, the classic "peek-a-boo" game is thrilling for your baby. He will giggle continuously during this play-time activity as if he's super surprised each time you reveal your face from behind your hands. Get a little creative during peek-a-boo to intensify the visual learning and brain development. Find a small towel and use it to cover your face. Change colors of towels. Cover a favorite toy with a towel and then flip the towel off to reveal the toy. Your baby will quickly try to pull off the towel by himself to get to the toy. This is also a perfect activity for siblings to play with baby, as they will delight in the positive reaction they receive from their little brother or sister.

Although your baby is fascinated with hands and toys, the mere discovery of his world doesn't end there. He is now able to locate an object, as well as determine its size and shape. The brain connections are now strong enough for these messages to travel from his brain to his hand, spurring him to reach for an interesting item, although he may not always grasp it the first time, as he is still learning to judge distances. Once he grasps the object, it will often be put into his mouth.

> ## The InfantSEE® Program
>
> InfantSEE®, launched by the American Optometric Association in partnership with The Vision Care Institute of Johnson & Johnson Vision Care, Inc., is a national program designed to provide no-cost eye and vision assessments to children under the age of one year. Former President Jimmy Carter and Former First Lady Rosalynn Carter are honorary spokespersons. Visit http://infantsee.org to find an optometrist near you who participates in the InfantSEE® program.

Here are some more games to encourage vision development after five months of age:

- Now's the time to get out those colorful toys that squeak, crackle, crinkle, rattle, and roll which you received at your baby shower. Lay these toys around your baby as he plays on the floor or in a bouncy seat. Let him examine them for a long time. Inside his brain, he is making an internal filing cabinet for the toys: one folder for yellows, one folder for purples, and one folder for soft, chewy ones. Pick up a toy that he has been studying and place it in the palm of his hand. Shake it gently and show excitement at the noise. Continue this a few times, and soon your baby will be doing it on his own.

- Place your baby under a gently whirling ceiling fan. His developed length of vision allows him to see this contraption, which blows soft air that he can feel on his face.

- Prop a baby mirror (not a heavy one that can fall over and hurt your baby) near your child during play time. He will be fascinated by the beautiful baby in the mirror. He will reach for the "playmate," talk to him, and laugh at him. Sometimes your baby will get mad or sad that the "playmate" doesn't respond.

- Take your baby outside in her stroller while you play ball with baby's older sibling. He will watch you and the movement intensely.

- Inside, roll a spool of thread to your baby from short distances.

- Put a little ball (watch for choking hazards) in a bowl and move the bowl to make the ball move while your baby watches. Give your baby a spoon so that he can develop eye-hand coordination and move the ball around on his own. This will work with a cake pan as well.

It's Toy-Dropping Time (7-8 Months)

It's not what you look at that matters; it's what you see.
~Henry David Thoreau

By this age, your baby has learned the game of "cause and effect." One only has to wait until mealtime to see this demonstrated by baby's annoying game of "drop the cup"! As your baby drops food, toys, cups, and blankets from her high chair, car seat, or stroller, she will actually watch the item float (or plunge) to the ground and see it land. Then she'll automatically look to you to rescue the ditched item. This game can go on seemingly forever. Keep in mind that baby's brain connections grow stronger every time this happens. She learns this cause-and-effect insight: *Toys drop to the ground. They might make a noise. I get a reaction from Mom. And then I can do it all over again!*

Janice knew it was time to invest in a drop cloth when her eight-month-old, Tessa, started making a game out of every meal. Pureed peas went straight to the floor. Mashed sweet potatoes made a beautiful mess. And Cheerios were great for feeding to the dog. At first, Janice got mad. Why did Tessa insist on making such a mess? But then she read that this was actually a learning activity for her daughter. Knowing that this fun—albeit messy—game was actually growing her baby's brain gave Janice a different perspective. With a "splat mat" and an organic cleaner in hand, Janice cheerfully cleaned up the signs that Tessa was a budding engineer!

Your baby is becoming mobile, and everything she sees is a treasure to inspect. She may be scooting along on her bottom, army crawling using her arms, and even pulling herself up. This means that she has access to many more things around the house: candles, books, vases of flowers, and dog food. It is time to update the baby proofing in your house. Don't forget to keep the bathroom door shut or baby-gated. The risk of drowning in the toilet or getting a hold of cleaners is high at this age. Toilet brushes, liquid soap, shampoo, and conditioner can create colorful mosaics when you turn your back for just a minute. Makeup is fun for baby, too. Mascara can be eaten, blush can be rubbed on the walls, and eye shadow can be crunched up for a beautiful picture around the sink. Also be sure to gate doorways leading to laundry rooms, stairs, the garage, and other rooms containing harmful items.

By seven to eight months, your baby sees the world almost as well as you do, and she can differentiate between even subtle colors.[3] Her short-range sight is

How the Doctor Checks Your Baby's Eyes

Your pediatrician should check for eye problems at every well-baby visit. The examination should include these procedures:[4]

- Asking you about your family's vision history (or the birth family's history, if your child is adopted and this information is known).

- Examining your baby's eyes with a penlight. The doctor should check the eyelids and eyeball, seeking signs of discharge, infection, disease, allergies, or blocked tear ducts, as well as the positioning of the eyes. The doctor will look to see if the pupils are the same size and that the eyelids aren't droopy.

- Tracking your baby's eye movement by checking her ability to fix on an object and follow it as it is moved. Your baby should be able to do this one eye at a time and with both eyes together (after the first few months).

- Observing the reflection of light from the back of baby's eyes. The doctor does this in a darkened room (which makes baby's eyes dilate) and uses a lighted instrument called an ophthalmoscope to look for a red reflex in the eyes. Abnormal reactions could be a sign of cataracts or tumors.

still better than her long-range sight, but she can recognize a favorite toy or family member across the room. This can lead to "stranger anxiety"—fear of people that she doesn't recognize. Her eyes are now about two-thirds their adult size. She is developing the neural connections that will support learning for the rest of her life. Her eye color will be close to its final color by now, although some small, subtle changes may still occur (see box "When Will I Know My Baby's Permanent Eye Color?").

Your baby will start to judge the size of objects up to three feet away. She is able to follow a sibling or pet as they walk by and may even squeal in delight. While feeding her, it is difficult sometimes to keep her focused on the job at hand because she's so busy looking at things around her. To develop perception during feedings, alternate the side you sit on. This allows for the "outside" eye to strengthen and see her hectic world. You may want to create a necklace using large beads strung on a sturdy shoelace to wear around your neck while you're feeding your baby. Using this necklace a few feedings a day will make her curious and hold her attention longer, as well as create an opportunity for developing the muscles in her fingers as she plays with it.

Baby play isn't the same as child or adult play. It is actually work for your baby! She is taking important developmental and cognitive steps. Play not only encourages vision development, but it also stimulates the learning process, creativity, language development, physical fitness, and even social skills.

Your baby will be sitting up, and that means she will be seeing many more objects to examine. Her attention span is lengthening along with her vision. Sturdy toys, snap-lock beads, take-apart toys, and nesting cups develop vision, fine motor skills, and intelligence. Play these games with your baby:

- Roll a ball back and forth.

- Stack a simple block structure together.

- Play a modified form of peek-a-boo, in which you hold up a blanket between you and your baby. This will also help your baby improve her body control, as she'll need to reach for the blanket and move it away to see you hiding behind it.

● Play pat-a-cake with your baby. At first, you may have to hold her hands and show her how to do the motions, but by the eighth or ninth month, she should be able to clap on her own. This exercise also develops "spatial awareness"—knowing where to put her hands.

Curiosity Grows the Brain (9-12 Months)

There is no end to the adventures that we can have
if only we seek them with our eyes open.
~Jawaharlal Nehru

At this age, your baby is extremely curious about everything he sees. He moves toward anything that draws his attention. He can follow rapidly moving objects like a dog running or a car driving. Stacking and take-apart toys create an opportunity to use eye-hand coordination. Very simple puzzles are great toys for baby to do with a sibling or grandparent. Remember to "moo," "baaa," or "growl" when playing with toy animals. Rumble like a diesel truck when playing with toy cars, motorcycles, and boats. Your baby will want to do this over and over again. But take heart! Each repetition is growing your baby's brain in multiple ways, such as improved vision, eye-hand coordination, fine motor skills, and verbal skills.

At this age, baby will be thrilled with remote controls. The tiny buttons are just the right size for his fingers and (ugh!) his mouth. (Pay close attention, because this is a potential choking hazard.) He will imitate you by pointing the controller at the TV (an intellectual development).

When Will I Know My Baby's Permanent Eye Color?

Most babies start life with either blue/gray eyes (in lighter-skinned babies with little melanin) or brown/black eyes (in darker-skinned babies with larger amounts of melanin). As your baby's body begins to produce melanin, it will change the color of his eyes. This can take up to three years, but for most babies, this change will be completed from around six months of age to one year. So it's possible that your blue-eyed baby could become a brown-eyed toddler. In rare cases, eye color in some people changes even in adulthood!

Your baby's ears will begin to appreciate music, and he can point to or act out the music that he wants to hear. Keep the empty CD cases in a special drawer at his level. He will study the cases intently and then choose one for you and him to dance to.

His vision at this point has become so acute that he can see even the tiniest crumb or rock. His eyes and his brain are coordinated and working together. He will crawl or scoot over to an item and, using his developing pincer grasp, promptly put it in his mouth.

Try these games with your nine- to 12-month-old to stimulate vision development:

- Playing "copycat" may be annoying to older children, but for babies, the performance is worth an Oscar. Get down on the floor and initiate a game of "Follow the Leader." At first, you follow your baby as he maneuvers around his play area. Then, encourage him to follow you. It may take a few tries for your baby to understand what you want him to do, but he will soon giggle happily and follow you around. Crawl through table legs, around the couch, and on hard floors as well as textured carpet floors. (You may want to invest in a set of knee pads for yourself with this exercise!)

- Get two non-breakable bowls and wooden spoons. First, demonstrate banging the bowl with a spoon, singing a familiar song while pounding to the beat. Then tell baby that you'll do it together. He will watch your actions and try to repeat them. Although this isn't the quietest game in the world (not recommended for apartments with thin walls), it increases eye-hand coordination, listening skills, and musical ability.

- Create a "hungry box" by getting a shoebox and covering it with brown paper. You and your little buddy can use washable markers and crayons to decorate the box. Cut a rectangular slot in the shoebox lid. Now gather up pretend food, toys, socks, brushes, etc., and teach your child to put the toys in the slot one at a time. Keep an ongoing dialogue: "Your sock is pink." "That brush fits perfectly!" Count the items as your baby puts them in. Identify the colors and the size (big, small, triangular, etc.). To bring this game to another level, find a picture of an animal or cartoon character that your baby likes, paste it on the shoebox lid, and cut a slot where the character's mouth is. Then you can "feed" Dora, Cookie Monster, or even the family pet!

*Karl sometimes felt bad that he spent so much time with his baby daughter, Lily, at the expense of his time with his older daughter, Monica, age four. But then he realized that they could now all play together! He showed Monica how she could play "Follow the Leader" with Lily. She pretended to be a kitty by pinning on a tail and having Lily try to catch it as Monica crawled around the room. Monica and Karl also looked through children's magazines together to find a picture of her favorite cartoon character, the Little Mermaid, to make a "hungry box" for Lily. They also went outside and played catch together while the baby watched from her stroller and clapped when Monica got the ball. Karl rejoiced in this newfound bonding with **both** of his daughters.*

Red Flags

The eye is the pulse of the soul.
~Thomas Adams

Fortunately, most babies' vision will develop normally, but it's good to keep your own eyes open for signs of these "red flags" that may indicate a problem. This is especially important if your baby was born prematurely or if there is a family history of childhood eye problems. Consult your pediatrician immediately if you see any of these signs:

- One of your baby's eyes moves and the other one doesn't, or one eye moves and the other moves differently.

- When your baby is older than one month, things like lights, toys, and faces don't catch her attention.

- Your baby never opens one eye.

- Droopy or bulging eyes or eyelids.

- Any kind of gunky, yellow, grey-white, or white material in the eye, or pus or crust in the eye.

- Redness that persists for more than a few days.

- Excessive eye rubbing when she isn't sleepy.

- Sensitivity to light.

- Any change in your baby's eyes from how they usually look.

After three months, the list of red flags lengthens. Consult your doctor if:

- Your baby's eyes turn way in or out and stay that way.

- You notice that your baby is unable to track a toy from side to side.

- Baby's eyes seem to jump or wiggle (almost vibrate).

- She seems to tilt her head in order to see things. This indicates that one eye is not seeing objects clearly and that she has to rely on the one good eye.

Your doctor can determine if intervention is necessary and can refer you to a medical eye specialist if appropriate.

Conclusion

Think about how many songs you know about eyes. Some well-known ones include The Who's "Behind Blue Eyes," Van Morrison's "Brown-Eyed Girl," and Peter Gabriel's "In Your Eyes." Why are there so many songs (and poems) about feeling love and admiration when looking into another's eyes? Why do animals instinctively look us in the eyes? It's because the eyes are the mirror for our feelings, our energy level, and our interests. They reveal when we're sad or angry, tell people when we're tired, or reveal our excitement for something in the environment. So be sure to keep those baby eyes healthy and sparkling. You may even write a poem or song one day about the love you see in your cutie's eyes!

Chapter 5
Hearing: Little Ears Do Big Things

Childhood is measured out by sounds and smells and sights,
before the dark hour of reason grows.
~John Betjeman

Do you remember the sounds that you heard when your baby was first born? Perhaps you heard the doctor's voice announcing your baby's gender, the shouts of joy from your spouse or your own lips, or the very first cry from your new baby's mouth. These sounds will remain in your memory forever, but your baby was not likely experiencing the same sounds at birth. Most likely, he still had some amniotic fluid in his middle ear tubes and was only hearing muffled sounds when he first emerged into the world. This may have been a blessing to him, though, as the noises outside the womb would probably have startled him at first with their intensity. To suddenly break free from spending nine months in a little cave to enter a world of bright lights, loud noise, and cold air is probably one of the biggest shocks he will ever experience! But your little one was listening to your voice in his watery world before birth. (Amazingly, he was able to hear sounds from outside your womb a mere 20 weeks after conception!) So it didn't take long before he recognized your same soothing, comforting voice after birth.

Researchers have found that babies can actually remember sounds that they heard in their mothers' wombs for more than a year after birth. According to a study by Dr. Alexandra Lamont of the Leicester University Music Research Group at the university's School of Psychology, one-year-old babies recognized a single piece of music played consistently while they were in the womb. The Child of Our Time study involved a small group of mothers playing a single piece of music to their babies for the last three months before birth. The music

Glossary

Auditory: pertaining to hearing or the ears

Congenital: present at birth

Eustachian tube: also called the auditory or pharyngotympanic tube; links the throat to the middle ear and serves to equalize pressure on either side of the eardrum

Genetic counseling: when people who are at risk of an inherited disorder are advised about the consequences and nature of their condition, the probability of developing or transmitting it, and their family-planning options

Otitis media: an inflammation of the middle ear; also known as an "ear infection" when classified as "acute"

Tele-location: identifying sounds from a distance

came from multiple genres, including pop, reggae, and classical. Some moms even reported that playing the same pieces of music for their infant that they played while the baby was in the womb actually decreased colic after birth![1]

If you're reading this book before your baby is born, think ahead to the day of your little one's birth. As soon as your baby is born, request that he be laid directly on your chest with blankets over him for warmth, and begin to talk to him softly right away. Tell him about the bedroom that you have ready for him, how long you have been waiting for him, and how beautiful he is. Your baby will be making strange faces at this time in response to the lights, sounds, and trauma around him, but these soft secrets between you and your baby will get his brain ticking and begin to build that important parent/child bond.

After you and your baby are rested from labor and delivery, continue to talk softly to him, and enlist another woman (like an aunt or grandmother) to talk to him at the same time. You may notice that your baby will most likely turn to *you!* As the amniotic fluid begins to clear from his little ears, you may also notice changes in what pitches and tones your baby responds to. The auditory (hearing) system is the most developed of all of the five senses at birth.

Of course, your baby is not accustomed to the sounds outside of the protective womb, and some noises can easily startle him. Imagine being in a foreign land and not understanding the language. Your baby is in a similar position, so he will stick close to the people who make him feel safe, and he will listen for familiar voices.

As your baby grows, "Mama" (or whatever word you use for "mother") will most likely be the first word he recognizes. When he hears the word "Mama," he soon knows who that is and that he is safe in her presence. Research shows that a baby will assign the word "Mama" only to his mother, not to just any woman. This works as well for "Daddy." Think about all of the words and sounds that he may hear thousands of times each day. Out of those millions of words, his first one will most likely be "Mama" or "Dada." (Some couples enjoy a little spirited competition in trying to get their baby to say "Mama" or "Dada" first, but don't worry—your little one will be yelling both "MOOOOOOM!" and "DAAAAAD!" for years to come!)

> *Even though her baby is now two months old, Kathy still gets a thrill every time he immediately calms at the sound of her voice. If Grandpa is holding Aidan and he begins to fuss, Kathy's "Come to Mama" is all that's needed to settle him down. It melts Kathy's heart that they already have such a beautiful bond—linked together by the mere sound of her voice.*

Early Hearing Assessment

When babies are born, it's easy to see if all exterior parts are present and accounted for: two arms, check; two legs, check; two eyes, check; two ears, check; and so on.... But it's not as evident whether all interior parts are present and functioning correctly. She has two eyes, but can they see? She has two legs, but will they walk? She has two ears, but will they hear? Fortunately, doctors have many ways of assessing these capabilities, as you've already seen in other chapters. In terms of hearing, every U.S. state and territory routinely screens hearing before newborns leave the hospital. The Centers for Disease Control and Prevention recommend that all babies be screened for hearing impairment before one month of age. Without newborn screening, hearing impairment usually is not diagnosed until two to three years old, resulting in the loss of valuable time for intervention.

Some babies are born with normal hearing but lose hearing later in their infancy or childhood due to high fevers, ear infections, injury, and even some medications, so hearing should be checked periodically, even if it is classified as "normal" at birth.

As you get to know your baby's personality, smiles, and routines, you can also pick up on her "baby language"—coos, giggles, wiggles, vocalizations, facial expressions, and gestures—that show that your baby is listening to you, other people, and the whole miracle of sounds in her new world.

If hearing loss or impairment is detected, early intervention is extremely vital because it can directly affect language development. According to the March of Dimes, three in 1,000 babies are born in the United States each year with significant, *congenital* hearing loss.[2] Detection of hearing loss before the age of six months can help prevent serious speech and language problems down the road. Babies as young as four weeks can be fitted with hearing aids.

Some hearing problems can even be predicted before birth through genetic counseling. If hearing defects run in either side of your baby's family, you may want to consider having *genetic counseling* to help prepare for any conditions that might be present in your child. Genetics are believed to cause 33% of cases of hearing impairments in infants and young children, but 90% of babies with congenital hearing impairment are born to parents who hear normally.[3]

Even if your baby's initial diagnosis reveals healthy hearing, it's important to promote hearing development in the brain by protecting her little ears. Doctors agree that "too loud" for your little angel is prolonged exposure to anything over 80 decibels. Sounds that are considered detrimental to your baby include a lawnmower or motorcycle (90 decibels), a rock concert (110 decibels), a jackhammer (130 decibels), and an ambulance siren or jet engine at take-off (119–140 decibels). Don't become alarmed, however, if you are in a loud area for a few minutes. Damage occurs when there is *prolonged* exposure to loud sounds.

Your pediatrician will continue to check your baby's auditory development at her well-baby visits. Be sure to mention any concerns that you might have, such as if she doesn't respond to loud noises like a pan dropping or the doorbell. (Other symptoms of hearing difficulties are listed later in this chapter.) If you have major concerns about your baby's hearing, schedule a longer visit with the doctor to ensure that you have enough time to get all of the information you need. (See Chapter 8 for more information on doctor visits.)

How the Ear Works

If the person you are talking to doesn't appear to be listening, be patient.
It may simply be that he has a small piece of fluff in his ear.
~Winnie the Pooh

Inside your baby's head, the Eustachian tubes connect his middle ear to the back of his throat, making a passage for fluids when he yawns or swallows. The tubes also protect the middle ear from germs that may enter into it via the throat. In addition, the tubes equalize air pressure, which will play a big part in your child's ability to balance later on. Unfortunately, babies are more prone to ear infections than older children or adults because their Eustachian tubes are short (about a half-inch) and horizontal. (Their immune systems are also less well-developed.) As babies grow, the Eustachian tubes will triple in length and become more vertical, which helps prevent ear infections as the fluid can drain more easily. But until that happens, your baby may be particularly vulnerable to infections. In fact, ear infections are the most commonly diagnosed childhood illness in the United States, second only to the common cold. More than 75% of children will have at least one ear infection by the age of three.[4]

The most common type of ear infection is formally referred to as *otitis media,* caused by fluid and bacterial buildup behind your baby's eardrum. If the Eustachian tubes are swollen due to a cold, allergy, or sinus infection, the

---

How Is a Newborn Tested for Hearing Impairment?

Two quick and painless tests are normally done on newborns:

Otoacoustic emissions (OAE) test: a small microphone connected to a computer is put in the baby's ear. It sends soft clicking noises into the ear and records the inner ear's response.

Automated auditory brainstem response (AABR) test: soft clicking noises are sent to the inner ear through little earphones. Sensors on your baby's head measure her brain-wave activity in response to the sounds.

If your baby fails to pass one of these preliminary screening tests, further testing by a hearing specialist is needed to determine if there is a problem. Up to 10% of babies will have abnormal results on their screening test but will later be diagnosed with normal hearing in follow-up tests.

fluid can become trapped in the middle ear. In this warm, wet environment, bacteria will thrive and produce pus, putting pressure on the eardrum. This pressure causes it to bulge and results in a very painful ear infection. If you suspect that your baby has an ear infection (see box "Signs of an Ear Infection"), be sure to take him to the doctor. The doctor may prescribe antibiotics or just monitor your baby's condition to see if it clears up on its own. Repeated ear infections may be treated more aggressively to prevent hearing loss (see box "Will My Baby Need Ear Tubes?").

Colds and allergies aren't the only causes of fluid buildup in the ear. Fluid can also be prevented from draining if you hold your baby in a horizontal position during feeding. Although it seems instinctive to completely recline your baby in your arms while nursing, this position actually brings more fluid into your baby's Eustachian tubes. During your stay in the hospital, you may notice nurses feeding bundled babies in an upright position, which helps reduces any "backwash" from feeding. So be sure that your baby's head is higher than his feet when he's being fed.

Signs of an Ear Infection

- Tugging on the ear
- Increased irritability or crying
- Trouble eating or sleeping
- Fluid drainage from the ear (this may be a result of the eardrum rupturing; seek medical attention right away)
- Lack of response to soft sounds
- Cold/flu symptoms, such as fever or vomiting

Early Listening (0-6 Months)

The hearing ear is always found close to the speaking tongue.
~Ralph Waldo Emerson

Your baby will spend a lot of time listening in the first few months. After all, she has a lot to figure out! *Where does one word end and another begin? Why are different tones and pitches used?* By talking with your baby, reading, singing, and playing with her, you can help her begin to unravel the hearing/language puzzle, which has many pieces and takes years to learn. Many people struggle with correct usage of language even into adulthood!

For the first few months, your baby will not be able to *tele-locate* sounds—that is, she will not be physically able to turn her head and use her eyesight to see if a sound came from a toy train or a dog barking. In the first few weeks of life, she is still a little tender and sleepy. As she "wakes up" more fully at about three weeks and her neck becomes stronger, you may notice her begin to turn her eyes slightly to one side or the other to locate a sound.

By four and a half months, your astonishing baby can recognize her own beautiful name, even if another name has the same number of syllables or stress patterns.[5] She loves to hear her own name, so when you talk to your baby, use her name frequently: "Keelin, let's put in the laundry." Or, "Keelin, you need some lunch." Or, "Keelin, the phone rang."

> *Juan's days off from the firehouse used to be quiet ones. When his wife Ilana was at work, he'd turn on the TV just for some noise. But now that he's caring for his six-month-old baby, Michael, Juan is amazed at what good company he is. Unlike his buddies at the fire station, Michael listens to every word Juan says. He giggles when Juan throws around Michael's toy dinosaur, blows bubbles when he's happy, and even pounds on his highchair tray. Juan delights in the sounds of his child playing in the house.*

As your baby moves toward six months of age and gains better control of her muscles, she is able to be propped up or to sit up in a high chair. This allows her to move her head and body to locate sounds. The ability to physically turn her body, head, and eyes toward a sound is related to motor development. As we've seen in other chapters, all of your baby's body systems are learning to work together, and each baby step is important.

Delightful Sounds (7-12 Months)

After six months of age, a baby can recognize a word that he often hears used in a sentence after his own name. He knows that "when Mama says my name, we do something." For instance, "When I hear, 'Nick, bath,' I know that it's warm, sudsy, fun time with Mama! When

Will My Baby Need Ear Tubes?

If your child has had repeated ear infections or fluid behind both eardrums for longer than three months, resulting in signif-icant hearing loss, he may be a candidate for ear tubes.[6] These plastic tubes are placed through a small surgical opening in your baby's eardrum to drain the fluid, keep infections from recurring, and restore hearing. They usually stay in for six to 12 months before falling out (or being surgically removed).

I hear, 'Nick, book,' I know that she wants to read! When she says, 'Nick, walk,' I know that it's time to go out in the stroller!" (These sentences are short to dramatize what your baby is hearing and understanding. Use full sentences when talking to your baby so that he can learn to understand correct speech.) Remarkably, in the above examples, it takes only *milliseconds* for your baby's brain to match sounds and words to images and feelings.

When you think of a cat, what words come to mind? Maybe "tail," "furry," "perky ears," "claws," and even "allergies"! As your baby nears his first birthday, he may "label" objects in his daily life, like "cat." He will understand the larger concepts of his world but is still learning the pieces and parts of objects, people, and his environment. He may not understand all of the parts of the cat, but he probably will be able to distinguish a cat's nose from a cow's nose!

Your baby's work is to play. While playing with you, or even alone, his brain is making connections between sounds and their sources: the toy car goes honk; the bell dings; the baby doll laughs. Remember that you are your baby's favorite toy! Facial expressions and actions express emotions for your baby to interpret and learn to understand. He gets to communicate with you throughout the day, which is beneficial for your baby's brain, and especially his auditory development.

Babies love to create their own sounds, and they delight in playing with objects that make noise. Let your baby bang blocks together or shake his toys around in a plastic bucket or pan. Encourage his interest in music by playing child-sized instruments with him, such as tambourines, mara-cas, and xylophones. Sing silly songs about animals and vehicles, and imitate the sounds that they make. Introduce your baby to all of the delightful noises in his environment!

Informal Hearing Check

We have two ears and one mouth
so that we can listen twice as much as we speak.
~Epictetus

When your baby nears the three month mark, add informal hearing tests into your weekly routine. This is an easy, effective way for you to see if any hearing difficulties may be present. Choose three to four noisemakers, like a bell, rattle, squeaky toy, etc. During active play time, put these toys behind your back. Don't let your baby see them, because then her play time will be spent trying to roll or scoot around you to satisfy her curiosity of what is in your hands.

While your baby is playing, or even in the middle of talking to her, unobtrusively put one hand behind your back and ring the bell or create other toy noises. Your baby should stop playing and turn toward the general direction of the sound. Look to see if: (1) she hears the sound, (2) she is able to locate the general direction that the sound is coming from, and (3) she can distinguish between different pitches and tones.

Keep a chart of these informal tests. Write down the date, what toys or sounds you used, and how your baby reacted. She may be able to hear some sounds or pitches but not others, and this will change as she gets older. Note whenever she has an ear infection, which can affect the quality of her hearing. In this way, you can accurately report any changes or concerns to your pediatrician, and the problem can be addressed at the earliest time possible.

Malika was devastated when her daughter was diagnosed with a hearing impairment when she was just a few weeks old. She pictured her daughter living in a silent world, never able to interact with her hearing parents or other children. But Malika's fears were put to rest when Jasmine responded well to her new hearing aids. At almost a year old, Jasmine is now babbling and laughing like Malika had always hoped she would. With appropriate and early intervention, Jasmine's prognosis is excellent, and her future is bright.

Signs of Impairment

Below are some signs of hearing impairment in babies. This short list is not all-inclusive. If any symptoms are a cause for concern, even if they're not on this list, be sure to report them to your doctor right away.

- *0-2 Months:* doesn't startle or cry at loud noises, like a siren, a dog barking loudly, or crashing thunder; doesn't stop moving or crying in response to your voice. Your baby will cry a lot at this early age, but you should be able to see him become somewhat relieved when you talk to him.

- *3-4 Months:* doesn't turn eyes in the general direction of a sound; appears to move his head, even slightly, to the right or left to hear; isn't soothed by your voice; doesn't gurgle or coo.

- *5-6 Months:* doesn't notice you until he sees you. If you are coming up the stairs to get your crying baby after a nap while calling his name, see if he settles down, knowing that your voice means you are coming to get him.

- *7-8 Months:* isn't babbling or trying to vocalize. Your baby should start making consonant and vowel sounds like "mamamama" or "babababa." Lack of attempts to vocalize may indicate that your baby has not heard these sounds and therefore isn't inspired to try to talk back.

- *9-12 Months:* hasn't said simple words yet, like "Mama," "Dada," "bye-bye," or a pet's name.

Earwax—What's That?

Earwax is a natural substance secreted by the ear to trap dirt, dust, and other particles that could damage the eardrum. After the smooth, damp earwax dries, it is moved toward the front of the ear where it can be removed with a washcloth or a clean fingertip. Sometimes earwax accumulates faster than the body can move it out of the ear canal. This produces earwax buildup, which can cause pain and affect hearing. If you suspect that your baby has an overabundance of earwax, never try to remove it yourself, as you can damage the inner ear. Have it removed by your pediatrician.

72

Conclusion

*If we can discover the meaning in the trilling of a frog,
perhaps we may understand why it is for us not merely noise
but a song of poetry and emotion.*
~Adrian Forsyth

There are so many wonderful sounds in our world—birds singing, frogs ribbitting, bugs chirping—but hearing our loved ones' voices is a gift that keeps on giving. The sound of your voice is the most beautiful music to your baby's ears! So be sure that she can hear you to the best of her ability by being alert to any signs of hearing loss or ear pain. And protect her little ears from loud noises that can damage her hearing. Talk to her, sing to her, hum to her, and even cry along with her! Fill your baby's world with delightful and soothing sounds.

Chapter 6

Motor Skills: From Crawling to Walking to...Watch Out!

The one thing children wear out faster than shoes is parents.
~John J. Plomp

You have probably heard all of the statistics and bad news about obesity in America. Adult and child obesity rates are skyrocketing. In many houses, there are TVs in almost every room. Rare is the family home without several computers, video game systems, MP3 players, and DVD players. We don't even need to leave the house to play our favorite sports, thanks to computer programs that simulate activities like tennis and golf. However, as is being reported, with this vastly entertaining technology comes a big price tag—the diminished health of our families. As games and activities are introduced in this chapter, remember that *you* are your child's first teacher and model in everything. If your child sees you being a "couch potato," what intrinsic value is he going to place on activity? If you have let the "active" part of you slide, now is the time to get busy—not only for your own health, but for that of your baby, who absolutely adores you and needs you.

What does physical exercise have to do with growing your baby's brain? Research indicates that regular activity "increases the number of capillaries within the brain, which, in turn, facilitate the absorption of nutrients and the elimination of waste products."[1] And with more ways to deliver nutrients to the brain, its performance is tip-top. Thus, helping your baby to be active and encouraging him to meet those milestones when it comes to developing motor skills will also help his brain to become as accomplished as his body! Plus, giving your baby an early start when it comes to physical activity can pay off in larger dividends down the road. The Robert Wood Johnson Foundation reports that "kids who are more physically active tend to perform better academically."[2] So playing is important for physical fitness and health, as well as for brain development.

> *Abby's sister called with great news: her 10-month-old daughter was already walking! Although Abby was thrilled for her sister and her precious niece, she couldn't help but be a little alarmed as well. After all, her little Dustin had just turned a year old, and he still hadn't taken his first step! Sure, he was cruising around the furniture like a madman, but when it came to independent walking, he just didn't seem ready. And now his younger cousin was already taking steps. Abby wondered if there was something wrong with Dustin. Should she call the doctor? Was there something that she could do to help him to walk faster? Was her darling boy normal? She couldn't help but worry that he was "behind."*

What Are Motor Skills?

> *Good, old-fashioned play and movement are the best contributors to brain development.*
> ~Rae Pica, *A Running Start*

Infant muscle development starts at the head and works its way down your baby's body. Her physical movement is classified into two categories: gross motor skills and fine motor skills. Gross motor skills involve the brain, nervous system, and large muscles working together to create an action like jumping, clapping, and throwing a bottle or food off the highchair tray. It includes the use of large muscles in the legs and arms. Gross motor skills are used to crawl, cruise, walk, and run.

Fine motor skills involve using small movements, like fingers grasping a piece of food, pushing toes to move toward a toy, rotating wrists and fingers to manipulate an object, and positioning the lips and tongue to babble and blow raspberries (that will eventually evolve into conversation!). Everyday endeavors such as buttoning buttons, holding a cup, turning a doorknob, tying shoes, and using utensils are all ways in which your baby will use her fine motor skills.

You'll see a very rapid development of both the gross and fine motor skills during the first year of life. At first, you will see your baby holding her head up unsteadily during tummy time or while you are holding her. While in your arms, she may push you with her feet as in a walking or stepping motion. Your little one will gain strength every day, which will be evident during dressing and diaper changes. She will be kicking and flailing her arms when she's just a few weeks old.

Glossary

Fine motor skills: involve the small muscles of the body, such as those used for writing, picking up small objects, and buttoning buttons

Gross motor skills: involve the large muscles of the body, such as those used for walking, kicking, and throwing a ball

Shaken Baby Syndrome: brain injury in babies caused by violent shaking that induces the brain to rebound against the skull, which can lead to swelling, bleeding in the brain, severe brain damage, and death

Exercise with Your Newborn (0-3 Months)

As a parent, you have an obligation to spend as much time as possible at play with your child. The sense of security, the self-confidence, the mental and physical exercise and the development of group spirit which these play sessions will encourage in your offspring are vastly important contributions to the child's general well-being.
~Stan & Jan Berenstain, *The Berenstains' Baby Book*

To maximize the development of these muscles, your baby and you both need exercise. Take things lightly at first, as your baby and you are both exhausted after birth and just getting used to each other. The house seems strange to your baby after the comfort of your womb, and there is no routine established yet. You're most likely feeling frumpy and lumpy as you gaze at your post–pregnancy body. So everything should be done very gently in terms of playing with your

Jiggling vs. Shaking Your Baby

Because of the publicity that has been given to Shaken Baby Syndrome—when a baby's head is whipped back and forth, resulting in brain damage and often death—many parents are fearful of moving their babies around too much. But there are major differences between "jiggling" your baby and shaking him aggressively. According to Dr. Karp in *The Happiest Baby on the Block*:[3]

- Healthy jiggling movements are fast but *tiny*. The baby's head only moves one to two inches from side to side, rather than flailing about.

- The baby's head always stays in alignment with the body during jiggling. With Shaken Baby Syndrome, there's a "whipping" motion involved—the body goes in one direction, while the head goes in another.

Small jiggling motions made when you are in a good mood (not angry) can help calm your baby and add fun to play time.

newborn. As the weeks and months pass, you can slowly add to the difficulty, duration, and intensity of your workouts together.

But even in the first few weeks, your baby will be taking "baby steps" toward building more strength and engaging in more activity. He will kick his legs in anger while waiting for a bottle. He may stretch and flail his arms and legs when getting out of a warm bath. You may even see him hold his head up by himself for a few moments! Perhaps Mother Nature knew what she was doing by getting mothers and babies off to a slow start. Imagine chasing around a newborn that is as busy as a toddler in your postpartum state! These early days are meant to get both of you accustomed to this post-pregnancy period before you launch into a full-blown cycle of action and activity!

Through the first three months of age, help your baby develop his muscles through baby sit-ups. When your baby is alert and happy, lay him on his back. His hands will grab your finger or thumb reflexively; then pull him up slowly so as not to jerk his head. (You may see your pediatrician do this to check out the strength of your baby's muscles.) Doing this exercise with your baby helps to strengthen his head, neck, and shoulder muscles. Just a few of these sit-ups sprinkled throughout the day does a tremendous amount of work for those bitty muscles. Plus, as your baby is pulled closer to your loving, smiling face, more bonding occurs.

Another muscle stretcher and strengthening activity is called hug-a-baby. Set your baby on your lap comfortably. Gently cross his arms over his chest, as though he is hugging himself. Try it yourself and feel the wonderful stretch between your shoulder blades. With baby balanced on your lap, gently pull his arms back as if opening them up for a huge hug from Daddy or Grandma. Adding words or a simple tune develops your baby's listening vocabulary, too. "Sooo big," "Give a big hug," or "Love baby" are all it takes for a baby at this stage of development.

Carrying your baby in different positions also activates different muscles. For instance, switching from using a baby car-seat carrier to a sling gives your baby more freedom to turn his head, hug Mama, and keep his head steady while looking at the world.

If the doctor gives you the "okay" at your six-week postnatal checkup, start planning your days around movement. That darling stroller you got as a baby shower gift is ready to go on an easy walk, which will eventually work up to one that includes hills. Your baby will love listening to your voice as you explain where you are going ("We are crossing the street"), what you see ("Look at the robin!"), who you meet ("There is Stephanie!"), what you are physically feeling ("The wind is blowing our hair," or "This road is bumpy!"). Go on a walk mid-morning when baby is clean, dressed appropriately, and alert. Depending on the strength you have, the walk could be an hour or more. Then, when you get home, it's time for lunch and (sigh of relief!) a nap!

If your schedule permits, consider joining a Mommy & Me class, which may keep you motivated to exercise with your baby. Check with your local community center to see if there's a class near you.

Let's Get Lively! (3-6 Months)

Since the dawn of time, perceptive parents have recognized the wonderful effect movement has on babies.
~Harvey Karp, M.D., *The Happiest Baby on the Block*

At about three months, you and your baby can begin more lively exercises. Spread out a soft, fuzzy blanket. Lay your baby down on her back. Hold each of her feet in each of your hands and "bicycle" your baby's legs and feet. Vary the speed of the imaginary "bicycle ride," always keeping in mind the fragility of your little pumpkin.

Now, hold your baby's hands. Gently move her wrists back and forth. You are working to strengthen and elongate muscles, just like a physical therapist!

As your baby grows strong enough to steadily hold her head and body, move on to more "mommy and baby" play time. Sit on the floor with your baby on your lap facing you (already this is exciting for your baby to have your undivided attention). Support your baby under her arms. Sing a Mother Goose rhyme, favorite song, or even just the ABC song. Gently bounce your baby with the cadence and rhythm of the song. Many of these songs and rhymes have actions that you can emulate. When Humpty Dumpty falls down, pretend to let your baby fall down (gently, of course). Giggles, giggles, giggles. This also strengthens the back, neck, and abdominal muscles.

In the well-known pat-a-cake rhyme, lay your baby down on a blanket or soft carpet. While saying the rhyme, "roll" out your "baby dough" back and forth, back and forth. Don't forget to mark your "dough" with baby's name, like "J" for Jaynee. When the bread is finished baking, it truly delights the baby when Mommy pretends to eat her little toes, blow raspberries on her tummy, or nibble on fingers.

Other games for babies older than three months include "Pop Goes the Weasel," where you "pop" the baby gently at appropriate times. Yankee Doodle allows for a "pony ride" on a lap with a surprise at the end when you can "drop" the baby's upper body down a bit during the "macaroni" part.

Parents often become concerned about their baby's safety when she is able

---

Are Plastic Baby Bottles Harmful?

Some studies have shown a possible link between a chemical called bisphenol-a (BPA), which is commonly used in plastic baby bottles, to possible cancers and reproductive problems later in life. A report issued by the U.S. National Toxicology Program stated that there was "some concern for neural and behavioral effects in fetuses, infants and children at current human exposures." And Health Canada has said that BPA is particularly harmful to infants. Industry insiders, however, insist that BPA is safe.[4] If you're concerned about the possible effects of BPA on your baby, consider using glass or BPA-free bottles. (If you can't find BPA-free bottles in the store, they are available on the Internet.)

to roll over. They have heard so many warnings and reminders to keep their baby on her back in an effort to avoid Sudden Infant Death Syndrome (SIDS). Some parents spend many long and sleepless nights watching over their baby, just so they can roll her onto her back again if she flips onto her tummy. But for a healthy baby, this is unnecessary. Pediatricians agree that once the baby is developed enough to roll over on her own, go ahead and let her do it! Just be sure that the baby crib is free of stuffed animals, extra blankets, and bumper pads. It's better for you and your baby if you get some sleep yourself!

Before she's able to sit up on her own, prop your baby up a few times a day while under supervision. (Babies can easily topple over during the early stages.) She will be thrilled to look you in the eye as you lie on your tummy and talk in silly rhymes or tickle songs.

Time to Dance! (7-8 Months)

*There are no seven wonders of the world
in the eyes of a child. There are seven million.*
~Walt Streightiff

Once your baby can sit (mostly) on his own, his best teacher (you) needs to have toy time that activates as many muscles as possible. Using a favorite toy or one that makes sound, grab your baby's attention. Place the toy slightly out of reach. Depending on where you set the toy, your baby may use gross motor skills to turn his body at the trunk, use core muscles to reach up high, and shift his weight in order to grab the toy. The more able your baby grows, the more activities you need to provide. Each time your baby zooms a car or throws a ball, the cells in his mind make connections, and then the connections become stronger. Remember, it isn't all fun and games for your baby's brain. The brain is constantly searching, comparing, and contrasting.

You have probably heard of "head banging," but have you heard of "hand banging"? You may notice your baby beginning to "pat" different items in your home, such as the coffee table, chair, wooden floor, or fireplace hearth. He is realizing the cause and effect of his actions;

he pats, he feels the object, and he decides if it hurts or feels good. Then, he continues this game all around his environment.

To bring this banging to a different level, hand your baby a squeaky toy. Hold baby's hand and toy together, and bang them on the floor. Baby will soon realize the different sounds that he can make on his own. He may begin to bang blocks, choo-choo trains, and any other toy to figure out what kind of sound it makes. This is a motor and intellectual milestone that all babies go through. Let him pat away (with non-breakable items, of course). You can even take a "patting tour" of the house or yard. Take his hand and pat-pat the kitty, pat-pat the grass, and pat-pat the tree trunk. All of these sensations and movements are making his mind fire up and make connections about cause and effect, as well as good and bad feelings about various textures. Run your baby's hand over different textures—smooth objects like a kitchen counter, rough objects like a rock, or a cool object like an ice cube. Don't forget to talk, talk, talk about what you're doing.

Forget "Dancing with the Stars"; dance with your own little star! Again, when your baby is sturdy, hold him on your hip and move to some music that is not playing too loudly. Take his little hand and move it to the beat or spin slowly. Face-to-face interaction in this mobile way will surely have both of you laughing and bonding. Don't forget to tickle his little belly or just under his chin. As your baby is able to stand on his own, hold his hands and try some simple moves back and forth, or just bop baby up and down on your legs. As with all things baby-related, easy does it.

Around seven months, your baby is ready to transfer objects from one hand to the other. The impulsive fist and hold that you adored in your newborn is gone. Your baby can now manipulate figures, reach and grasp toys, and hold objects between his hands. To encourage your baby to transfer objects from hand to hand, choose three toys, such as blocks or large Legos. Give your baby one toy, then offer another toy in the empty hand. With lots of praise and kisses, enjoy this for a moment. Now, pick up the third item. Hold it out to your baby. Position the third toy just a bit away from your baby and in the middle of his chest. This way, he has to decide which hand to use to grab the third toy. Give your baby some thinking time. Chances are, he will drop one toy and grab the new one, or even transfer the first two toys to one hand and grab for the new toy with the now-empty hand. Play this game often, and you may even see some signs of hand preference.

Create a "Yes Environment" (9-12 Months)

A characteristic of the normal child is he doesn't act that way very often.
~Author Unknown

Between nine and 12 months, sit on the floor with your baby. Put some low-sugar dry cereal in a paper cup. Pour the cereal from the cup into an empty cup and repeat several times until you think your baby can try it. Of course, she will spill the cereal, eat it, and transfer it imperfectly, but that's okay. Give it a lot of time and practice. You can also do this exercise with cups and water in the bathtub, pouring water from one cup into another.

Now that your baby has mastered rolling over, pushing herself along with her toes, and pulling herself with her arms and hands, she will enter "pull-up time." If all of the neural pathways are strong and fat (myelinated), so to speak, thanks to all of the play time and exercises that you've been doing with your baby, she cannot help but think of new ways to move. A coffee table or couch is at the right level for baby to put her little hands on and attempt to pull herself to a stand. Sometimes you can help her, again playing the role of physical therapist, boosting her bottom and steadying her legs. The more you encourage and aid in her movement attempts, the happier your baby will be, and the more delighted you will be! Feel the bond strengthening between you as you work together to get baby in motion. Soon, she'll be off and running away from you!

Baby-Proofing Your Home

We could write a whole book with tips, instructions, and products on how to baby-proof your home. But since there are plenty of resources out there already, we just want to encourage you to use them. Cover outlets. Keep cords out of reach. Put breakable items away. Put locks on doors, drawers, and toilets. You want your baby to feel free to explore her environment without constant fear of harm or being told "No." Start making lists now of all the ways in which you can make your home safer for your little one.

How does baby know to pull up or cruise along a couch? The mind is truly an amazing thing. With no prior experience or modeling, your baby's brain tells her body to try something new. The brain creates curiosity, challenges, and trials over and over again. If your baby could speak, she would probably not be able to tell you why she wants to cruise along the dining room chairs. It is just a gigantic urge that she *must* accomplish. Her "window of opportunity" is wide open with nothing in the path of baby moving. This is the ideal time for her to develop control of her movements.

Now is the time to rearrange your house just for a little while. Create a "yes environment" that allows her to move around freely and safely. Remember, your baby is growing fast, and each phase of babyhood goes by as quickly as a shooting star. So plug those outlets, fix those curtain and blind cords, and resign yourself to the fact that the coffee table will be the center of puzzle-making, coloring book drawings, and teddy bear beds instead of designer knickknacks for many years to come. Learning in a safe environment makes your baby's brain stronger and faster. If you are telling your baby "no" every time she reaches for a forbidden object, her curiosity will be curbed. She wants your praise, your smile, your laughter, and your love. With a "yes environment," you can relax a bit in knowing that most dangers are out of the way of your precious muffin. (However, your baby should never be left unsupervised, even in a "safe" room. You never know what ways she can figure out to get into trouble that you never even anticipated!)

Even plants that are deemed "non-poisonous" can be dangerous. Do you know what types of pesticides and fertilizers have been used on the soil? Babies put everything in their mouths beginning around six months, so think about your curious baby discovering a big pot of dirt. What a mess! What an accident waiting to happen!

Put away light-weight objects in baby's play areas, as she has no concept of what can hold her weight or what she's strong enough to pull over. Example items include a basket of clothing, kitty's scratching post, a fax machine on the table, light chairs and benches, and floor lamps. You are her knight in shining armor. Be the brave mommy and clear the path for your baby!

Don't be alarmed when your baby gets a few bumps and bruises. Many parents fear that the Division of Family Services will come knocking at their door during this learning phase, as they observe the various colored bruises on their baby's head and legs. Accidents are going to happen, but make sure to always supervise your moving baby. Be there to catch her if she falls. Hover in the area where she has chosen to play. Knowing that you have done everything you can to make your house baby-safe is a good feeling, even when baby bonks her head or tips over.

Another danger for babies is slippery floors. Toes are generally colder than the rest of the body, as there is less blood flow to extremities. Our obvious maternal reaction is to keep those tootsies warm by putting on socks or shoes, but for a little tot trying to manipulate and balance her body across a floor, slipping is a serious concern. Take off your baby's socks and shoes. Set her up for achieving a crawl, scooch, or step without the threat of slipping.

When baby-proofing the house, get down on your hands and knees to see what your rolling, crawling baby sees. A paint chip? A spider's nest? A lost earring? A dust bunny? Yummy in baby's tummy! Put candles, lighters, and medicine high up in a cabinet. This includes cough drops, vitamins, even Band-Aids. Colognes, makeup, lotions, car keys, purses, and cell phones can also be dangerous.

Dustin is now 14 months old, and Abby can hardly believe the change in him since his first birthday. It seems that he went

Every Child Is Different

Did you know that Albert Einstein was a very late talker? Accounts vary on when he began to speak (anywhere from age three to seven), but most records show agreement in saying that his parents were very worried about him! The point is that every child matures at his or her own rate. You'll find plenty of guidelines indicating the month when your baby should be rolling over, sitting up, crawling, standing, or walking, but remember that these are just approximations. There is a wide range of "normal" when it comes to mastering certain motor skills. Let your child progress at his own pace. If you're still concerned, please be sure to check with your doctor. After all, if there's a real problem, it's best to seek out early intervention. But if the doctor assures you that all is well, enjoy the "baby steps" that you see in this first year of life. It may seem like forever before your little one walks, but you'll soon be struggling to remember a time when he wasn't going full steam!

straight from hanging onto the furniture to running across the room! Abby realizes now that Dustin just had his own timetable. Once he decided to take that first step, there was no stopping him! Now that he is walking, she has to watch him even more carefully to make sure he's not headed toward a staircase or tripping over the coffee table. But the extra vigilance required is worth the pleasure in seeing Dustin explore his world even further than before. Abby is already thinking about the places that she and Dustin can visit together—on their feet!

Conclusion

Achievements in the motor skills area of your baby's expanding mind and body are much easier to see on a daily basis than some other areas of growth. It is thrilling and rewarding to see your baby working on a new movement or skill every day. Some parents even cancel business trips to stay home and see their baby's momentous first steps! The amount of energy and mind power involved in learning to reach a toy or bang two blocks together cannot be overstated. Each day is a grand adventure for your baby and a huge challenge for you to outsmart your little one with safety measures.

As right as rain, your little one will learn to walk around age one. Then, don't expect him to walk again for many years, as he will run wherever and whenever he can until he hits puberty! At that point, he will be walking mostly away from you—to his friends, his sports, and his room. This thought tugs at any parent's heart, but empowering your baby for success and health is what parenting is about. So brush those thoughts aside for now. Baby delights in you. Focus on how tear-jerking those little bitty hugs are with little bitty arms and hands. File that profound feeling away in your mind and heart so that you can pull it out when baby is old enough to slip out the door and away from you for his first day of preschool, kindergarten, high school, or college.

Chapter 7
Temperament: Is Your Child a Shrinking Violet or a Thorny Rose?

Only those who respect the personality
of others can be of real use to them.
~Albert Schweitzer

Is personality formed in the womb and biologically dictated, or is it the result of what the child has learned from her environment, how she was treated by caregivers, how rich of a life she has? This question has been debated since researchers started doing psychological studies on the development of personality. Are the favorable character traits seen in a very young baby simply wishful thinking on the part of parents? Are newborns merely a collection of reflexes—primitive organisms that require time for their personalities to develop in response to the environment?

After many years of research and debate, most experts agree that one's personality—also known as temperament—is created by both *nature* and *nurture*. From a nature standpoint, your baby's personality is made up largely from how her brain was formed in the womb. As soon as the first day of her life, you may notice her unique personality. Right away, it seems that you can tell how anxious or happy or laid back she is simply from hearing her newborn cries. Those first signs of your new baby's disposition are usually right! It isn't just your imagination—she really does have preferences from the first moment. And your baby's temperament will be with her for the rest of her life.

After her birth, Baby Rilee lay perfectly still on the warming table. Her arms were stretched over her head, and her legs were cast out straight. Her eyes were wide open, and she looked all around her. She seemed to be taking in all of the newness and then deciding how she would act. She was evaluating the area in perfect calm and stillness. Rilee is now nine years old, and her family reports that she still checks things out thoroughly before engaging. She stood by her mom and dad's side for a little bit before deciding to join the ballet lesson. She held onto Mommy's hand extra long on the first day of preschool while viewing what was going to happen and how the teacher was going to act.

However, your baby's temperament is also influenced by her environment—particularly by how people react to her. During her first year of life, your baby is learning about herself, her family, her surroundings. Pediatrician Cindy Kirby-Diaz reports that, during the first year of your baby's life, it is simply up to you to "deal with" how your baby reacts to stimuli.[1] She is simply letting her needs be known to you in the only way that her brain dictates (often by crying). It is up to you to modify her environment, routines, and exposures in order to strengthen the bond of trust between you and your baby, and also to decrease factors and stressors that may inhibit brain growth. Your baby is not developmentally able to understand discipline at this age; she cannot understand the cause and effect of behavior modification. Toward her second birthday, you may be able to start teaching her how to deal with frustration, loud noises, social interactions, and other areas that might be a source of stress due to her temperament. But during that first year, she's not going to be able to figure out that "honey" (good behavior) brings more positive results than "vinegar" (poor behavior).

> ### Glossary
>
> *Nature versus nurture debate*: the importance of people's innate qualities (*nature*) versus their personal experiences (*nurture*) in shaping differences in behavioral or physical traits
>
> *Temperament*: personality or disposition; a person's inborn mental, emotional, and physical traits

Uncovering Your Baby's Temperament

Understanding your baby's temperament may give you clues to solving some behavior problems that you find particularly frustrating during the first year of life. It can also encourage greater bonding between parent and child. Psychologist Mary Ainsworth and her

Twins and the Nature vs. Nurture Debate

Scientists have been using twins in research for thousands of years. Charles Darwin's cousin, Francis Galton, was one of the first to suggest in 1875 that studying twins could offer valuable insights into the study of nature versus nurture. Are we more influenced by genes or the environment?

Identical, or monozygotic, twins share 100% of their DNA. Thus, when scientists compare a particular trait between sets of identical twins and sets of fraternal twins (who are no more alike than any other siblings), they can determine that any additional likenesses between the identical twins are most likely a factor of their genes, rather than the environment. But the research isn't always fool-proof. For the most part, scientists have found that intelligence is a heritable trait. However, when identical twins were raised in vastly different socioeconomic backgrounds, the twin placed with the poorer family had a lower IQ. So environment may have an impact on the expression of particular genes.

Twin studies have provided valuable information on human behavior and health-related issues. Some of these studies suggest that autism is largely inherited, a comfort to parents who were told in the past that it was caused by "aloof parenting." Many twins consider it a privilege to be able to help scientists better understand diseases and behavioral issues that affect the human species.

colleagues have found that "the infants of sensitive, responsive mothers have stronger attachments than infants of insensitive mothers or mothers who respond inconsistently to their infants' needs…. Difficult infants who fuss, refuse to eat, and sleep irregularly tax their mothers, which makes it hard for the mothers to be properly responsive."[2] It's a two-way street. As we explained in Chapter 2, responsive mothers enable babies to better bond with their caretakers, resulting in a more well-adjusted infant. (Remember, you can't spoil an infant!) However, babies who are particularly fussy may discourage their mothers from responding consistently because they're worn out from repeated attempts. It's a catch-22 that parents need to address.

As we noted, some personality traits will be obvious from birth, but others may not be as readily apparent. How can you determine your baby's temperament—and respond accordingly? Researchers Stella Chess, Alexander Thomas, and associates in the New York Longitudinal Study identified nine different temperamental traits in babies and children.[3] The study followed the emotional and social development of 133 children for 30 years, starting with their births in the mid-1950s and extending into the '80s. This resulted in a "temperament test" that parents can use to determine their baby's dominant personality traits. Temperament characteristics can be measured through behavioral observation. Study the behaviors in the list below and determine where you baby fits in. Share your findings with other caregivers.

The Temperament Test

> *There is no personal charm so great*
> *as the charm of a cheerful temperament.*
> ~Henry Van Dyke

For each of the nine traits listed below, select option (A) or (B) according to how closely it describes your baby. Then follow the advice beneath your selection to determine how you can best accommodate your child's particular personality traits.

Trait 1: Regularity

(A) Does your baby sleep and eat like clockwork? Does he thrive with routines and tight schedules?

(B) Is it difficult to keep your baby on a routine? Does he play longer or eat later from day to day? Is your baby content to catnap during the day as needed rather than take a consistent nap?

If you selected A: Schedules for bedtime, naps, meals, and play need to be followed as closely as possible every day. Write down routines as soon as you become aware of them. Be prepared for each part of baby's day with the appropriate items: PJs, clean blankets, bottles, and books. It is especially vital to be consistent with bedtimes and naps. A tired baby is a grumpy baby. During sleep, the brain actually grows and absorbs all of the day's lessons into baby's mind.

If you selected B: Take deep breaths and allow your baby to decide what he's ready for. If he balks at feeding, move on to another activity.

Reassure yourself that he isn't trying to manipulate you. He just needs more flexibility in his life!

Trait 2: Activity

(A) Is your baby content just to watch life go by from her stroller or bouncy seat? Does she play quiet games like looking at books or rolling a quiet toy back and forth?

(B) Was your baby a mover and a shaker even in the womb? Does she wriggle in the crib? Is there a wrestling contest at every diaper and clothing change? Does she kick her feet and bat at overhead objects for an extended period of time?

If you selected A: These babies use their fingers more than their legs and tend to develop fine motor skills earlier, such as coloring, painting, stringing beads, and printing. Don't overwhelm her with physical play. She may be studying the world, new people, and interesting smells. Be aware of your baby's environment, and change it at various increments as she dictates to continue appropriate activity.

If you selected B: Crawling, walking, climbing, etc., will likely begin sooner than for less active babies. Keep up on childproofing the house. If there is an unsafe spot, this might be the little one who would find it. Never leave her alone in a bouncy seat, highchair, or exer-saucer. Sometimes active babies can tip these over by their movements and leg kicks. An interest in running, kicking, and jumping will increase with age. This child will be very happy in soccer, basketball, jumping rope, trampolines, etc.

---

*The principle of all successful effort is to try
to do not what is absolutely the best,
but what is easily within our power,
and suited for our temperament and condition.*
~John Ruskin

Trait 3: Sociability

(A) Is your baby a mini-social butterfly who coos and smiles at everyone he meets? Does he make eye contact with others? Is he curious about new visitors? Is he approachable?

(B) Does your baby seem to have perpetual "stranger anxiety"? Does he cry in fear if passed to Dad or Grandma? Is he withdrawn in social situations?

If you selected A: Take your baby with you on errands. He will be in heaven with all of the people to "visit" with. Set up play dates so that your baby can be around more people. (However, be conscious about the spread of germs with your sociable baby. Encourage people who want to hold him to use hand sanitizer or wash their hands first. Keep baby's hands clean with the wet wipes in your diaper bag.)

If you selected B: Hold your baby close. Have a blanket (light or heavy, according to the weather) to wrap around his legs while you are holding him. Well-meaning friends may want to touch baby and say "hello." This is a sure way to make him very upset. Don't force him into new situations. Add extra adjustment time when dropping your baby off at daycare or a sitter's house.

Trait 4: Adaptability

(A) Is your baby laid back? Does she go with the flow? Does she quickly get used to new people and play areas? Does she change activities easily? Does she handle the unexpected well?

(B) Does your baby refuse to sleep anywhere but in her own crib? Does she take weeks to settle into a new routine? Does your baby act like it's the end of the world if a friend plays with one of her favorite toys?

If you selected A: It's tempting to leave the laid-back baby alone in her sea of contentment, but she still needs plenty of human interaction. Make sure that your adaptable baby gets lots of "face time" with you.

If you selected B: With this type of temperament, "slow and steady" should be your mantra. Introduce new foods slowly, a little bit at a time. Introduce friends slowly, and have play dates with maybe only one other child. But don't give up on making changes—life is all about changes! Just bring life on in a slow and steady manner.

Mankind adapts rapidly to innovation,
often in spite of itself. We are amazingly adaptable,
which is why we survived—our progeny
will not only adapt, they will excel.
~Mark Reed

Trait 5: Intensity

(A) Is your baby a "shrieker" when angry? Does he break out in huge belly laughs when something is funny? Does your baby show high levels of emotional expression? Would you sometimes describe your household as "mental chaos"?

(B) Is your baby quiet? Does he have a sweet, gentle laugh? Does he only grimace or whimper when he has a dirty diaper? Does your baby show low levels of emotional expression?

If you selected A: Your baby will be happier when happy, sadder when sad, and angrier when angry. If you are worn out from dealing with your intense baby, you may need a 15-minute "mommy time-out." It will help you think more clearly and allow time to think about how to handle a difficult situation.

If you selected B: Pay close attention to your baby's manner. The clues to his emotions may be very subtle, but as a parent, you have to meet his needs, even if he isn't having a grand fit or showing annoyance at a certain stimulus.

The intensity of your desire governs
the power with which the force is directed.
~John McDonald

At three months, Megan was already known as a "drama queen"
and a "diva." When she got mad, she'd kick her feet in rage, and
her face would turn beet red. When she was happy, the giggles

just spilled out of her. Megan's parents, both easygoing types, learned to cope with Megan's emotional extremes by having a sense of humor. Instead of getting upset when she had a tantrum, they'd joke, "Our little volcano is about to blow her top!" Megan soon began to respond to her parents' soothing responses and learned how to manage her frustrations better as she got older.

Do You Have a Feisty— or Gifted—Baby?

If your baby is a poor sleeper or demands a lot of attention, this doesn't mean that she's a "bad baby." According to Deborah L. Ruf, Ph.D., in her book *Losing Our Minds: Gifted Children Left Behind,*[4] your baby may actually be showing early signs of giftedness! In Ruf's studies, parents of gifted children reported that their children "had a high need for eye contact and direct, continual interaction almost from birth.... Although some might suggest that babies will become spoiled or overly demanding if parents give into them, the opposite appears to be true. When the need for interaction is consistently met for an infant or young child, that child is more confident and trusting and demands less attention later."[5] Ruf also reported that "20% of gifted children seem to need less sleep than average children.... Many parents said that their very young gifted children simply weren't content to stay in their crib."[6] She advises that parents "learn how to work with them—not fight against them,"[7] in order to encourage cooperation.

Trait 6: Disposition

(A) Is your baby a happy little one? Does she seem to enjoy every bit of life? Does she giggle happily at a puppy and adore playing silly tickle games?

(B) Is your baby's face constantly in a scowl? Does she whimper and whine? Does she get grouchy easily?

If you selected A: Your baby may be happy-go-lucky most of the time, but be aware of the times when she isn't her happy self. This may be an indication of an illness, ear pain, or fever.

If you selected B: Model happiness. Play silly games that make your baby laugh. Be very affectionate to help lighten her mood. Check your schedule. Some babies seem like they have a negative disposition, but what they really need is a few more hours of sleep or an added nap.

Trait 7: Persistence

(A) Does your baby have "stick-with-it-ness"? Does he reach and reach and reach for a toy until he finally figures out how to maneuver himself to be

When Parents' and Children's Temperaments Clash

Sometimes parents think that their child is being "bad," when the problem is that they don't have matching temperaments. If a parent is very high-achieving and intense, and his child is easygoing and gentle, the parent may perceive the child as lazy or may pressure him to achieve more. Conversely, if a parent is mild-mannered, his high-strung child may appear to be naughty or overactive to the parent.

When you realize that your temperament is different from your child's, it can give you a better understanding of why he acts the way he does and make it easier for you not to blame your child for behavior that might just be in keeping with his personality. You can also learn new parenting strategies to adapt, as well as help your child to modify behavior that might be difficult to tolerate.

Also remember that certain personality traits that might be difficult in the baby and toddler years—such as being strong-willed—might be modified into something more tolerable and beneficial in later years—such as being self-confident. With the right attitude and understanding, you can steer your child in more positive directions, despite his inborn tendencies.

Finally, learn to accept your child for who he is. "Different" doesn't necessarily mean "bad." Never make your child feel negatively about himself because he's not like the other family members. Cherish and celebrate his uniqueness!

able to get it? When he wants someone else's toy, does he constantly try to grab or trade for it?

(B) Does your baby get frustrated and give up easily? When reaching for a book, does he give it one or two tries and then give up or look to you for help? Does he only enjoy a toy for a brief time and then grab the nearest new toy for additional play?

If you selected A: Be aware that your baby will feel a need to achieve things in his life. He could be persistent in getting a game of soccer going or in coloring a page. When possible, build in time for your child to have ample opportunity to reach his goal. Give him an "end time" for his play, like five more minutes; this gives him a mental map to show that play time is ending and he needs to speed up his activity.

If you selected B: Offer simple activities that your baby can accomplish quickly and easily. Have many toy and book choices available. Otherwise, when baby gives up, he will want to be entertained by you!

At the core of every true talent there is an awareness
of the difficulties inherent in any achievement,
and the confidence that by persistence and patience,
something worthwhile will be realized.
~Eric Hoffer

Trait 8: Distractibility

(A) Is your baby easily interrupted by sights and sounds? While nursing, is your baby more interested in the noise and activity around her? While playing, does the sound of the phone or siren stop her from her play? Is she soothed easily by a new book, a look out the window, or a quick step out the back door?

(B) Does your baby focus simply on what she wants—a special "lovey," a particular toy, or a person? Will nothing else please her but that particular thing?

If you selected A: Keep in mind that your baby will divert her attention to many things. Be ready with safety measures to ensure that her curious wanderings will be safe. Create a "yes environment" through baby-proofing so that she doesn't become frustrated with "no's" when exploring. Distractibility is a trait that, in the future, will be obvious in the classroom, and her teachers will most likely mention it many times.

If you selected B: Buy doubles or even triples of special "loveys." Have extra pacifiers. Create a mini-photo album of favorite people— Grandma, Daddy, pets. Sit baby on your lap when she may be missing these special people. In a soothing voice, "read" through the book, pointing to the people. Repeat this over and over while your baby is upset. The sight and sound of this activity will become predictable for her, and that predictability is comforting to her.

Trait 9: Sensitivity

(A) Does your baby fuss and whine when you vacuum? Does he become cross while wearing an itchy or tight outfit? Do bright lights or sunshine make your baby squint, turn away, or fuss? Does a strong wind upset him? Is he bad-tempered when hearing noise from a TV, radio, dog, or lawn mower outside?

(B) Is your baby seldom bothered by a change in the environment? Is he happy listening to all kinds of music at various volumes (keeping in mind baby's fragile ears)? Does he react positively to the smells of different people or food?

If you selected A: Try to safeguard your baby from sights and sounds that disturb him. Share this information with caregivers or during a visit to Grandma's. He may actually feel pain when continuously exposed to these stressors. Be prepared to check out early at noisy parties. Find a babysitter if going to a basketball game.

If you selected B: Remember that your baby may react very little to a dirty diaper or even pain. Keep a mental or actual list of things to check on a consistent basis. For instance, every time you change his diaper or bathe him, check for diaper rash; belly button cord inflammation; splinters in the hands, knees, or toes (when your baby becomes more mobile); hangnails; erupting teeth; fever; and cold symptoms.

Conclusion

I swear my kids were each fully themselves
from the moment they opened their eyes.
~Shoshana Marchand

It's important to recognize that all personality traits have their advantages and disadvantages. Understanding that many of your child's temperamental characteristics are inborn can help alleviate your anxiety about, "Am I doing something wrong?" or "Did I do something in the past that 'made' my baby this way?" The goal of understanding your baby's temperament is to help her make the most of who she is in the easiest manner possible.

Sometimes culture and family structure play large roles in determining whether a child's temperament is likely to cause difficulties. For example, in Lawrence Kutner's book *Parent and Child*, he cites findings by Dr. Michael W. Yogman, assistant professor of pediatrics at Harvard Medical School, that American parents encourage children to be active, while Chinese parents consider a placid temperament to be far more desirable.[8]

You may also want to assess your own temperament. Where do *you* fall in the behavioral continuum? If you and your baby are opposites, you need to work extra hard to understand and meet your baby's needs (see box "When Parents' and Children's Temperaments Clash"). Babies thrive best with "goodness of fit"—a reasonable match between their temperament and the environment (which includes the parents' personalities and response to baby's behavior).

If you feel that you are lacking the appropriate "tools" to deal with your baby's personality, consider asking your pediatrician for resources for parenting classes offered in your area. Check out parenting books from the library. The more you learn about your baby, the happier and better her—and your—life will be.

Chapter 8

Going to the Doctor: Why the Doctor/Patient Relationship Is So Vital

---

Never go to a doctor whose office plants have died.
~Erma Bombeck

In your baby's first year of life, you're going to get to know the pediatrician's office like the back of your hand. Some parents complain that it begins to feel like it's their second home, between well-baby visits and all of the assorted viruses and ailments that your baby will pick up in that first year. So it's important for your baby's welfare—as well as your own mental health—that you have a healthy and trusting relationship with your pediatrician.

It's best to shop around for a pediatrician *before* your baby is born so that your chosen doctor will be able to make her first visit with your baby at the birthing hospital. If this is your first child and you haven't yet selected a pediatrician, word of mouth is usually a good source. Most parents are more than willing to share their recommendations with you. Ask if their doctor is patient about answering questions, is reachable 24/7 (or has coverage if she's out of town), and has a pleasant office staff. Make an appointment with doctors who come highly recommended and meet them. Don't be shy about interviewing several doctors.

Of course, you'll want to think about some practical considerations, too. Is the doctor close enough to your home that you can get your child there in good timing if he needs to be seen suddenly? Does the doctor accept your insurance? Is she authorized to practice at a hospital of your choice if your child must be hospitalized? Does she have the proper qualifications? Does she share her after-hour calls with other doctors?

And ask potential doctors about their parenting philosophies. Do they practice preventative care? Do they support breastfeeding? How often do they prescribe antibiotics? Make sure that you are in agreement on issues that are important to you.

Think about whether you'd prefer an older doctor, with more years of experience, or a younger doctor, who might be more knowledgeable about newer medical techniques. Do you feel more comfortable with a male or female doctor? Do you like a large practice or a small one? These are all things to take into consideration.

If, after your baby is born, you find that you're not so happy with your choice after all, be proactive about finding a new pediatrician. Remember, you're going to have a long relationship with this person—it might as well be a happy one!

Conversation with a Pediatrician

In the sick room, ten cents' worth of human understanding equals ten dollars' worth of medical science.
~Martin H. Fischer

In learning more about what constitutes a healthy patient/doctor relationship, it can be helpful to look at some of the issues from the other side of the examining table—from a doctor's point of view. Co-author Holly Engel-Smothers sat down with Dr. Cindy Kirby-Diaz to gain more insight into how parents can maximize their visits with the pediatrician. Dr. Kirby-Diaz received her medical degree from the University of Nevada School of Medicine and did her residency at Children's Mercy Hospital in Kansas City, Missouri. She now works with Cockerell and McIntosh, a group practice in Blue Springs, Missouri. Because of a lifelong love for children, Dr. Kirby-Diaz always knew that pediatrics was her special calling, and she loves to educate parents about how to take the best care of their kids. Here's what she had to say about visiting the pediatrician with your child—and much more.

Windows of Opportunity: How do you teach parents about windows of opportunity for meeting certain milestones—that this is the most vital time for their child to learn—without scaring them?

During the well-baby visits in the first year of life, pediatricians really reinforce the parent's role in stimulating brain development and growth. We take the opportunity to teach and try to encourage parents to take an active role in their children's lives.

At each visit, I do a developmental assessment. If the baby is on target, I say, "Okay, great! Let's look at what's coming next. You need to work on these developments for the next time." Similarly, if there is a delay, I discuss it with the parents so that we can hopefully address it early.

The American Academy of Pediatrics has something called "Anticipatory Guidance." For each age, there are certain things that pediatricians need to talk about and address with parents. It's not mandatory, but any good pediatrician will abide by these and discuss them with patients.

Brains well prepared are the monuments
where human knowledge is more surely engraved.
~Jean Jacques Rousseau

Packing Your Bags: What should be packed in the diaper bag to go to the doctor for the first appointment and beyond?

The first visit to the pediatrician is usually the first time parents leave home with their infant, and it's pretty daunting to get everything ready. Almost everyone is late! One of the most important things to bring is the hospital record. The hospital should give you a paper that has the baby's birth weight, his weight when he went home from the hospital, and the bilirubin level, which tests for jaundice in a newborn. Too much jaundice can affect brain development later on, so we monitor that in every baby so that it doesn't reach a harmful level.

Pack your diaper bag with diapers (more than one, because baby is having lots of stools), wipes, and a change of clothing because babies are frequently spitting up and ruining an outfit or two.

What Is Jaundice?

Bilirubin is a yellow chemical produced in the blood from the normal breakdown of red blood cells. It travels to the liver, where a chemical reaction takes place to remove it from the blood. Sometimes the liver cannot remove enough bilirubin from the blood, and the extra bilirubin travels to all parts of the body through the bloodstream. This causes the skin to turn yellow. More frighteningly, the brain can become damaged by prolonged exposure to the extra bilirubin, possibly resulting in cerebral palsy, mental retardation, problems with vision and hearing, and even death. Fortunately, jaundice is easy to detect and cure. A baby with jaundice is placed under special warm blue lights or wrapped in a "bili-blanket" that helps remove bilirubin from the blood. This treatment is not at all painful or uncomfortable for your baby.

Bring a list of how baby is doing with his feedings—when baby is eating, how many poops and pees he has, how much he is eating. This gives us an idea of how he is doing overall. Another thing to include is a list of questions. It's usually better to write the questions down so that you can remember them.

If you have a question or concern about your baby's behavior or health when you're home, pick up phone and call the office! Pediatricians are available 24 hours a day, seven days a week. We want parents to contact us if there is a concern with their baby. We expect it.

Vaccinations and Screenings: Tell us more about vaccines and tests performed on a newborn.

Sometimes the hospital record will show the date of the baby's Hepatitis B vaccine. This is the only vaccine that babies get in the hospital right now.

The heel prick is a newborn screen that is mandatory on every baby born. This test screens for a variety of disorders that may not be picked up until later and could present a lot of problems, such as thyroid issues, PKU, cystic fibrosis, and sickle cell anemia. If picked up early, something can usually be done to change the overall outcome of these conditions. This test has different requirements from state to state. Any baby born in a hospital has to have a state blood screen.

Vaccine records are kept on file with the pediatrician's office, so if you lose your copy, you can always call the office for a replacement. If you move to a different office or state, you can call and get your vaccine information for your new doctor, school, and daycare. This information is in your file and medical records. It includes when you got the vaccine, what lot number, where it was administered, and what place it was given on the body. There are universal vaccination recommendations for the entire United States. There is a little leeway for the time period in which to get vaccinated for certain vaccines, like 15 to 18 months, so babies may get a particular shot at the beginning of that time period or at the end, but as far as which vaccines you need for which age group, those are pretty standard.

Authors' Note: Vaccination and screening requirements may change over time. *Please check with your pediatrician for the most current recommendations.*

The First Visit: What is a pediatrician's expectation of newborn baby doctor visits? Some moms are worried about taking too much time or using appointment time to feed or change the baby.

If baby needs to be fed at the first appointment, feed her. If baby is screaming and crying and I'm trying to talk to the parents, they're not going to be able to hear what I'm saying. Plus, if the baby is fussy, I am not going to get a good exam while listening to her heart. Try to have your baby happy and fed for the appointment. Of course, you can't always plan or schedule when a baby wants to eat. Sometimes we may have to examine baby during her feeding time and will have to interrupt her for a moment, but then just continue feeding afterward. We want to work around the baby's needs. We know that parents are sleep-deprived and tired. We expect them to be late, and that's just part of being a new parent. Pediatricians are not there to judge you or think that you're a bad parent because you don't have makeup on or your baby is hungry during visits and may need to eat.

The Newborn Screening Saves Lives Act

In 2008, the national Newborn Screening Saves Lives Act was enacted. According to the March of Dimes, "this legislation lays the groundwork to establish national guidelines on what conditions should be tested and authorizes funding for states to strengthen their existing newborn screening programs.... Newborn screening is a vital public health activity that provides early identification and treatment for 29 treatable metabolic, hormonal, genetic, and/or functional disorders.... Failure to screen for these conditions puts every baby at risk because if untreated, a seemingly healthy newborn with an undetected condition can become seriously ill, resulting in brain damage, lifelong disabilities, coma, or even death."[1]

Finding a Doctor: How would you suggest that a family find a pediatrician?

Talk to your friends, other people you trust, families who have kids already to see if they have somebody who they really like. It may be a little more difficult when you are new in the neighborhood. Talk to people at church or synagogue. The most important thing in finding a pediatrician is finding someone you are comfortable with—somebody who you feel you can sit down with and discuss your worries and stresses. You want to feel that you can open up to your doctor and he isn't going to chastise you or criticize you. In order to have a good relationship with the doctor, you have to be able to talk with him.

A lot of offices will have a website that you can visit, which may include a brief synopsis of the doctor's philosophies. Another factor that determines if you have the right pediatrician is, when calling the pediatrician's office, is somebody going to answer the call with "Hello, how are you?" or is it going to be an automated recording in which you have to "press 1 for this and 2 for this"? Many times, people will leave an office, not because they don't like their doctor, but because they can't stand the front office. They can never get to who they need to talk to. Sometimes you just have to go to the office and see how comfortable you are.

> ## Assessing the Doctor's Office
>
> When you make your first visit to the pediatrician's office and you're in the waiting room, look around you. Is the waiting room clean? Do the toys look like they're washed regularly? Are the magazines up-to-date?
>
> Is the waiting room packed? Are people sighing and looking at their watches or complaining about the wait?
>
> Witness the staff interacting with patients. Do they have smiles on their faces? Do they seem to be happy at their jobs? Do they maintain an even demeanor with a difficult patient? Do they appear to be overworked or stressed out? Are they rude?

Male or Female? Does it matter if the doctor is male or female?

At first, when you have a newborn, it's just whatever the parent feels comfortable with. When you have an older child—say 10, 11, 12—then you need to ask your child if he has a preference.

Doctor Interviews: What about interviewing the pediatrician before the baby is born?

Most pediatricians have what is called a "prenatal visit," in which you can come in and talk with the doctor. If it's a very busy office, it can sometimes be difficult to grab a time slot, so call ahead. The prenatal visit—or interview—will give you a feeling of how comfortable you are with the doctor. You'll want to know if she is going to be very staunch or if she is going to say, "Let me help you out. Let me be a teacher, a guide. Let's build a good relationship."

Brothers and Sisters: How do most pediatricians feel about siblings during baby visits?

We love it. Sometimes it depends on the age and the needs of the sibling, but for the most part, we like to have siblings come along because they are part of the family dynamics and interactions. Pediatricians can model how to incorporate new babies into a family with siblings. However, if parents have a lot of concerns and issues with the new baby, then it might be better to leave the sibling at home so that we can concentrate one-on-one on the baby.

Medication Samples: What medication samples does the office have?

It's basically what the pharmaceutical representatives bring. We don't have much say about what's in our sample closet. Usually we have a new medicine that is a name brand and a company's "newest, greatest" medicine. Offices like to have samples of medicines that are difficult for insurances to approve. That way, we can give you some samples to tide you over until the insurance kicks in. Also, we can have some samples for parents who say they can't afford the co-pay. We try very hard to get something that will work through looking at insurance websites to find compatible medicines at a cheaper co-pay.

Most sales reps are moving away from giving actual medicine samples to providing "vouchers," where you just get a little card that you can take to the pharmacy for a free certain amount or discount off of your co-pay.

Getting Sick at the Doctor's: How concerned should parents be about going to the pediatrician and picking up another virus?

It should be a very big concern for parents. Some practices have separate waiting rooms for sick and well children in an attempt to try to keep the sick and well apart, especially for babies less than two months old. If we see a baby less than two months of age with an illness and a fever, oftentimes this will send her into the hospital for several days. Keep infants and babies in their car seat, and don't put them on the waiting room floor and let them play. Try to keep them confined to a "well area" where there are not a lot of other people and things around. Some offices, size-wise, just can't have a separate room. Keep a blanket over the car seat so that those germs aren't going directly to the infant. Parents should use hand sanitizer. Bring some things from home for your child to play with.

Sunscreen for Babies: What do pediatricians think about sunscreen for little babies?

Guidelines say that sunscreen should not be used on children under six months of age. The best thing to do is to try to keep babies out of direct sunlight. Their skin is so new and so fragile that getting a large amount of sun is not recommended anyway. We advise that the baby wear a wide-brimmed hat, a long-sleeved shirt, and long pants (corresponding with the season and temperature) when outdoors. Sunscreen can be absorbed through the skin, and it may contain some toxins that can be absorbed

Screening for Autism

Parents and doctors are now conscious about screening children for autism at well-baby visits. The earlier a diagnosis is made, the earlier that intervention can begin. According to WebMD, "Evidence over the last 15 years indicates that intensive early intervention in *optimal educational settings for at least 2 years during the preschool years* results in improved outcomes in most young children with ASD."[2]

Behaviors associated with autism spectrum disorders may be apparent in a baby's first few months or may develop over the next few years. Ask your doctor to perform a "developmental screening test" to help screen for autism. If any concerns show up on the initial screening tests, you will be referred to other professionals for diagnosis. This usually consists of a team that may include a neurologist, a psychologist, a psychiatrist, and/or a speech therapist. These specialists will perform thorough testing to determine if your child has an autism spectrum disorder, and they will recommend appropriate therapies.

more easily in a baby than a toddler or adult because our skin is a lot thicker. It has not been proven that there is any harm in applying sunscreen to babies, but there is the theoretic possibility.

Stranger Anxiety: What do you tell parents to expect as far as stranger anxiety?

Stranger anxiety shows that the baby has formed a good bond with the family because he can actually recognize who belongs to his family and who doesn't. This is a positive milestone that we look for at six to nine months of age. The baby should look for Mommy when I pick him up, as he needs to be sure that Mommy is still there. If we are not seeing a lot of that, it could indicate a problem with bonding.

Each patient ought to feel somewhat the better
after the physician's visit, irrespective of the nature of the illness.
~ Warfield Theobald Longcope

Surfing the Web: What do you think about parents getting information from the Internet?

I think that it's very helpful, and I encourage it, but it's important that parents check that they are getting it from a reputable source. There are two organizations that monitor medical information on the Internet. High-quality sites and articles will have an organizational stamp on the bottom of the website: HON, for Health on the Net. This is a non-profit organization that looks at the information to see if it is of good quality.

The second organization is the ACIP.

Authors' Note: The Advisory Committee on Immunization Practices (ACIP) consists of experts in fields associated with immunization that provide guidance to U.S. government health agencies on the control of vaccine-preventable diseases. They develop the written recommendations for administration of vaccines to children.

If you don't see one of these stamps, then the information could be questionable. Some parents will visit chat rooms, etc., and it is a great source of communication, but take the advice for what it is. Just because it's on the Internet doesn't mean that it is accurate. Some of the things you read are just opinions unless you see verification.

I recommend websites like those from the American Academy of Pediatrics (www.aap.org), Centers for Disease Control and Prevention (www.cdc.gov), WebMD (www.webmd.com), and large children's hospitals like Children's Mercy (www.childrensmercy.org). They give a lot of information for parents to follow up on a certain diagnosis that we may have talked about for five to 10 minutes in the office. Sometimes, parents bring in an article from the Internet that talks about one of their concerns in regard to their child. I review it and look into its findings, and then I get back to the parents on what I find and whether it is reputable or not.

Getting Face Time: How can I get my doctor to spend more time with me?

If you have extra concerns, make an appointment for a well-visit, but let the office know that you want to discuss additional concerns during the visit. If you let us know that, we can schedule more time or schedule you for two visits. One of the biggest complaints that most parents have is the wait time for a visit. There are a variety of reasons for this, but mainly it's because parents want you to spend more time with them but are afraid to say that and schedule in advance for a consult. This situation is going to frustrate both the parents and the child—no one wins. Some parents have a problem because they can't afford the additional co-pay. They don't have the time or the transportation. It may be a case in which a family faces the problem of going to the doctor versus getting food on the table.

Common Concerns: Are there any concerns that parents have over and over again?

Sleep, sleep, sleep! Probably the biggest concern we get for children from about nine months to two years is: "My child won't sleep well at night; my child is having problems with sleep." It stems from what the parent has taught the child. Most parents don't realize that sleep in children has to be *taught*. A child doesn't naturally just lie down and sleep very nicely, especially when she is used to being right next to Mom and hearing her heartbeat. A lot of parents don't teach their child good sleep habits—for example, they rock the baby to sleep; they make sure the baby is completely asleep before they creep out of the room; they put baby to bed with bottles. Just like you have to teach them to read and not run out into the middle of the road, you have to teach them how to go to sleep on their own. Parents need to start this at an early age—by this I mean two to three months of age, *not* newborn.

How Much Sleep Does My Child Need Each Night?[3]	
Age	Hours
1-4 Weeks	15.5-16.5
4-12 Months	14-15
1-3 Years	12-14
3-6 Years	10.75-12
7-12 Years	10-11
12-18 Years	8.25-9.5

The other big mistake that parents often make is trying to be their child's good buddy and friend. Parents want someone to love them, but they don't want to set limits or guidelines; they want to be the "good guy." Kids do well with structure, routine, and knowing the consequences in a consistent manner. If they know that every time they pull hair they will get a certain consequence, pretty soon they are not pulling their brother's hair. It *has* to be consistent. Being a parent is not equivalent to being your child's best friend. These are two completely different things. Being a parent is not just about protecting the child's physical being; it's about teaching the child and developing her emotional self, her intellectual self, and making her into the best child that she can be.

Another thing I see a lot is that children are not allowed to just play—free play time. Everything has to be scheduled out to the minute. Kids really need the opportunity for free play, and so do the parents. All of the structure and scheduling in today's society isn't good for kids.

Play provides a wide variety of skills
necessary for success in school and life.
~Rae Pica, *A Running Start*

Early Discipline: What do pediatricians recommend regarding discipline from newborn through age one?

In the first year, babies don't quite have the intellectual ability to know cause and effect. The baby can't think, "If I do this, I get this consequence." In the first year, they are in the process of learning this. One of the best discipline techniques for this age is distraction. Distract your child into doing something positive. When the baby is doing well—playing quietly with toys, looking at a book—parents need to reinforce the activity. Point out the action that the child is doing well and cheer for him or say how proud it makes you feel. Positive feedback from a parent will make the child repeat those things.

The concept of time-out is one that children won't understand until they get more toward the age of two. If the child is doing something wrong, like biting, say a stern, "No!" and move him away from the spot. We don't recommend spanking in the first year.

Babies are just learning, just practicing. Parents need to be proactive with them. Create an environment that will not produce a lot of "no's." Make sure there are enough toys if two kids are playing; put cabinet locks on; put up the baby gate. The baby will realize that the way to get Mommy's attention is by doing the "right" thing—when he's quiet, when he's playing, when he's happy.

Unsafe Products: Is there anything else you want to add or tell parents about?

Don't use walkers! Walkers move at four times the speed that the child can developmentally keep up with. Also, babies in walkers are able to reach things that have been out of their reach while they were on the floor but can now reach because of the walker. They can pull things over on themselves. And walkers can hit a bump in the carpet and flip over (see box "Are Walkers Safe?").

A second thing that parents need to know is not to get bumper pads for the crib. They look pretty, but that's all they

Are Walkers Safe?

The American Academy of Pediatrics advises that you *not* use walkers with your baby. The walkers of previous generations allowed babies to walk/roll along as fast as their little toes could go. The problem is that "what goes forward must also stop." Studies have shown that babies knocking into walls or furniture have actually sustained neck injuries, some as serious as whiplash. Further, baby can get out of your sight in a silent instant and be headed for a staircase, which could be deadly. Third, walkers do not allow for normal walking positions. The height and pose of the seat only allow for babies' little toes to do the moving. We don't walk on our toes, but rather in a heel-to-toe fashion, elongating and using our Achilles' tendon. Walkers and overuse of exer-saucers contribute to "toe walking" and actually shorten the tendon at the back of the heel. Using an exer-saucer is okay as long as the seat is lowered enough so that your baby's feet can stand flat, but as with most things, moderation is key to healthy usage.

do. Children don't need them at any age. It is important not to have bumper pads as a precaution to SIDS.

Getting Emotionally Attached: You may see 20 to 30 patients a day. You have a lot of emotion packed into your daily life as a pediatrician. How does that affect you?

I cry a lot. I cry when diagnosing a life-threatening illness. I cry with happiness, rejoicing. Part of being a good physician is being emotionally attached. It pulls on a lot of emotional aspects. I think the biggest honor that somebody can give is bringing their little infant to you and saying, "Help me." The trust that a parent actually gives you by handing you their child is overwhelming. Physicians need to take this very seriously.

References

American Academy of Pediatrics. (2001, February). Children, adolescents, and television. *Pediatrics, 107*(2), 423-426.

Arnold, C., Bartlett, K., Gowani, S., & Meral, R. (2007, March). *Is everybody ready? Readiness, transition and continuity: Reflections and moving forward* (Working Paper 41). The Hague, The Netherlands: Bernard van Leer Foundation.

Berenstain, S., & Berenstain, J. (1983). *The Berenstains' baby book.* New York: Pocket Books.

Blakemore, C. J., & Ramirez, B. W. (2006). *Baby read-aloud basics: Fun and interactive ways to help your little one discover the world of words.* New York: Amacom.

Breus, M. J. (2008, May 29). *How much sleep do children need?* Retrieved July 23, 2008, from www.webmd.com/parenting/guide/how-much-sleep-do-children-need

Burgess, K. (2008, April). *Talented toddlers: Identifying and enriching the gifted toddler.* Retrieved May 1, 2008, from www.toddlerstoday.com/articles/development/talented-toddlers-5765

Burnham, M., & Lawler, J. (2006). *The complete idiot's guide to sleep training for your child.* New York: Alpha Books.

Chess, S., & Thomas A. (1996). *Temperament: Theory and practice.* New York: Bruner/Mazel.

Cone, L. (n.d.). *Swaddling babies: Ancient practice comforts infants and parents.* Retrieved July 27, 2006, from www.babiestoday.com/articles/basic-care/swaddling-babies-3657/3

Daley, B. (2008, April 23). *Puzzle, precaution over plastic.* Retrieved July 23, 2008, from www.boston.com/lifestyle/green/articles/2008/04/23/puzzle_precaution_over_plastic

Diagnosing autism spectrum disorders. (n.d.). Retrieved July 23, 2008, from www.webmd.com/brain/austim/diagnosis-autism-spectrum-disorders

Duke University Medical Center. (1998, April 9). *Extra choline during pregnancy enhances memory in offspring.* Retrieved July 23, 2008, from www.sciencedaily.com/releases/1998/04/980409080807.htm

Fitzpatrick, M. (2002, Sept.). Theories of child language acquisition. *Child Language Acquisition.*

Focus on eye exams. (2007). *Parents,* 44.

Glass, P. (2002). *What do babies see?* Retrieved July 23, 2008, from www.lighthouse.org/medical/childrens-vision/what-do-babies-see

Golinkoff, R., & Hirsh-Pasek, K. (2005). *Five minute linguist.* Retrieved July 23, 2008, from www.cofc.edu/linguist/archives/2005/05

Golonka, D. (2007, Feb. 28). *Tubes for ear infections.* Retrieved May 22, 2008, from www.webmd.com/cold-and-flu/ear-infection/tubes-for-ear-infections

Gookin, S. H., & Gookin, D. (2002). *Parenting for dummies* (2nd ed.). New York: Hungry Minds.

Gunnar, M., & Quevedo, K. (2007, Jan.). The neurobiology of stress and development. *Annual Review of Psychology, 58,* 145-173.

Judge, M. P., Harel, O., & Lammi-Keefe, C. J. (2007, June). Maternal consumption of a docosahexaenoic acid-containing functional food during pregnancy: Benefit for infant performance on problem-solving but not on recognition memory tasks at age 9 months. *American Journal of Clinical Nutrition,* 1572-1577.

Karp, H. (2002). *The happiest baby on the block.* New York: Bantam Books.

Knorr, C. (2003, Feb). *Your child's growing brain.* Retrieved July 23, 2008, from www.parenthood.com/article-topics/article-topics.php?Article_ID=3603

Kutner, L. (1994). *Parent and child: Getting through to each other.* New York: Avon Books.

Leppo, M. L., Davis, D., & Crim, B. (2000, Spring). The basics of exercising the mind and body. *Childhood Education, 76,* 142-147.

March of Dimes. (2007, August). *Hearing impairment.* Retrieved May 23, 2008, from www.marchofdimes.com/professionals/14332_1232.asp

March of Dimes. (2008, April 24). *President signs into law March of Dimes-supported Newborn Screening Saves Lives Act.* Retrieved May 11, 2008, from www.marchofdimes.com/printableArticles/22684_29860.asp

Marchand, S. (2008, May). Destiny's child. *Wondertime,* 84-89.

Margulis, J. (2008, May). Why do babies look so keenly at faces? *Wondertime,* 38.

McLellan, T. K. (2007, Sept.). What can he see? *Parenting,* 150.

National Scientific Council on the Developing Child. (2005). *Excessive stress disrupts the architecture of the developing brain* (Working Paper No. 3). Retrieved July 23, 2008, from www.developingchild.net/reports.shtml

National Institute on Deafness and Other Communication Disorders, National Institutes of Health. (2002, July). *Otitis media (Ear infection).* Retrieved March 6, 2008, from www.nidcd.nih.gov/health/hearing/otitism.asp

Perlez, J. (1996, March 25). *Romanian "orphans": Prisoners of their cribs.* Retrieved July 23, 2008, from http://query.nytimes.com/gst/fullpage.html?res=9B06E7D71439F936A15750C0A960958260

Pica, R. (2006a). *A running start.* New York: Marlowe & Co.

Pica, R. (2006b, June). *Skinship: Better bonding with baby.* Retrieved September 7, 2007, from www.movingandlearning.com/Resources/Articles24.htm

Ratcliff, K. (2008, March). Raise a reader. *Parents,* 118-121.

Roberts, J. E., & Zeisel, S. A. (2000, July 26). *Ear infections and language development.* Retrieved March 6, 2008, from www.ed.gov/offices/OERI/ECI/earinfections.pdf

Ruf, D. L. (2005). *Losing our minds: Gifted children left behind.* Scottsdale, AZ: Great Potential Press.

Sattler, J. M. (2002). *Assessment of children: Behavioral and clinical applications* (4th ed.). San Diego, CA: Author.

Sattler, J. M. (2008). *Assessment of children: Cognitive foundations* (5th ed.). San Diego, CA: Author.

Sears, M., & Sears, W. (2000). *Why breast is best.* Retrieved May 9, 2008, from www.enotalone.com/article/3603.html

Skinner, W. (2007). *Infinity & zebra stripes: Life with gifted children.* Scottsdale, AZ: Great Potential Press.

SparkNotes Staff. (2008, Aug. 13). *SparkNote on stress, coping, and health.* Retrieved July 23, 2008, from www.sparknotes.com/psychology/psych101/stress

Stamm, J., with Spencer, P. (2007, Sept.). Talk to me. *Parenting,* 89.

Thurston, A. F. (1996, April). In a Chinese orphanage. *The Atlantic Monthly, 277*(4), 28-41.

Trost, S. (2007). *Physical education, physical activity and academic performance* (Research Brief). Princeton, NJ: Robert Wood Johnson Foundation.

U.S. Department of Health and Human Services, Office on Women's Health. (2005, April). *Depression during and after pregnancy.* Retrieved July 23, 2008, from www.womenshealth.gov/faq/postpartum.pdf

Whiteman, B. (2001, July 11). *Birth of musical protégés? How music heard in the womb is remembered by the child.* Retrieved July 23, 2008, from www.le.ac.uk/press/press/babiesmusic.html

Willis, J. (2008). *Building better brains: Brain research-based strategies to enhance learning for gifted middle school students.* Scottsdale, AZ: Great Potential Press.

Wood, M. E. (2005). *Reactive Attachment Disorder: A disorder of attachment or of temperament?* Retrieved July 23, 2008, from www.personalityresearch.org/papers/wood.html

Zilberstein, K. (2006, Jan.). Clarifying core characteristics of attachment disorders: A review of current research and theory. *American Journal of Orthopsychiatry, 76*(1), 55-64.

Endnotes

Chapter 1

1   Knorr (2003)
2   (2008, p. 246)
3   Duke University Medical Center (1998)
4   Judge, Harel, & Lammi-Keefe (2007)
5   Sattler (2008, p. 249)
6   Sattler (2008, p. 249)
7   (2008)
8   (2002, p. 357)
9   (2007)
10 Burgess (2008)
11 (2005)

Chapter 2

1   As cited in Knorr (2003)
2   Perlez (1996)
3   (2006b)
4   Zilberstein (2006)
5   Wood (2005)
6   National Scientific Council on the Developing Child (2005)
7   (2005)
8   Gunnar & Quevedo (2007)
9   (2006b)
10 Sears & Sears (2000)
11 Margulis (2008)
12 Cone (n.d.)

Chapter 3

1   Fitzpatrick (2002)
2   Stamm (2007)
3   (2006)
4   Ratcliff (2008)

5   (2001)
6   Roberts & Zeisel (2000)
7   Arnold, Bartlett, Gowani, & Meral (2007, p. 6)

Chapter 4

1   Glass (2002)
2   Margulis (2008)
3   McLellan (2007)
4   *Focus on eye exams* (2007)

Chapter 5

1   Whiteman (2001)
2   (2007)
3   March of Dimes (2007)
4   National Institute on Deafness and Other Communication Disorders (2002)
5   Golinkoff & Hirsh-Pasek (2005)
6   Golonka (2007)

Chapter 6

1   Leppo, Davis, & Crim (2000)
2   Trost (2007, p. 2)
3   (2002)
4   Daley (2008)

Chapter 7

1   Personal communication, April 25, 2008
2   SparkNotes Staff (2008)
3   (1996)
4   (2005)
5   (p. 200)
6   (p. 200)
7   (p. 201)
8   (1994)

Chapter 8

1   March of Dimes (2008)
2   *Diagnosing autism spectrum disorders* (n.d.)
3   Breus (2008)

Index

About the Authors

Holly Engel-Smothers is a former Parent Educator for the Parents as Teachers early childhood program and continues to work as a consultant for Parents as Teachers, especially for families with twins. To qualify for this certification, Holly participated in hundreds of hours of training and workshops to study a brain-based curriculum that benefits both educators and parents. Since 1990, she has been an educator specializing in teaching parents and their children up to age seven. She works in a Title I program teaching low-level students and is on her district's Communication Arts Committee and Literacy Team. She has a Master's Degree in Teaching Reading. Holly's writing credits include "The Read and Respond" series, consisting of six curriculum guides based on children's literature. She has also written "The Real World" series—three books for practical applications of reading, math, and science. Holly has had numerous articles published in magazines, including Missouri's National Education Magazine *Something Better*, as well as *Mother and Child Reunion: A Parenting, Education, and Health Resource*. She is a contributing author to the books *Chicken Soup for the Soul: Living Catholic Faith* (2008), *It's Twins! Parent-to-Parent Advice from Infancy through Adolescence* (2007), and *Twice the Love: Stories of Inspiration for Families with Twins, Multiples, and Singletons* (2007).

Susan M. Heim is an author and editor specializing in parenting, multiples, and women's issues, and she is a former Senior Editor for the bestselling Chicken Soup for the Soul series. Susan's books include *Oh, Baby! 7 Ways a Baby Will Change Your Life the First Year*; *Twice the Love: Stories of Inspiration for Families with Twins, Multiples, and Singletons*; *It's Twins! Parent-to-Parent Advice from Infancy through Adolescence*; and the upcoming *Chicken Soup for the Soul: Twins and*

More (2009). Susan's articles and essays have appeared in many books, magazines, and websites. She writes a regular online column for *Mommies Magazine* called "Loving and Living with Twins and Multiples," as well as a blog for parents called "Susan Heim on Parenting" (www.susanheim.blogspot.com). She has been on numerous radio shows, including BBC Radio, Colleen Miller's "Lighten Up" show, the Michael Dresser show, Parent's Journal, Parent Talk with Susannah Baldwin, and Share Your Mission with Winn Henderson, M.D. Susan is also an expert on twins and multiples for AllExperts.com and ParentsConnect.com, as well as a parenting expert for SelfGrowth.com. She is a member of the National Association of Women Writers and the Southeastern Writers Association and has a degree in Business Administration from Michigan State University. Susan maintains websites at www.susanheim.com, ababywillchangeyourlife.com, and www.twinstalk.com.

Other Publications from Great Potential Press

www.giftedbooks.com

How to Parent So Children Will Learn
By Sylvia Rimm, Ph.D.

Dr. Rimm provides practical, compassionate, no-nonsense advice for raising happy, secure, and productive children, from preschool to college. Chapters include easy-to-follow parent pointers, sample dialogues, and boxed step-by-step strategies.

ISBN 978-0-910707-86-2 / 352 pages / Paperback / $21.95

A Parent's Guide to Gifted Children
By James Webb, Ph.D., Janet Gore, M.Ed., Edward Amend, Psy.D., and Arlene DeVries, M.S.E.

Raising a gifted child is both a joy and a challenge, yet parents of gifted children have few resources for reliable parenting information. This four-time award-winner, deemed a "must-read," provides practical guidance in numerous areas.

ISBN 978-0-910707-52-7 / 415 pages / Paperback / $24.95

To order GPP books or request a catalog, contact:
Great Potential Press
PO Box 5057, Scottsdale, AZ 85261
Toll-Free: 877-954-4200 ~ Email: info@giftedbooks.com ~ Website: www.giftedbooks.com

Other Publications from Great Potential Press
www.giftedbooks.com

Parenting Successful Children
By James Webb, Ph.D.

The frequent breakups of families, the fast pace of technology, the information explosion, and other changes in today's evolving world make parenting more difficult. Learn more than two dozen practical strategies to set successful limits, avoid power struggles, minimize sibling rivalry, promote self-esteem, and much more. Available in both DVD and Audio Book format.

ISBN 978-0-910707-36-7 / 52 min / DVD / $29.95
ISBN 978-0-910707-85-5 / Audio Book & Pamphlet / $21.95

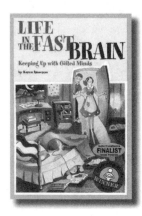

Life in the Fast Brain: Keeping Up with Gifted Minds
By Karen Isaacson

As a sequel to the delightfully entertaining and award-winning *Raisin' Brains: Surviving My Smart Family*, this book will keep the laughs coming! This mother is living proof that the journey of raising five gifted kids is full of surprises. Enjoy comical stories of the things gifted kids do and say, and discover the wit and wonder of this mother all over again!

ISBN 978-0-910707-82-4 / 176 pages / Paperback / $16.95

To order GPP books or request a catalog, contact:
Great Potential Press
PO Box 5057, Scottsdale, AZ 85261
Toll-Free: 877-954-4200 ~ Email: info@giftedbooks.com ~ Website: www.giftedbooks.com

Other Publications from Great Potential Press

www.giftedbooks.com

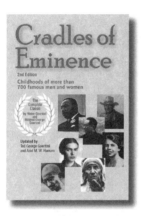

Cradles of Eminence: Childhoods of more than 700 Famous Men and Women
By Victor Goertzel, Ph.D., Mildred Goertzel, B.A., Ted Goertzel, Ph.D., and Ariel Hansen, B.A.

Get acquainted with the childhoods of several-hundred famous people, including Walt Disney, Elvis Presley, Lucille Ball, Oprah Winfrey, and Michael Jordan. Discover how they lived, the struggles they faced, and the roads that led them to stardom.

ISBN 978-0-910707-57-2 / 492 pages / Paperback / $24.95

Infinity & Zebra Stripes: Life with Gifted Children
By Wendy Skinner

The author shares her family's story of struggle and eventual success in working with the school system to meet her children's needs. Enlightening anecdotes demonstrate strategies for minimizing parent-school conflict and for building trusting relationships with teachers and administrators.

ISBN 978-0-910707-81-7 / 184 pages / Paperback / $16.95

To order GPP books or request a catalog, contact:
Great Potential Press
PO Box 5057, Scottsdale, AZ 85261
Toll-Free: 877-954-4200 ~ Email: info@giftedbooks.com ~ Website: www.giftedbooks.com

Other Publications from Great Potential Press
www.giftedbooks.com

Helping Gifted Children Soar
By Carol Strip Whitney, Ph.D., with Gretchen Hirsch

This reader-friendly book describes "the world's biggest, highest, and longest roller coaster"... the one called parenting a gifted child. Discover how to survive the ups and downs by learning about important gifted issues such as types of gifted programs, helping parents and teachers work together, meeting social and emotional needs, and forming parent support groups.

ISBN 978-0-910707-41-1 / 288 pages / Paperback / $19.95

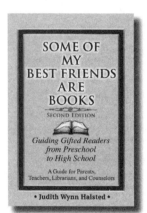

Some of My Best Friends Are Books
By Judith Wynn Halsted, M.S.

This annotated K-12 reading list comes complete with summaries of nearly 300 titles for bright students. Recommended books will both challenge and stimulate young minds. Cross-indexed by author, title, topic, and reading level, Halsted also includes questions for each book to promote discussion and understanding.

ISBN 978-0-910707-51-0 / 552 pages / Paperback / $26.95

To order GPP books or request a catalog, contact:
Great Potential Press
PO Box 5057, Scottsdale, AZ 85261
Toll-Free: 877-954-4200 ~ Email: info@giftedbooks.com ~ Website: www.giftedbooks.com

"Until I began rowing indoors several times a week at age 53, I never believed what I had always been told, that you have more energy when you exercise. Almost immediately after taking up indoor rowing, I noted a significant change in my sleep pattern. I was able to fall asleep easily and when I awakened I felt more rested than I had in years. **In addition to relieving stress, rowing has improved my memory function and I have experienced a reduction in chronic neck and back pain, better control of my hypertension, and less dependence on prescription medications.** I find that mornings are the best times to work out on my rowing machine. Rowing first thing in the morning gives me a chance to clear my head and plan my day. **For the first time ever, I actually look forward to exercising. I'm hooked."**

Diane E. Goller, J.D.
Crew Parent, Domestic Relations Attorney.

"Great motivation for both the novice and the lapsed athlete to adopt a healthy and balanced approach to daily exercise, **this book has the potential to change and lengthen your active life."**

Jo A. Hannafin, M.D.
Professor of Orthopaedic Surgery, Weill Medical College of Cornell University, Hospital for Special Surgery; Olympic Team Physician, 2004; Member, International Federation of Rowing Associations ("FISA") Sports Medicine Commission; Former collegiate rower, three-time National Champion (double and quad), and current recreational rower.

"Filled with positive energy, encouragement, and sound advice, Ordway **shows the way to improve your fitness and quality of life through rowing."**

Marlene Royle, OTR
Rowing Coach; Author of Tip of the Blade: Notes on Rowing; Founder of Roylerow Performance Training Programs, www.roylerow.com.

"To go from moderate fitness to elite, Olympic-level fitness requires vast amounts of time, effort, willpower, and a certain genetic potential, with little or no effect on health or longevity. But to go from a sedentary lifestyle to moderate fitness requires surprisingly little time, realistic amounts of effort and will power, and no particular genetic potential, while the effects on health and longevity are enormous. **Rowing is a simple and enjoyable activity from which virtually anyone, regardless of initial fitness level or innate athletic ability, can benefit.** If you give it a chance, rowing may improve not only your fitness, but your whole outlook on life. This book provides a simple program that, consistent with fundamental principles of kinesiology (the study of the mechanics of human motion), anyone can use to improve their health and fitness. **I use the principles in this book to help train people to become Navy SEALS; you can use them to improve your fitness at your own pace, whatever that may be.**"

Michael Caviston, MS (Kinesiology); Director of Fitness, United States Naval Special Warfare Center, Coronado, CA (www.sealswcc.com); Former Rowing and Conditioning Coach (University of Michigan); CRASH-B Indoor Rowing World Record Holder and World Champion (2002, 2003, 2005) (Senior Lightweight Men [ages 40-49]) .

"Mr. Ordway offers a wonderful perspective and approach to rowing via discussion of concepts and principles that also apply to good living. This book is like **a 'golden gateway' to the sport of rowing for those who know nothing about it and a demonstration of how easily you can find better health and a better life through rowing!**"

Victoria Draper
Founder/CEO, Rowbics Indoor Rowing, Inc., www.rowbics.com.

"To competitive rowers, the idea of rowing in their 'comfort zone' is heresy. 'No pain, no gain' is the rule. If you want to be a competitive rower, this book is not for you. But if you want the health benefits of exercise without the pain and suffering, you just need to move more and move more often. Ordway explains how **anyone can use the same rowing machines as Olympic rowers, but use them at their own pace to improve their health and energy. This book outlines a practical program that everyone can do every day.**"

John G. Everett, PhD
Member, United States Eight (World Champion, 1974; Olympic team, 1976 and 1980); Four-time winner, CRASH-B Sprints, Masters Division.

"Use this book for essential encouragement as it lights the pathway to improved physical and mental health through rowing. As a 60-year-old, non-athlete psychologist, I am thrilled to see this wisdom on the benefits of rowing being shared with a wider audience. **In my experience** and that of people I know from rowing in Austin, Texas and at Craftsbury Sculling Camp, **rowing is an effective and enjoyable way to turn back the effects of osteoporosis and returns many other health benefits. Hooray!**"

Jean Ehrenberg, PhD
Clinical Psychologist, Recreational Rower

Row Daily, Breathe Deeper, Live Better

Row Daily, Breathe Deeper, Live Better

✦

A Guide to Moderate Exercise

D.P. Ordway
(Use Indoor Rowing to Build Muscle
Mass and Wind to Enhance Your
Vintage Body's Performance)

iUniverse, Inc.
New York   Bloomington

Row Daily, Breathe Deeper, Live Better
A Guide to Moderate Exercise

iUniverse books may be ordered through booksellers or by contacting:

iUniverse
1663 Liberty Drive
Bloomington, IN 47403
www.iuniverse.com
1-800-Authors (1-800-288-4677)

ISBN: 978-0-595-43437-4 (pbk)
ISBN: 978-0-595-69537-9 (cloth)
ISBN: 978-0-595-87764-5 (ebk)

Printed in the United States of America

iUniverse rev. date: 11/20/08

Dedicated to Kim, Sam, Elsa and Sophie

Acknowledgments

John, for introducing me to rowing.

Tom, Pete, and Mike for their coaching, leadership, and love of the sport.

Mike, Jere, Greg, Andy, James, John, Doug and many others, for the pleasure of rowing and competing together.

Doug, Dickie, Mike, Lisa and many others for growing Michigan Crew at a critical time.

Grant, Sharon, Christine, Susan, Linda, Kent, Kevin, Ed, Bob, Colleen, Paul, Amy, Tom, and many others for their efforts to support Grand Rapids Crew.

Todd, Regina, Sophie, John, and other friends and family who have read and commented on drafts and revisions.

Sarah Wimer and Sandy Kendall for their editorial insights. All mistakes are mine.

"Never go to excess, but let moderation be your guide."

—Cicero

"A sound mind in a sound body
is a short but full description of a happy state in this world."

—John Locke

Contents

Preface

Writing this book has felt at times like a fool's errand. There are several reasons for this. The core idea of daily adaptation seems so obvious to me that it should not have to be stated. It goes against the grain for a competitive rower and rowing coach to advocate "moderate" rather than competitive rowing. Exercising every day seems extreme rather than moderate to many people. And rowing on a machine is not perceived as fun. As Dr. Henry S. Lodge, co-author of *Younger Next Year*, wrote about this idea, "while I wholeheartedly agree with the overall concept, . . . [rowing machines] do seem sadly to be the least used machines in the gym."

I felt I had many good reasons to continue in spite of these concerns. One reason was to overcome the many misconceptions about rowing and healthy exercise. Many people mistakenly think rowing is not for everyone because it has to be strenuous and is inaccessible. The common idea of limiting exercise to three days per week also must be reconsidered. These two misconceptions bracket what this book is about. The many other reasons are the parents of teenagers I have worked with and the adults of all ages I have seen benefit from rowing. The parents recognize the value of rowing in their children's lives, but rarely see what it can do for them. Many adults learning to row look for basic direction. I hope this book helps them get something valuable out of rowing in their own way without feeling they need to emulate competitive athletes.

A few notes about my background may help explain my perspective. I first heard about rowing when I was a freshman at MIT. I was lucky enough to row with some great athletes in a growing intercollegiate program. In 1972, we won a fall race, in the process beating some members of that year's Olympic silver-medal rowing team. The Olympians may have approached that race as a pleasant diversion between the rigors of international competition and the following Spring's college championships. For us, however, the experience of gaining on and defeating them in a three-mile race was a tremendous experience. During the summer after that autumn victory, our boat competed in England and Switzerland. My senior year, we placed second at the year-end championship. After having been neither an athlete nor a competitor in high school, I was learning first hand the value of using year-round training for achieving competitive improvement, a relatively new idea at that time.

After I graduated from MIT and before I started to practice law, I learned more about training for competition while coaching rowing at Brown University and the University of Michigan. I worked with a lot of great people in both programs. One of the best learning experiences I had was sitting down after each practice to discuss rowing with Vic Michalson, then the head coach at Brown. Mike was an exceptionally dedicated and focused person. Although he may not have said it this way, a core message that came through again and again was, "Figure out what works and do it; acknowledge what does not work and discard it."

Years later, when I began coaching kids in our community, I encountered a new challenge. How do you instill in a new team, with no experienced rowers who can set an example, the importance of being at practice every day? I learned a lot from working with the kids and their parents.

While I was coaching the junior rowers, I was also trying to recover some of the fitness I had lost over the years. I found as I got older that, if I did not exercise for a few days, I began to feel like I was starting over the next time. I would feel bored, tired, and winded after just a few minutes. I began to realize that the most important part of my own physical training was fitting the workout into my schedule each day.

Then, one of our children who was rowing began to complain if the gym was closed or she could not get on the rowing machine that day. She had internalized the principle of exercising every day. Her workouts had become an essential part of her day. What a breath of fresh air! And her fitness improved tremendously as a result of her diligence.

I found myself answering questions from parents and team contributors about how adults could use rowing for their own fitness. And I came to see that someone who had no interest in rowing on the water or in competing as a rower could still benefit from using the indoor rowing machine for fitness.

I also began to pay more attention to the many articles in the popular press on health and exercise. All too often, the columnist notes the benefits of exercise but assumes it will be ineffective. For example, in her April 22, 2008 column in the *New York Times*, Jane Brody quotes an expert on hypertension, Dr. Marvin Moser, saying that although improving exercise habits can help lower blood pressure, "most people can't adjust their lifestyles enough to normalize" it. As a result, the medical focus is on minimizing the side effects of medication. We are certainly lucky to live in this age of modern medicine. But I believe it is possible for the average person to do something medicine cannot achieve, to use exercise effectively to help "normalize" his or her health. Let me know whether you agree.

D.P. Ordway

Introduction

This book is based on a simple, self-evident truth: Your body adapts to how it is stimulated every day by tuning itself to do more of the same, only better.

A second basic idea supports what follows: Your body is designed to be used more actively than occurs in the average, sedentary modern lifestyle. A simple conclusion follows from these two fundamental notions: A daily routine of breathing more deeply with moderate exercise will stimulate your body to develop greater fitness and energy.

We all know that something as simple as taking a walk each day can help us feel better. This book explains a self-directed, non-threatening method of using rowing (along with walking and other exercise, if you wish) to enhance your fitness and well-being—it's a simple guide to moderate, daily exercise that can work for anyone.

The book is not intended to motivate you. There are many sources of motivation within and around each of us, including:

- I want to lose weight.

- My doctor says I need to exercise.

- I am not sleeping well.

- I need relief from stress (have high blood pressure, etc.).

- My cholesterol is high.

- My wind and energy, even for simple daily tasks, are too limited.

- Osteoporosis runs in my family.

- I want to get in better shape to improve my basketball (insert your own interest: running, cycling, soccer, swimming, and so on).

The list is nearly endless. Exercise is often recommended as a curative or helpful measure to deal with many maladies, including the effects of aging. We all, whether active or out of shape, have our reasons to become more fit.

The plan I set forth here is simple: Start rowing today on an indoor rowing machine. Do it easily, without pushing. And then continue to do it moderately every day, to the extent you can. Learn from this book and from your own experience as you go.

The rest of this book is about why that works and how to get more out of it. If you decide later that you want to explore differing perspectives on exercise and health, you should. But do not put off exercising in order to study.

Daily rowing is an exercise for everyone. Anyone can do it without any special background or training:

- You do not have to be a rower (someone who has learned to row on the water or who has been trained in rowing technique).

- You do not need to know anything about the sport of rowing.

- You do not need to *become* a rower, or even want to.

- You do not have to be athletic, fit, or thin.

- You do not need to become competitive or to push yourself to your limits.

- You do not have to join a club or group.

- You do not have to row at a time that suits anyone's schedule but yours.

- You do not have to go to a central facility to row.

- You will not have to deal with weather or seasonal changes.

The biggest challenge about daily rowing is simply to make it happen each day, to fit it into your schedule and make it a habit.

Take that challenge on: Try it yourself today. Go to the Y and spend a few minutes on one of the rowing machines there. Keep at it each day. Over time, you will find your body is responsive to this healthful stimulus. You will gain muscle mass (and strength) and improve your wind.

Some critics may say that starting without proper coaching will result in bad habits. And they may be correct from the point of view of perfect technique. But consider this competing point of view: *The worst bad habit is not to exercise.* The most important good habit to develop is to exercise every day. You can take steps as you proceed to improve your technique. You can ask questions. You can hire a personal trainer if you wish. But start rowing today.

What Does Daily Stimulation Mean?

The body responds daily to the activity it experiences whether we exercise it or not. For example, my body responds not only to the weight-lifting I do on Monday but also to my sitting at my desk, in airports, in the car, and in front of the computer and television on Tuesday through Thursday. Thus, using this example, by Friday my body has reacted to one workout on one day and three days of inactivity. This translates into daily instructions to store fat and be sedentary. If I then lift weights again on Friday thinking, "I should feel strong because I just did this earlier this week," I am likely to be disappointed with the results. My body has been instructed for the three most recent days that I want to store energy, not use it.

The body does not know work schedules, excuses, or good intentions. Each day you spend working at the desk or puttering in the garden without exercising provides the body instructions just as surely as the day you work out for an hour of deeper breathing.

If you pay attention to the instructions you give your body every day, will you find you are giving it consistent instructions to improve your fitness? Inconsistent, confusing instructions undermine the body's ability to perform.

Consistent, appropriate daily stimulus will improve your fitness over time to an extent that will amaze you. Consider the expression "Rome wasn't built in a day." One building block and paving stone at a time, a city and an empire were built out of nothing. On any given day or week, Rome did not look much different than before. Yet over time, tremendous change was achieved. In the same way, what you can achieve over time at a moderate pace far exceeds what a brief, all-out effort or inconsistent training can produce.

Become Winded; Gain Wind

Too often, we judge our fitness and health based on a single, narrow criterion like body weight, arm strength, or muscle definition. Fitness is a state of the body as a whole, including how all of the body parts function, not just how some of them look. Do not become trapped into believing you are becoming fit overall based only on the number of push-ups you can do. That and similar indicators are too narrow to be your guide.

Instead, look for a broader indicator. How your lungs function may not be as simple to monitor numerically as how many push-ups you do, but it is a far more meaningful measure of fitness. You need effective oxygen exchange (getting oxygen from the air into your blood) for all of the work your body performs (not just while you exercise, but twenty-four hours a day). You improve that exchange by stimulating your lungs while you exercise.

You do not need complex technical information from stress tests and the measurement of "VO$_2$ max" (how much oxygen your lungs can exchange while working to your limit) to gauge how you are doing. Simply ask yourself, *"How do I feel* when I take a walk, go for a jog, run for a cab, or walk up a flight of stairs?" Do you feel powerful and eager to do more, or are you struggling for breath? For almost everyone, the answer is "struggling." It does not have to be that way; our bodies are designed to do better. Your body works better when it is more active some of the time rather than resting all the time.

Learn to get out of breath intentionally in a controlled way as you exercise instead of fearing the feeling of being winded. Every day that you engage in exercise that safely and effectively causes you to breathe more deeply (but still comfortably) for thirty to forty-five minutes or more, your body will reward you with better lung power. Better lung power is the foundation of better fitness and that translates into yet more effective exercise. It is a cycle you will learn to use to your benefit.

Keep in mind that every day you skip, every day you do not engage in some exercise that causes you to breathe more deeply, you are instructing your lungs to become less efficient. The body does not coast; it declines without positive stimulus. When you struggle for breath after walking up the stairs because you do not exercise (or, worse yet, you avoid taking the stairs altogether), you are reaping the "rewards" of your lack of daily stimulation (or your stimulation to be sedentary, if you will).

Make your motto *"Spirare est Vivere"* ("To Breathe is to Live"). Pay attention to your breath. Enjoy deeper breathing and watch it improve your life.

WHY ROWING?

The beauty of indoor rowing as an exercise, apart from the easy access, is that it is a non-impact exercise that can be done at any age and *at any level of effort.* It can be done moderately, as I advocate here, and does not have to be painful or intense. As a result, it can be used in a way that is responsive to your needs and condition, whatever they may be.

The rowing motion involves sitting down and generating resistance based on how hard you choose to work. Since you control it, you stimulate your breathing to the degree that is right for you. Exercising in your comfort zone, you can do it every day. Using the monitor on the rowing machine, you can keep track of and record your improvements over time. Since rowing uses nearly the whole muscle mass of the body, it has the added benefit of stimulating heart and lungs more efficiently and completely than most other exercises. And since you row sitting down on a stable seat and without joint impact, it is safer and easier for many of us to undertake as beginners than most other forms of exercise. In short, it is one of the safest and most effective ways to stimulate your whole body each day to greater health.

WHY DAILY?

I suggest you row daily based on how our bodies function. In my experience, the body responds well to being given reasonable stimulation each day. Daily rowing transforms the way your body works by using its natural abilities to adapt and to function more efficiently.

My focus on rowing daily does not come from a scientific study but from experience and common sense. We live on a twenty-four hour cycle of activity and rest. It seems sensible to make the activity during each cycle well-suited to optimum functioning. Consider the extreme opposite, complete inactivity. Most of us are not bedridden and at risk of developing bed sores. But a day of sitting most of the time can have harmful consequences for our bodies, nonetheless. Most of us cannot change the need to work at a computer or to commute. But we can insert into the day a period of exercise that gets the heart pumping and the systems of the body working more actively than when we are at rest.

It is also useful to plan to exercise daily because, inevitably, there will be days you cannot exercise. Planning to exercise every other day will lead to exercising three days a week (or two, or fewer) instead of four. Planning to exercise six days a week will lead to five or four or three. Plan to exercise every day. You will do better for that attempt and can only gain more if you succeed.

Among the many books and studies on exercise, there is much information available about how long and how often to exercise. For example, someone training to run a marathon can get a weeks-long schedule of training runs. I am not aware of any that promotes exercising every day. However, I believe that stems from the fact that most exercises other than rowing involve pounding or twisting or other impacts on the body. You need rest to recover from that. In addition, most training regimens focus on training for competition. If you are training for health rather than competition and do not overdo it, you can row every day and benefit from it.

USING THIS BOOK

Here are some suggestions to help you enjoy this book:

First, the book begins with an explanation of the principles. Following a second chapter on the implications of those principles for the body, chapters three through five provide information on how to row. Start with the principles if understanding the reasoning appeals to you. Ignore the principles and go right to the rowing instruction in chapter three if you prefer. You can look back at the principles at your convenience. *Most importantly, do whatever helps you start now and helps you keep at it every day.* Thinking about it does you no good; doing it is what counts.

Second, you may want to explore the resources in the Appendices first for background information on rowing. On the other hand, I put that information in the back because you do not need it for now; look at it later if you like. For example, you do not need to know the difference between sweep rowing and sculling to have your own beneficial indoor rowing experience.

Third, feel free just to scan the book at first, start rowing right away, and then turn back to it for reference as you work on your rowing. Many of the tips, such as those in chapter five, may be more useful for you to read as you proceed, rather than serving as preparation to begin. You are not required to read and incorporate anything in the book to get started.

Here are a few ways to start quickly:

- Take five minutes to read sections 3.1 through 3.3; go to your local YMCA and begin. When you get home, return to the book for more pointers.

- For more technical background, scan through chapters three through five; get on a rowing machine and begin. You can fill in the blanks day by day as you proceed.

- Read section 3.2 on rowing machines; go on-line and call and order your own rowing machine. Read the book while it is being shipped and get started when it arrives.

Here are synopses of the chapters of the book to help you pick and choose:

- Chapter One: Two key principles are that the body responds to its daily activity and that the body is designed to function actively. The beginning of this chapter discusses these two principles. The rest discusses the fact that rowing daily is an optimum way to apply the two principles to improve your muscles mass, your wind, and your health.

- Chapter Two: What happens to your body when you exercise? This chapter offers a lay person's perspective on how rowing is good for the systems of the body, with a few brief technical notes to illustrate what happens inside the body when we exercise and become more fit.

- Chapter Three: Start rowing with a simple set of instructions, with information about rowing machines and where to find one.

- Chapter Four: Daily rowing is good for other activities in your life; and, other exercises can supplement your rowing. Evaluate your success using a variety of methods to score yourself.

- Chapter Five: Rowing is a simple motion. There are many ways to vary your movements and to work on effective technique. Here are a dozen suggestions.

- Chapter Six: Aches, pains and other complaints will occur. Acknowledge them and deal with them rather than letting them interfere.

- Chapter Seven: The biggest challenge with rowing each day is fitting it into your daily life. Here are some thoughts concerning different aspects of daily life and how to manage them to help you row.

- The Appendices contain background information about rowing, terminology, and information resources, as well as some ideas on working out the conflicts between other demands in your life and your attempts to row daily.

In sum, even if you intend to read this book cover to cover and engage in a dialogue with a personal coach to help set up your rowing program in an organized way from the start, it is not necessary to do all of that before you begin. My advice is to *get started. Find or buy a rowing machine today and start rowing now.*

CAVEATS

If you already exercise often: Please keep in mind, those of you who are already fit and competitive, that the thoughts here are primarily for those who should exercise more. Some of us are already applying the principles described here by regularly stimulating our bodies toward better fitness. If you are doing that and pushing yourself for competition, you actually *should* take a day off once in a while. Do not take the basic rule as license to overdo it. *Get the rest you need and listen to your coach.*

Non-technical: I am writing for people with no knowledge of rowing who do not want to have to study technical information to row. I am not a doctor or physiologist and make no pretence to special expertise except what

I have learned from rowing and coaching. There are many other resources for athletes who want technical explanations about how the body works, how to use their heart rate to manage their workouts, development of a personal workout regimen to improve performance, and more.

Your responsibility for your health: This book does not offer medical advice or an individual training program. You must consult your physician for medical advice.

What this book does offer is the suggestion that by rowing daily you can experience again the enjoyment you had playing as a child, breathing deeply, full of energy.

Happy rowing and deeper breathing!

1

First Principles:
The Body Responds Daily

o o o o o o o o o o o o o o o o o o o o o o o o o o o o o

"Principles are the main ingredient of courage. A man with principles can get the better of fear."

"I thought you doubted the existence of principles."

"Touche," she answered, and gave me a fleet impish smile. "I do not doubt the power of principles, Dubin. I say only that it is an illusion that they are the first thing in life. It is an illusion we all crave–better principles than the abyss–but an illusion nevertheless. Therefore, one must be careful about what he deems issues of principle. I despise petty principles, obstinate principles that declare right and wrong on matters of little actual consequence. But there are large principles, grand principles most men share, Dubin, and you have them, as well."

—Gita Lodz talking with David Dubin

Ordinary Heroes
—Scott Turow

1.1 WHY ROWING EVERY DAY WORKS: USING THE BODY'S DAILY ADAPTATION

This is not a traditional exercise program in which you work on certain muscles or skills for a particular game or function. Most importantly, it is

1

not an exercise program in the sense that you need to become athletic or push yourself. It is simpler than that. It requires no skill or background. It is intended to be performed at your own pace.

Understanding the mechanism behind the program will help you focus on the goal of exercising daily in a moderate way. Your focus should be on rowing daily, not on pushing yourself hard or setting performance goals. Start now and make exercise a daily habit. That is the hardest part of this program; the rest will follow naturally.

The body is a dynamic, responsive system. If we use our hands a certain way repeatedly, calluses form. If we walk regularly, we notice it becomes easier to walk faster and farther. These are basic examples of the responsiveness of the body that is the foundation of this program.

We also know that adaptation is a two-way street. If we are sedentary and eat more than we need, our bodies downgrade our functioning. The muscles thin. When we do not use our lungs, we find that we become more easily winded.

For competitive rowers (and cyclists and other endurance athletes), the principles play a key role in their training. By pushing themselves during a workout, they tell their bodies to become ever more efficient. Over time, the body maximizes its efficiency at transferring oxygen from the air we breathe into the blood, pumping more blood to the muscles, storing and using more energy in the muscles, and taking away the waste products of strenuous effort more efficiently.

The same type of benefit on a more modest scale is available to the average person who rows moderately. Rowing daily causes our bodies to respond by becoming more efficient and more energetic. With a consistent, daily program, you can row at your own comfortable pace based upon your present fitness. And you will improve.

Keep in mind that this program is based on both my experience and *your* own observations each day as you proceed. Your observations of the effects on your body as you row each day and as your body changes month to month are important. Learn to pay attention to what you are doing physically, how you feel, and how your body is working. No book or trainer can get inside your mind and observe for you how and what you feel. Your paying attention will allow you to reap benefits from your personal observations.

While coaching rowing at Brown, I had the opportunity to learn more about the mechanics of motion from one of the track coaches. He was immersed in the study of physiology and kinesiology. He wanted to guide his athletes to shave seconds from races and add inches to their jumps with the same effort by moving smarter. The details of how the body works, and in particular how it can work more efficiently, are fascinating to study. Like his athletes, you do not have to study to gain the benefit of basic exercise. Yet observing what you do will help you do it better.

Fig. 1
Exercising daily on a rowing machine is simple, can be done at your own pace, and involves no joint impact. Photo of rower on Concept2 Model D indoor rower by Chris Milliman, courtesy of Concept2.

Most importantly, I want to keep the focus on your efforts to row daily, with all other information being secondary. If additional information supports that central goal, then it may be good. It may help keep you going. It may help reinforce your confidence in how you are proceeding. It may help you get more out of what you do each day. What this book should not become, however, is a burden that delays or interferes with your making it a daily practice to row.

1.2 THE FIRST PRINCIPLE: AUTOMATIC ADAPTATION OF THE BODY TO DAILY DEMAND

The human body is made to adapt automatically. You can use that capability. The principle is simple:

Your activity each day sends a message to your body that it should expect more of the same. Your body adapts to enhance your ability to maintain that level of activity the next day and thereafter.

Most people recognize the application of this principle to the body builder or the professional athlete. We acknowledge that they have trained their muscles to perform. We usually do not think of the same principle applying to us, too.

Yet the same principle works for each of us. And it applies not just to the strengthening of a set of muscles but in a broader sense to our overall cardiovascular fitness, our wind, our ability to breathe more deeply and to use our bodies physically for work and play.

There are two core concepts in this principle. One is the concept of activity, demand, or stimulus to which the body will respond. The second is the concept that the body responds daily.

Let's take the second concept first. Why daily? The idea of doing something every day is not common. There are three aspects of "daily" you should think about.

- First, consider the proposition that your body responds on a twenty-four –hour cycle. Pay attention to your own experience and decide for yourself what cycle your body follows. You can do a physical activity once a week, three times a week, or even twice a day. Your body will respond to each of these patterns, so why focus on the body's daily responsiveness? I submit that there is an adaptive pattern that follows the natural twenty-four– hour cycle of activity and rest. Try it and see what you think.

- Second, when thinking of the word *daily*, note that its meaning includes today. If you are going to row daily, you are going to row today. Focus on today. Include exercise in what you plan to do today. Whether it is a matter of making time, finding the place to do it, remembering workout clothes, or developing a positive attitude so you do not avoid it, take steps to include exercise in your life today.

- Third, *daily* includes the concept of action repeated *each* day. Do not just row today; row every day. Plan it into your routine. Watch for the cumulative results of your daily activity over a longer period of time.

Put together, the three aspects of "daily" focus your attention on acting now and repeatedly, while looking for cumulative benefits over a period of many days or months.

What about the second core concept of this principle, the activity you engage in, the demand or stimulus you apply to your body each day? Consider three aspects of the "stimulus" you should apply.

- First and perhaps most contrary to our usual way of thinking, consider that inactivity is just as a much a stimulus as activity. In terms of your body receiving instruction how to adapt, it will take what you do each day as the stimulus or instruction no matter what you do. If you are stuck at your desk and in your car, and then you rest physically over a meal and with a book or in front of your computer or TV at night, you will have instructed your body to adapt to inactivity. You know what that means.

- If you do push-ups every night before bed, you may train a small portion of your body to develop. But if you incorporate a daily row into your routine, you will stimulate your whole body to become more fit. This is the second aspect of "stimulus," that positive daily stimulus of the *whole* body has a broader positive effect than exercising parts of the body.

- The third aspect of "stimulus" to consider is that you should stimulate the body in a way and to a degree that is appropriate for your present level of fitness. Use your breathing to help you identify what is an "appropriate stimulus" for you. It is not your goal to push so you are gasping for breath. Row at a pace you can comfortably maintain.

Caveat: It is worth emphasizing that the principle of daily stimulus and adaptation applies to reasonable and healthy demands and should be used with reasonable expectations. This principle is not about undertaking harmful activities, ignoring injury, or going to excess. Nor does it imply that everyone can eventually become a Roger Bannister and run a four-minute mile or set other world records. To the contrary, the focus is on what works at your present level of fitness and moderately raises your heartbeat while you breathe more deeply and use your whole body.

Some would argue that exercising every day can be bad for you and that you should exercise only five days per week or three days per week or every other day. For example, weight lifting coaches may explain that weight lifting breaks the muscles down and so you need a day off for your muscles to recover. There's sense in that. But the exercise I am suggesting you do daily is well within the boundaries of comfort. The intent is to gain a maximum benefit over time by stimulating your body daily at a level that is just above your norm and does not cause strain. You might call this exercising within your comfort zone.

When you exercise above your sedentary level but within your comfort zone, you can gain fitness. You can burn fat. You create an improvement. As the basic building block of long-term cumulative gain, daily exercise is the sure path to success.

1.3   The Second Principle: Higher Natural Level of Functioning

Our bodies are made to walk the earth, not to fly through the air or to live underwater. But are we made to walk or to run? Are we designed for physical activity or to sit at a desk? Do our organs function more efficiently when we breathe deeply or when we barely breathe at all? Do our hearts remain more healthy if we rest them or raise our pulse? Some people joke that you should take life easy because your heart only has a pre-determined number of beats. I don't think so. I think our hearts are built to support activity, to beat more actively than when they are in a resting mode. Too much rest without daily stimulation robs your heart and the rest of your body of its potential.

The second principle is that our bodies function optimally when they are active:

The body is designed to function at a higher rate of physical activity than the usual, modern sedentary lifestyle. The lungs need to breathe deeply a significant amount every day. The heart is built to pump more blood on a sustained basis. The other systems of the body, such as the digestive system and energy conversion systems, function more effectively when we experience physical activity each day.

Staying in a rest phase all day is like never driving a vintage car. It is simply not good for it. The fact that we get weaker and accumulate fat without exercise does not indicate that that state (being weaker and heavier) is normal for us. Our bodies are built to function more effectively on a diet of regular exercise. Just as the car is designed to recharge its battery through use, through reasonable daily activity our bodies function in a healthier way. In short, the body not only has the ability to adapt but is healthier when we give it a higher level of physical activity than has become normal for most of us.

When we are constantly inactive rather than active some of the time, we put strain on the body because the systems in our body do not have an opportunity to perform normally. It is like crimping a water hose to reduce the flow of water or, back to the car analogy, like letting the filters clog up with accumulated dirt. While you may have to replace the filters on an automobile, your body cleans its "filters" automatically. The point is to optimize that automatic maintenance.

To say that we naturally function at a higher level is not to say we are all meant to perform at top competitive levels. It does mean that we are meant to be more active (not "at rest") at least some of the time each day.

When runners talk about the "high" they get from long distance running, it is usually interpreted as the result of the body's manufacture of certain chemicals during the training. Just as common, though perhaps less glamorous or "sexy" than the special chemical concept, is the simple fact that someone who runs or gets other exercise regularly feels better generally during the day. Ask people you know who run, walk, swim, bike, or row at 6:00 AM every day how it makes them feel. They may joke about how good it feels when they stop, but the simple fact is that they will admit feeling worse *during the day* if they are forced to miss it. The body works better 'round the clock when it gets a boost of higher level functioning once a day.

The highly competitive athlete will notice after a championship that as soon as he or she stops the intensive training regimen, fitness starts to fall away. It is not possible to maintain peak fitness without peak training because the body naturally loses conditioning (and peak training cannot be maintained all the time). When, at a more basic level, our bodies become sedentary because we sit and drive and barely use them day after day, the same effect is occurring in us. It is simply occurring at a more fundamental level. Our bodies do not know to maintain and cannot automatically maintain an optimum level of functioning. Call it a weakness in our design, if you will. When we do not give our bodies sufficient daily stimulation, they become less efficient and less ready to perform when you want to take a walk, climb stairs, or perform other activities.

Tangents to the Principle

- Some people tend to approach a point like this principle by wanting to consider or debate how our bodies got this way. For example, is it a product of intelligent design or the result of evolution? It is not important for your purpose at this time to decide between the two (or to explore some other alternative, such as the possibility that evolution is intelligently designed). Just recognize that your body has this capability and use it. If you must think about such things, do it while you are stretching or as you warm down at the end of your row.

- It is natural to ask how fit you can become. Can you become a champion for your age group? What is your ultimate capability? Can you achieve that potential? However, it is not important to assess ultimate capability; it is important to rise above the routine state of fatigue, weakness, and unfitness that is the norm in a sedentary society. Focus on your starting point and move daily from there. You will have ample opportunity to consider how far you can go in the future as you continue. Don't let daydreaming substitute for your row today.

1.4   THE THIRD PRINCIPLE: ROW DAILY TO ADAPT THE BODY TO OPTIMUM FUNCTIONING

Daily cardiovascular exercise of the whole body that maintains a need to breathe harder than normal through a workout of forty-five minutes or more is the best way to use the first principle (innate automatic adaptation in response to daily stimulus) to achieve the benefit of the second principle (our bodies naturally function better at a higher level).

Rowing is a whole body exercise, using the major muscles of the legs, as well as the core and back, the shoulders, and the arms together in a continuous motion. By using all major muscle groups simultaneously, rowing demands more of the heart and lungs in a shorter time, providing an efficient stimulus to improve your body's condition.

Rowing also involves a range of motion that incorporates more muscle stretching and more muscle use than most activities. Imagine going for a walk and lowering your body close to the ground and then raising it again with each step. Rowing moves the large muscles through a wide range of motion, something that does not happen with walking.

Rowing is a non-impact activity, without foot-falls on the ground, sideways pressure, or start-and-stop motion, so there is a reduced risk of strain. Rowing is easy to do at home or at health clubs with modern indoor rowing machines.

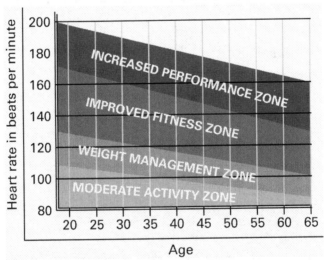

Fig. 2

This chart is taken with permission from Concept2's May 2001 indoor rower manual, where it was reprinted with permission from Polar Electro, Inc. It summarizes general ranges of heart rates based on averages during exercise at varying levels of effort. Your heart rate zones may vary from these averages

Most importantly, you can row at your own pace.

This heart rate chart illustrates the tremendous potential of moderate exercise.

This chart illustrates the important point that *exercise can effectively burn fat and improve fitness with a much lower heart rate than a competitive athlete would seek during his or her workouts.*

Imagine, as an example, that you are sixty years old. The rule of thumb is that a person's (theoretical) maximum heart rate is approximately 220 beats per minute minus his or her age. So in this case, we would assume that your maximum heart rate would be 160 (220 minus sixty years). You can see in the chart above that your "increased performance zone" would involve raising your heart rate from over 130 to more than 160 beats per minute (your "maximum" rate). This is what most people who take their pulse pay attention to. How high can I get my pulse and maintain it? How hard can I work? Can I hit my maximum rate?

But let's look at the rest of the chart above. For the sixty year old, there is a broad range, from a heart rate of just over 100 to slightly above 130 beats per minute, that is labeled the "improved fitness zone." As you can imagine, it is much easier to exercise with a pulse of 110 or 120 than to get it to 160 and keep it there! By raising your pulse during your daily exercise into this zone, you can improve your fitness without pushing yourself to a higher heart rate.

Look at the chart again and note that at even lower heart rates than in the "improved fitness zone" there is a range that is labeled the "weight management zone." For an average sixty year old, if you raise your pulse to a point from less than ninety beats per minute to just over 100, you can help to manage your weight. In doing so, you will also be doing some good things for the rest of your body.

Thus, the lesson of this chart for most people is not the same as for the competitive athlete, namely how hard to push yourself. The lesson is that we will receive benefits in weight management and fitness with a much lower heart rate and, thus, a more comfortable pace in our daily row. Moderate exercise will yield results.

I suggest that, knowing this, instead of focusing on your heart rate, simply pay attention to your breath. You do not need any instruments to help you monitor your breath. If you are a little bit out of breath, you are doing well. If you are out of breath so you know you will want to stop eventually, but not so much that you feel you must slow down right now, you are doing even better. Of course, if you are gasping for breath or are uncomfortably winded, you are pushing too hard. In that case, ease off to a pace you feel you can comfortably maintain. Alternatively, if you are not out of breath or winded at all, push the legs down just a little quicker.

For those who wish to learn more about the technical background for these conclusions, there are numerous studies on optimum heart rate, VO_2 max, and other technical bases for evaluating the appropriate level of performance. For the rest of us, the lesson is apparent: Working to intensify your breathing to a level that is comfortable yet deeper and maintaining it for forty-five minutes is a simple, self-directed way to achieve the core requirement for significant improvement over time. You will find if you occasionally check your heart rate that you are usually within the weight management and improved fitness zones.

1.5 Corollaries to the First Principle: The Effects of Daily Stimulus

A corollary is a statement or proposition that follows naturally from another. The corollaries in this and the following sections are observations about what to expect based on the three principles.

The first corollary is that *a day of inactivity* such as sitting at an office desk, driving to and from work, and sitting at home *is in fact a "daily demand" and will have a daily adaptive effect.* The result will simply be that fitness deteriorates instead of improving as it can with activity. It would be a challenge to quantify the effect of a day off from exercising, but the basic point is plain: You should not expect to feel fit if you do not give your body the exercise to make it fit. You should not expect to come back after a day off performing at the level you achieved before. Unless that break was needed to incorporate improvements based on a significant demand, you should expect to have fallen back. More generally for the beginner, note that if you have not been exercising regularly, your present lack of fitness reflects not your potential but your body's cumulative response to daily instructions to adapt downward.

The high performance athlete may need an occasional day of rest. But the normal person who exercises moderately each day should not need to skip days. We normal folks are more likely to miss a day or several days in a row not because we need rest but because we have not planned carefully enough. That problem, not the issue of whether we need a rest, is our primary concern.

The second and most welcome corollary is that *modifying a sedentary lifestyle in a regular way will send a signal to our bodies that leads to results.* This is why an action as simple as developing a habit of taking a twenty minute walk, for example, can have a noticeable, positive effect on our body's condition over time. Determining what level of stimulus is right for you will be part of your program. The key to determining that is to act each day and to observe the results.

The third corollary is the point just noted: *The effects occur over time.* What your body does in a given day or week to adapt may not be noticeable to you or large in scope. The factor of time is one reason so many ignore this obvious principle. They go for a walk and do not see the benefit right away. They run for a week and have not lost the weight they want to lose. They work out hard and just feel sore, not more fit. The benefits take time to become noticeable. The technique to assure they accrue is to make your daily row a habit.

The fourth corollary goes with the above: *The changes will vary from person to person* not only with what you do but also with the condition of your body to start. Everyone has the same capability in the sense that they can become more fit. But everyone is different in body makeup and current conditioning. You have to start with what you have and work from there, developing the right intensity for you.

Although later chapters offer more about what to do each day, a few observations about daily stimulus may be in order here. Remind yourself that this daily stimulus should be moderate. You should not push yourself because you will then want to take the next day off to avoid the discomfort you experienced from pushing. Your starting point should be that taking a day off is the primary error to avoid. Anything that interferes with your successfully getting in your daily row is to be dealt with and removed like any other obstacle. Thus, row comfortably instead of pushing yourself.

Another way to think about moderate daily rowing is to recognize how it is the opposite of the weekend warrior syndrome in more ways than one. The weekend warrior takes several days off and then expects to perform at a high level on the weekend. It is based on an unthinking belief that you keep what you have, that your body stays the same. It also reflects the belief that it is OK to push to a performance level that has nothing to do with your day-to-day inactivity. The point here is the opposite. If you wish to achieve a particular performance, prepare for it every day. Proceed moderately on a daily basis within your comfort zone. That appropriate stimulation will, over time, lead to tremendous improvement.

When starting out, you may find yourself using muscles that simply have not fired in a long time because you were not using them. It is easy, even with little effort, to end up with sore muscles in this situation. Two areas where you will likely discover muscles you did not know you had are among the muscles around the upper leg and in and around the core of the body.

Minimize the initial muscle soreness by holding back consciously for the first few days when you do something you have not done before. Perform the motion but do it lightly, easily, fewer times than you feel you can do it. This can apply to exercises such as sit-ups as well as your rowing. If you find that you have overdone it and end up feeling very sore, know that it will pass; and it will pass faster if you continue to use those muscles each day.

For the more experienced rower, the issue will not be avoiding these start-up pains but dealing with soreness from long rows or other repetition. The development of a sore joint, for example, may be an indication that you have overdone it. For example, when I worked up to consecutive days of eighty-minute rows, I found that one of my knees began to feel sore under the knee-cap. It may be that the tendons that connect the thigh muscles across the knee under the knee-cap had become slightly inflamed. If something like this becomes extreme, it may be necessary to take days off. Instead, catch it in time by paying close attention to what you are doing. Reduce the demand for a day or two to allow it to go away.

1.6 Corollaries to the Second Principle: The Body is Built to Be Active

The first corollary to the second principle is that *overall energy and health will tend to be better if we are using our bodies actively rather than living a sedentary life.* Because the body is built to be active, it runs better when moderately active and worse when inactive. One extreme example of failure is pneumonia in the inactive elderly. The lungs fill with fluid. This result is less likely to occur the more the individual is able to stay active because a more active body contributes to keeping the lungs clear. When the problems of age force one to become inactive, the resulting lack of use of the body may sometimes create greater risks or even hasten death. Fight it now while you can by becoming active and staying active. Focus on the energy you feel after exercising and the growing muscle mass as your body adapts.

The second corollary is that *a more active body can lead to a healthier mind.* A healthy, active body offers a better environment for a healthy mind. At the most basic level, more blood to the brain is a good thing. In this sense, rowing daily may be even better than the brain exercises now being suggested to keep us alert as we age.

The third corollary follows from both of the first two principles: *The body will adapt gradually in relation to both its individual potential and its present state.* Whether fit or not, it is not wise to make an unreasonable demand on the body. Start with what you have. Work on it regularly but moderately. Just as neglect begs for breakdown, an extraordinary demand can overtax the body. The more out of shape your body is to begin, the more patient you need to be. Even those who are exceptionally fit have their limitations. The goal is gradual but lasting change. Let it happen over time.

Finally, the corollary most want to hear: *Rest at an appropriate time is a useful part of adaptation.* For most, the basic rule to exercise every day is completely foreign and there will inevitably be many days of "rest" as they learn to make exercise a daily habit. For those training intensively, the need for rest should become obvious and will have to be factored into a routine of demand-and-response. What the beginner needs to overcome is the idea that basic exercise is better doled out on alternate days. Rest at the right time is good; rest as frequent as exercise undermines the message to the body to become more fit. The best rest is to get adequate sleep each night. Make sure your daily rowing is moderate instead of stressful and repeat it every day.

Consider the opposite of an active lifestyle. I use the word *sedentary* to describe a relatively inactive lifestyle. A sedentary lifestyle means having a slow pulse all the time, with the exception of the occasional moment, like running for a cab. You can be living a sedentary life even with some activity such as gardening or mowing the lawn. During these types of activity, the action is brief, stop and go. You use only part of your body. You use a limited range of motion. You do not breathe more deeply in a sustained way. The fact that it may include some strain does not help. Each of these attributes tends to make the activity insufficient to help you rise above a sedentary lifestyle. Can someone get good, beneficial exercise doing a chore, perhaps chopping wood? Probably so. But can you do it every day and create a mechanism that allows the body as a whole to restore its natural state of fitness? Probably not.

Activity should involve continuous motion because then the systems of the body stabilize at a higher level of functioning instead of accelerating and decelerating in response to stop and go activity. Preferably, activity will use much or most of the body. Ideally, activity will be smooth and without strain. And it should be in your comfort zone, using a level of effort that is within your existing capacity without overdoing it.

1.7 Corollaries to the Third Principle: Row Daily to Tune Up Your Body

There are a number of practical corollaries to the third principle. Central is that rowing works well, perhaps better than any other activity, to stimulate the body to use its natural ability to adapt. That is not to say something as basic as taking a walk will not also help. The benefit you receive is a matter of degree.

First, *use a sustainable exercise regimen to be effective.* Many forms of exercise that are fun are hard on the body. Exercise that cannot be sustained because it involves potentially harmful impact (such as running for some people's knees, for example, or racquet sports or basketball for others' ankles) will not work as well. If you cannot do it every day because of injury or soreness, that undermines your program. Rowing is a non-impact activity you can do entirely at your own pace. As a result, you can repeat it every day.

Second, *exercise that involves start and stop activity* (such as weight lifting, tennis, basketball), even though demanding while in the active mode, *is simply not as effective as rowing* because it does not sustain the demand upon the body. A sustained lower intensity activity like rowing is a more effective stimulus for the heart and lungs than a stop-and-go activity like basketball. If you go for a bike ride and coast, you rob your body of some of the benefit. If you play soccer, it is too easy to slow down or stand around briefly when you get out of breath. Playing games like basketball and soccer can also be less effective because when you play you run *too* hard. While sitting on a rowing machine can seem less fun than interacting with others on the field of play, it is continuous and you can manage it instead of responding to teammates' demands. Keep it moderate to be most effective.

Third, *exercise that uses less of the body's muscle mass (such as bicycling or running) is not as effective as rowing* because it draws blood primarily to portions of the body instead of causing it to be pumped more vigorously throughout the body. With less muscle mass in play and less lung efficiency demanded, exercises using smaller portions of the body limit the beneficial effect under the first principle. When you row, you use almost all of your muscles because you engage both legs, both arms, and the trunk of your body in one continuous motion. Since your range of motion is almost from one end of your reach to the other (bending the knees and reaching beyond your toes at one end; straightening legs, extending back and pulling arms in at the other end), you also use more range of each muscle.

Fourth, *the feeling* we all hate and avoid *of being out of breath*, a feeling that too easily occurs during normal daily activity, *can be used effectively as a measure of the success of a daily exercise regimen.* Exercise that does not make you winded to a reasonable degree for a sustained period will not be as effective. Instead, it will reinforce the status quo. Learn to breathe harder without overdoing it. At first you may find this a difficult suggestion to follow. The challenge of dealing with uncertainty may account for many heart monitors being sold. But, while instruments are helpful, you will find you can also learn something useful by paying attention to how deeply you are breathing. At the most basic level, the task is simply to ask yourself when you finish whether you were breathing hard.

- If you know you did breathe hard and yet you were not uncomfortably out of breath, you were fine.

- If you are not sure, but you broke a sweat, you were fine.

- If you got too winded or if you know when you are done that you did no work at all, you need to moderate your effort the following day between those two extremes of overwork and no work.

Fifth, *being moderately out of breath can be a more effective stimulus if you sustain it for a longer period of time.* That middle range of moderate activity (your comfort zone) can represent a broad bandwidth of possible work. Focus to begin with on finding your comfort zone. Do not worry about determining what works in one day. And do not feel you need to push yourself, to drain yourself, or to breathe so hard that you feel concerned about catching your breath. Keep it moderate and, over a period of days or weeks, increase the total time you row.

Overall, the points that follow from the third principle relate to using the most beneficial method of stimulating your whole body that you can. The extreme opposite would be to focus on one set of small muscles such as the biceps. A middle range would be to do some general activity such as a game (tennis, basketball, soccer) or aerobic work (walking, running, cycling). All are positive, but simply not as effective.

1.8   The Corollary on Aging, and More

The body is designed so that, if we care for it like a vintage automobile as we age, our lines can still be good, the carburetor still breathes clearly, and the engine chugs along smoothly and powerfully. *It is not a natural state of aging to get out of shape, to feel tired, or to be overweight. Staying fit helps the bodily systems function better, the way they are meant to function, which in turn helps us age more gracefully, with more energy, in better health, with a more positive outlook on life.*

The importance of the principles to aging is that the body adapts to how we live. Choose to live actively and your body will respond with a greater ability to remain more active. However, choosing to give your body daily stimulus that says "slow down and do less" will result over time in reduced ability to perform and even reduced functioning. The natural path of the body without exercise is to decline. This is not just a matter of muscle strength or tone or outward physical fitness, but of the level of functioning and health of your organs and all systems in your body.

As we get older, it is increasingly important to exercise daily to fend off the accelerating decay which otherwise results from inactivity. As someone once said, the challenge as we age is to slow down less than the other guy. If you are already fit for competition, that adage may apply to you. If you are like most of us, however, there is a tremendous gap between your present fitness and your potential. You can improve, achieve more of that potential, and enjoy the results.

Stop and think about what causes aging and ill health. Suppose that illness, ill health, and death come about not only because of external causes such as viruses and bacteria but also, perhaps more so, due to the body's reduced fitness. If a sedentary lifestyle reduces your ability to grow white blood cells and filter out and expel waste products, you are facing the aging process with one hand tied behind your back. Use and enhance the body's general ability to heal itself using its own natural mechanisms by exercising daily.

Whatever your age or fitness or goals, you can apply the same principles and corollaries to what you are attempting to do. My goal may be to get into shape and improve my health. It may be to slow down my loss of fitness. It may be to improve my conditioning to prepare to compete in an event. It may be to lay the foundation for some other activity or sport. In all these situations, what I do each day to stimulate my body can help create a positive effect.

Here are some more thoughts on additional implications of the three principles for different age groups and levels of fitness.

- Youth (under twenty-two years old): As the body grows, the capacity for physical accomplishment grows with it, if stimulated. In the years the body is growing and developing, daily stimulation can extend the body's future capacity.

- Mature Beginners (twenty-three to over thirty years old): These are the peak years for physical performance. Work on the frequency and intensity of exercise to obtain optimal stimulation. Work with a capable and attentive coach.

- Middle-Aged Beginners (thirty and up): From young adulthood through middle age, the norm is to slow down and deteriorate, especially in response to the demands of work and family. Our bodies are capable of doing better. The effects of aging can be moderated and postponed by staying fit (or becoming more fit) as we proceed through middle age.

- The Developing Athlete (at any age): Many developing athletes, young and old, take lessons in the skills needed to play a particular sport but do not focus on the importance of regular exercise. The key to improvement at any age is to apply a reasonable daily stimulus instead of handicapping yourself with inconsistent exercise.

- The Young Competitor (junior, college, and open): Competitive athletes focus on pushing the envelope (the limits of their performance) and peaking without becoming stale. By paying attention to your daily exercise and how your body reacts as a competitive athlete you can better gauge what more you can do to achieve your goals. Whether that involves extra workouts, harder workouts, more rest, or other factors will depend on you and your coach's advice.

- The Older Competitor (masters): The major difference between the older competitor (especially those over forty-five) and the younger competitive athletes is lifestyle more than age. Certainly, there is a downward slope in peak capability as we age and, as a result, your expectations should change. But the principles work in the last several decades of life just as they do in the first three.

1.9   Variations on the Human Design: The Principles Apply to All

The human body comes in many shapes and sizes. Some conclude from that simple variety that some of us can be fit and others can not. That is wrong. We are all capable of being fit. More importantly, we are all capable of becoming more fit than we are right now. That fact is independent of each person's height, weight, bone structure, fat content, arch height, past exercise history, dress or hat size, or other body shape parameter.

It is true that some are naturally leaner and some naturally heavier. Some are taller, others shorter. Some are better at sprinting, others better at distance. Do not be distracted by those variations. Instead, put your attention on what we all have in common, a body that responds to its daily activity by adapting to it.

Think back to the question whether a glass is half full or half empty, and consider instead the many sizes and shapes of glasses. Whatever the size or shape of your glass, start refilling the glass, and focus on the following: Every person can be more or less fit. The level of fitness of any individual is not necessarily represented by that person's weight or body type. Fitness is a matter of a person's achieving more of his or her potential strength, flexibility, coordination, and wind or stamina.

Comparing yourself to others holds traps for the unwary. One of the worst traps is to look at someone who is more fit and conclude that he or she is naturally so, somehow innately more capable of fitness than you are. Instead, think about the amount of exercise that person has engaged in to become that fit or to maintain it. Better yet, simply focus on your own daily routine. Give yourself a period of months to see what daily exercise does for you.

The human body is designed to be fit. It is not designed to be out of shape, overweight, or inactive. Fitness involves improving your wind, muscle tone, and all bodily functions through reasonable daily stimulus. Remind yourself that you are capable of becoming more fit and make it a daily habit to work on it.

2

Daily Exercise is Good for the Body

○ ○

"Our bodies are our gardens to which our wills are gardeners."

—William Shakespeare

"Exercise ferments the humors, casts them into their proper channels, throws off redundancies, and helps nature in those secret distributions, without which the body cannot subsist in its vigor, nor the soul act with cheerfulness."

—Joseph Addison

"Underlying these ideas, of course, are the traditional essentials of health that have always had a strong place in medical canons—proper nutrition, adequate exercise, enough sleep, good air, moderation in personal habits, and so on."

—Norman Cousins

2.1 LOOK FOR ADAPTATION IN MULTIPLE SYSTEMS THROUGHOUT THE BODY

If you want to restore a vintage automobile, you do not just wash and wax it. You get the engine running better. You make sure the generator is working. You check the battery. Work on the body and suspension improve the look and the ride. The project is not as simple as adding fuel and turning the key; it takes time.

If as we age we become sedentary and give in to habits that do not promote a healthy body, we see our capabilities start to wane. Muscle tissue weakens and thins. Strength dissipates. Fatty tissue accumulates. The lungs,

19

the heart, and systems that control digestion and energy are all affected. Our bodies stop telling us what fuel they need (or we stop listening). Illness becomes more common, more random, more of a threat.

Part of the success of rowing daily is that, over time, you will begin to see multiple improvements because the activity of rowing is affecting a broad array of bodily systems. One day, certain muscles will tire or ache or tighten more than you are used to and you will focus on them. Perhaps you will make a point of stretching those muscles more or doing some additional strengthening of them. Or you may ease off the next day to rest them and simply row with less effort. Over time, the fatigue or soreness will pass and you will realize you do not notice those muscle aches interfering with your row.

Another day, your muscles may feel strong, but you will feel especially winded while rowing and you will focus on your lungs. Work on that feeling over a period of days or weeks. Work a little less hard and see how you breathe and how you feel. Are you still winded? If you are less winded, are you still breathing deeply? If you row easily for the first few minutes, do you find you can then work harder and breathe more deeply without that feeling of being uncomfortably winded?

Another week, you will notice that your digestive system seems to be working differently. You may also find your appetite is affected. At yet another time, one spot on your body will come to your attention. Your attention may be on a stomach cramp, tightness in your lower back, a pain in your shins, tightness in one wrist or the other, shoulder tension, or some other localized sensation. These may be reactions to your rowing or to other activities in your daily life. Your back may be sore because you shoveled snow that day, not because you rowed. When I play basketball, my ankles become sore. Then I look forward to rowing to clean out and restore the aching muscles and joints.

You will also notice positive developments like increased muscle mass and strength, better wind, clearer lungs, an ability to continue longer without fatigue. Pay attention and keep track of what you are experiencing.

And there can be many effects that you cannot or will not notice with your own senses, but which your doctor might notice during your annual physical. When you exercise regularly, your resting heart rate will tend to go down. Your doctor may comment on that. You may find blood levels changing.

You may want to change your diet with your exercise; most people exercising every day eventually decide they want high quality fuel that complements their exercise. You may adjust when you row in relation to when you eat in order to enhance the feeling of power as you row. And you may find you are less hungry after you row, less likely to overeat than you would be if you skipped rowing and sat down to a meal. Rowing daily affects many bodily systems.

2.2   DEEPER BREATHING AND THE LUNGS

The use of maximum muscle mass while rowing creates a greater demand throughout the body for oxygen. This is why rowing can seem harder than you expect at first. By creating a greater demand on the lungs by using almost all muscles at once, rowing does more good for the lungs in less time. As all major muscle groups work together, the heart must send an increased flow of blood to all of them simultaneously. This requires the lungs to develop more effective oxygen transfer. Then, as the blood returns more waste to the lungs to be expelled from the body, the lungs are ready with more oxygen from the air you breathe.

Technical Note: "Large, highly trained endurance athletes, such as rowers, can have maximal pulmonary ventilation rates … fully twice the rate typical of untrained individuals," according to Jack Wilmore and David Costill in Physiology of Sport and Exercise *(see pages 226 to 229). In other words, rowing helps increase your lung capacity. In fact, Willmore and Costill report, a sedentary individual who trains at seventy-five percent capacity for thirty minutes three times per week can achieve a fifteen percent to twenty percent increase in their ability to transfer oxygen from the air they breathe into their bodies in six months. Since, as they note, "available oxygen supply is the major limiter of endurance performance," rowing increases your endurance or "wind" for daily activity.*

When your exercise calls for your body to perform oxygen transfer and waste removal through the lungs, the natural result is to feel out of breath. If you get so out of breath that you want to stop, ease back to a level you can maintain. Better yet, start slowly enough and pay close enough attention to your progress that you will not find yourself gasping for air at any time. Rowing is especially efficient because of the simultaneous, full-body demand and the effect that has on the lungs. But because of the scope of the demand, it is easy to overdo it without feeling like your individual muscles are working hard.

By continuing to work the whole body over a period of weeks, the body's efficiency in oxygen/waste transfer increases and you feel your "wind" improve. What is happening in your lungs to cause this feeling of increased well-being? Is it the fact that you are using more of the lungs' structure? The lungs are essentially a sophisticated membrane. The more membrane you can use, the more air you can process. You have to breathe deeply to be able to use the full capacity of the lungs. The more "good air" you get in and "bad air" you remove, the more blood you can refresh before the heart sends it through the body. You may also increase the efficiency of the transfer of oxygen and other chemicals. Greater efficiency and greater capacity together combine for significantly improved performance.

Think of the lungs as a dynamic, responsive organ and you will have a basic incentive to breathe more deeply. If you do not use the lungs fully and, as a result, they tend to become less efficient, you lose out. If your inactivity causes you not to use portions of the lungs at all, you may risk losing the benefit of those portions as they go unused. Consider what may happen to portions of the lungs that are inactive or even completely unused. It cannot be healthy for them. For example, if you do not breathe deeply with the diaphragm pushing downward and the stomach moving out as you breathe in, then the lobes of the lungs at the bottom are unlikely to fill with air. Think of the lungs as many tiny balloons at the ends of other balloons like tiny gloves on the fingers of larger gloves, each of which has to inflate in order for the next one to inflate. If you do not breathe deeply, fewer balloons inflate. If some portions of the lungs are unused or less used, imagine them becoming fouled like a spark plug that does not get power to ignite the fuel so that it eventually becomes ineffective.

In contrast, the result of each day's exercise is that you can work a little harder the next day, week, and month. You also can maintain that effort a little longer, continuing the cycle of improvement. Obviously, you cannot see your lungs improve in fitness the way you notice your arms or legs getting bigger or firmer as the muscles become stronger. But it is happening all the same and is a central part of your increasing fitness. Observe it through how you feel and how you breathe.

As you continue with the daily stimulation of the lungs, you will notice that you experience an enhanced feeling of energy and quicker recovery when you walk stairs, do chores, run for a cab, carry the groceries, and so on. The improved ability of the lungs to deliver what you need is felt as greater energy because your blood is well-oxygenated. The more efficient oxygen delivery (and waste removal) system allows the whole body to be more productive and efficient like a well-maintained carburetor getting air to all cylinders, with wires getting power to all spark plugs. It also reflects the greater health of the body as a whole, including the organs, all of which benefit from the increased blood flow from the daily exercise.

Once you learn to pay attention to your breath as you row, you will become more aware of a broader range of comfortable breathing and its relationship to your performance. It is simple to pay attention to your breathing. You do not need to maintain constant attention on each breath. However, by noticing your breath occasionally during a workout and after exercise, you will become more attuned to how hard you are working. Similarly, paying attention during the day when you are not exercising, you will become more aware of progress with this one important aspect of your fitness.

Another effect of deeper breathing is stimulation of the digestive system. When you breathe deeply, the diaphragm moves up and down. Picture the diaphragm as a set of muscles resting like a small table beneath the base of the lungs. As you exhale, the table formed by the diaphragm rises to push up on the lungs and squeeze the air out of them. As you breathe in deeply, the diaphragm moves downward, making a larger space for the lungs for the intake of more air. This has the effect of using the lungs more fully whereas shallow breathing does not allow air into the whole volume of the lungs in the same way. Also, you will notice when you breathe in deeply that the stomach area tends to move outward. The muscles of the diaphragm are just above the core of the body where the liver, kidneys, intestines and other organs are located. When you breathe in deeply and the diaphragm moves down, it moves or massages the mass of internal organs beneath it.

2.3 THE HEART AND DELIVERY OF BLOOD TO THE BODY

As you row, the pulse quickens. The heart is pumping more blood to the lungs for the removal of impurities and the addition of more oxygen. The heart is also pumping more blood from the lungs throughout the body to deliver oxygen and nutrients. The volume of blood flow to the body per minute increases. The body attempts to direct flow to the areas that are working. But as the heart pumps harder and faster, more blood also tends to go to the extremities of the body, to the organs, to areas of potential infection, and to the brain.

Each of these examples of enhanced delivery of blood provides a mechanism to improve health. For example, maintaining highly efficient blood flow through the brain will tend to keep the blood vessels of the brain healthier and support the brain with better delivery of oxygen and nutrients.

Consider also the network of blood vessels in the body. Blood vessels branch off again and again until they are mere capillaries. A capillary is tiny, barely wide enough for blood cells to pass through single file. This is how the heart gets nutrients to individual cells. With exercise, the blood will tend to move more blood cells through the capillaries. The result is more successful delivery of oxygen, antibodies, and other healthful benefits carried by the blood, as well as more effective removal of waste from all cells.

*Technical Note: The heart pumps blood throughout the body using miles of arteries and veins. This includes a lengthy system of microscopic, single-cell–carrying capillaries that deliver nutrients to and remove wastes from each cell of the body. Exercise improves oxygen delivery to the cells because it leads to "increased maximal blood flow and increased muscle capillary density in the active tissues," according to Jack Wilmore and David Costill (*Physiology of Sport and Exercise, *page 229). Blood is pumped away from the heart at a relatively high speed, and slows down as the arteries branch off and ultimately separate into millions of capillaries. At any given time, while nearly three-fifths of your blood is returning to the heart in your veins, five percent is moving through your capillaries, almost one-sixth is in your arteries, twelve percent is moving between heart and lungs to be regenerated, and approximately nine percent is in your heart. (See* Know Your Body: The Atlas of Anatomy, *introduced by Emmet B. Keeffe, MD, page 95.) This highly complex system both expands and becomes more efficient as you exercise.*

We usually think of the blood vessels as if they were HVAC vents in a building: They are there. They are open. When the heart pumps, the blood flows everywhere. This simplified image is fundamentally flawed for at least three reasons:

- First, blood vessels can expand or constrict, affecting blood flow to particular areas.

- Second, when we are sedentary, our remaining in one position and our worsening posture both tend to limit blood flow to some areas.

- Third, unless we get the heart pumping more powerfully as it does when we row, the blood pressure does not tend to deliver blood to all areas in a sufficient flow for optimum health.

When blood flow is improved with exercise, there are many potential benefits throughout the body. Imagine you have an area of infection. It could be where you scratched your skin, in an organ, in the gums. When the blood flow increases to the whole body, it can deliver more white blood cells to any area of infection and more easily remove waste products that might otherwise accumulate.

Imagine your system of blood vessels is like a highway (the main veins and arteries), with a network of feeder roads and local streets eventually branching off to one lane roads and driveways (capillaries). If traffic on the highway is not moving (whether because traffic is stalled or simply because there is little traffic), then the flow of vehicles to the local streets and eventually to the individual driveways is minimal or non-existent. If the highway flow is increased (as the flow of blood increases during moderate full-body exercise), that increases the flow along the highway to all destinations and, thus, to the local roads. Imagine the difference between having limited or restricted blood flow that may not reach all parts of your body effectively versus having a period of increased blood flow each day. Which do you think would be better for your overall health? Which would you prefer?

2.4   The Effect of Rowing on the Muscles

Focus for a moment on the muscles. Muscles are what most people think about primarily or even exclusively in connection with exercise.

When muscles are not used, they become not just weak but thin. Thin in this sense is not necessarily good. Take note whether you see defined, toned muscles when you see a "thin" person. Too often, someone who is thin is actually in poor condition.

Checking skin-fold thickness is one simple way to observe how much of an area of the body is fat and how much is muscle. When you lightly pinch together a fold of skin in a particular area, the thickness will show you how much subcutaneous fat you have in that area. For example, if you pinch the skin on your thigh and find it is only a fraction of an inch thick, you can tell that the size and shape of your thigh beneath that folded surface layer is due to muscle. If the folded skin and fat is two inches thick, then you will have some sense of how much space remains for muscle beneath the one-inch layer of fatty tissue.

You will find that the skin-fold thickness varies from place to place on your body. For example, the skin-fold thickness on my gut is quite large compared to other areas of my body, while it is smaller on my sides and thinner still on my thighs and arms. See what your measurements are. Watch how they change over time.

When muscles are not used and therefore not stimulated to develop, energy that could be put into the muscles goes instead to waste or fat. The latter may add bodily size but not strength, fitness, or energy. When the muscles are used regularly, their natural response is to grow. They develop more power. They store more energy in each muscle cell to support the power. (The body uses energy to do work with the muscles.) And the network of blood vessels and support systems for the muscles grows to provide improved endurance as well as power. In other words, the muscles get bigger because they are adapting to the demand. You become fitter and your ability to row and to perform everyday tasks improves.

Technical Note: Exercise physiologists have found that aerobic training increases the number of capillaries in each muscle fiber. In addition, aerobic training results in more and bigger mitochondria (the cellular structures that help convert food to energy) in skeletal muscles. (See Physiology of Sport and Exercise, *by Jack H. Wilmore and David L. Costill pages 147 to 148.) In short, you feel better and stronger when you exercise because your body responds and adapts. It actually changes on a cellular and sub-cellular level in a way that prepares your muscles for more exercise the next day.*

As you row each day, pay attention over a period of months to the changes in your muscles. Which ones become sore and then lose the soreness? Which muscles tone up and become stronger? Which muscles did you not know you had before, but now use? What physical activities can you do more easily? Which muscles seem to be little affected? Which muscles provide you more power than others? Which muscles are tight, which relaxed? There are many observations you can make. You will find that what you observe changes over time.

The ability of the muscles to adapt is great. Make use of that ability with a daily row.

2.5   THE HEALTH OF YOUR BONES

Many people are aware of the health benefits of breathing deeply and stimulating the muscles, and recognize the terms *aerobic exercise* and *cardiovascular exercise.* But the common perception is that aerobic exercise simply helps with wind and muscle tone and burns off calories. There is more that happens in the body when we stimulate the heart, lungs, and muscles. One important additional effect is the increased blood flow to and through the bones. (Much is made of the use of weight-bearing exercise to maintain or improve bone density. That may occur with rowing, but focus for now on the simpler concept of blood flow through the bones.) Increased blood flow strengthens the bones. And the bones help the body in multiple ways.

Technical Note: The bones of the body are not dead tissue, like hair, finger nails or tooth surfaces, but rather are living and changing and are nourished by the flow of blood through and around them. In addition, a key source for the manufacture of new blood cells in the body is bone marrow, which "produces all types of white blood cells, red blood cells and platelets [the "tiniest cells in the body" responsible for making the blood clot]." Keeffe, at page 87-89.

Rowing can help maintain bone density because the additional stimulus of lungs and heart enhances the delivery of nutrients to the entire body, including the skeletal structure. This is important for all ages; but it is an especially good example why exercise is increasingly important as we age. Bones can weaken and become more susceptible to damage from otherwise normal activities (like a minor fall) as we age. Bones can also lose density to such a degree that posture and health are threatened. Regular exercise is widely regarded as an important part of preventing this physical weakening as we age.

Since blood flow tends to lessen as we age, increasing the flow of blood improves the delivery of calcium and other nutrients. The bones, like the muscles, can then remain strong and provide the physical frame your body needs. Similarly, daily exercise can improve the delivery of blood cells manufactured in the bone marrow to the rest of the body.

2.6   OTHER ORGANS AND SYSTEMS OF THE BODY

Consider the other parts of the body. How might improved blood flow affect them? Here are a few other thoughts about the potential benefits of full-body exercise on areas, organs, and systems of the body.

The Brain and the Nervous System: The brain and nervous system are essential to our health. Parts of the brain control automatic systems in the body. Other parts allow us to control the body consciously. The nervous system connects the brain with the organs, muscles, skin, and other tissue (such as structures in the eyes and ears) to enable the five senses to perform. It also provides a communication pathway for the assessment of pain and for balance. Consider how many diseases and daily problems can occur when one or more of these systems fails or is impaired.

Consider a more extreme example. Only a few minutes of depriving the brain of oxygen results in death. Loss of blood to the brain can cause unconsciousness in seconds. Obviously, getting a healthy supply of blood to the brain with the nutrients it contains is critical. Improving that supply is beneficial.

The Joints: We have many joints in the body. The joints most of us commonly think of are in the hips, knees, ankles, shoulders, elbows, and wrists. But there are also joints connecting the ribs and in the spine. The joints often contain a variety of tissues and other materials, including tendons, ligaments, cartilage, membranes, and fluid.

Earlier, I noted one positive benefit of rowing on joints is that there is no impact. Unlike the jumping of basketball, the repetitive pounding of running, and the twisting and turning of soccer and tennis, the joints are held in place without impact while you row. The body moves but you are sitting down. There is no hitting or other motion that causes an impact against a surface so as to create a potential for strain, as there can be with these other sports. At the same time, rowing strengthens the muscles that hold the joints in place.

A second benefit of rowing for the joints comes from the increased flow of blood throughout the body. As you row and your heart pumps more blood, you will tend to improve the flow of blood to and around your joints. With so many types of tissue and fluid involved in the healthy functioning of a joint, you can imagine that increased blood flow to these areas can be beneficial.

Rowing offers the joints a third benefit. When you row, you move many joints through a range of motion. This moderate use through a more complete range of motion can have positive benefits compared to not using your joints or using only a limited range of motion. Use without abuse is a good thing.

Kidneys, Liver, Other Organs and Glands: There are many organs and glands in the body, all performing important functions that depend on the flow of blood. Many are located in the abdomen. Some manufacture important chemicals to help our bodies to function well. These include, for example, chemicals for digestion and hormones to regulate how our bodies perform. Some organs are critical parts of the extensive system our bodies employ to remove impurities from our cells by filtering our blood.

The body is an interconnected set of responsive systems. When we are sedentary, the systems respond one way. When we exercise daily, we stimulate the body a different way. When we use full-body exercise that effectively increases breathing and blood flow, we tend to maximize the stimulation of the whole body.

Imagine a car that would automatically change the oil when it needed it. Would a system like that work as effectively if you did not drive the car, or if you only drove the car to the store to shop? The oil does not circulate in a parked car. A sedentary body does not circulate the blood and stimulate the organs as effectively as an active one.

The Skin: The skin is sometimes called the largest organ of the body. It is part of an active and interactive system the body uses to regulate temperature, manage chemical balances, balance fluid levels, and remove impurities from the body. When you exercise, you heat up your body. Blood flow to the skin changes. You begin to perspire. You activate a system that is otherwise relatively dormant.

As with other organs and systems of the body, a great deal of space could be devoted to how the skin works, what good it does you, and how exercise can enhance those benefits. For now, simply take note that it is a good thing to perspire. Think of it as your skin breathing more deeply.

2.7   ROWING, STRESS MANAGEMENT, MENTAL HEALTH, AND THE COMMON COLD

Many authorities recommend exercise as one tool to use to manage stress and even to combat depression. This makes sense. The stress of modern living can leave us tired and tense. Moderate exercise helps the muscles loosen up and strengthen, and can actually give us energy. Exercise gets the blood flowing and can serve as a form of recreation in which the mind can turn away from the demands on it. The body can perform instead of sitting shackled to a desk, if only for a short time.

In addition to creating a sense of peace and accomplishment from exercising, physical activity offers other benefits. The increased blood flow helps many functions within the body work more effectively, as noted in the preceding sections. It also can boost your energy simply because the stronger heart and greater lung efficiency works for you all day. Just as the body can enter a cycle in which being inactive fosters a more dormant state, initiating activity helps foster a desire for more.

Consider how daily rowing could affect your outlook on life. You will do something that is good for you each day. You are going to continue it day after day. You are observing how you feel over a long period of time. It is not difficult, yet it provides a real benefit to you. You are setting goals. You will feel more energetic. You are going to see significant changes over a period of months. All of that creates an anticipation of what additional changes can occur in the future. The act of rowing daily is a building block not only for your improved physical fitness but also for your outlook for the future.

There is a common belief among some rowing coaches that a good workout can burn off germs. They would say that a member of a rowing team should come to practice and work out even if fighting a cold (unless the team member is very ill or contagious). The exercise will raise the body temperature. The athlete will sweat out impurities, breathe in lots of good air, and clear the lungs of waste accumulating there. The heart will pump blood containing antibodies and white blood cells more thoroughly throughout the body to overcome areas of infection. The exercise will generally enhance the body's natural ability to overcome viral infection. It may not kill the cold once the cold has taken hold, but many believe it is a good preventative tool. See what you think.

Note how you feel when you begin your daily row and how you feel at the end. You may be surprised how often you start feeling lethargic and end your row feeling energized. Try rowing even if you feel like you are coming down with a cold and see what happens. Note in your log if you skip a row or do less because you feel ill, as well as when you start slowly because you are coming down with a cold, only to have a good workout. Keep track of how quickly you get back on the rowing machine after catching a cold and how your rowing has been affected. Over time, pay attention to whether you come down with a cold as often as you had in the past.

3

Begin Indoor Rowing Today

o o o o o o o o o o o o o o o o o o o o o o o o o o o o o o o o

"A journey of a thousand miles begins with a single step and a lifetime of fitness begins with a single row."

—Modified Chinese Proverb

"Dragons steal gold and jewels . . . wherever they can find them; and they guard their plunder as long as they live . . . .

"Far over the misty mountains cold
To dungeons deep and caverns old
We must away, ere break of day,
To claim our long-forgotten gold."

The Hobbit
—J.R.R. Tolkien

(Tolkien explains in the symbolism of fantasy adventure the need for a journey to recover a lost or stolen treasure. If this tale were an allegory for the search for lost breath or fitness, what would the dragon and trolls represent, and what are the dwarves, the elves, and the other characters? Keep in mind that when Tolkien wrote this book indoor rowing machines were not as available as they are today, so it may have been necessary to go down to the river "ere the break of day.")

3.1 START TODAY: THE PLAN

This chapter offers information on where to get a rowing machine and basic instruction on how to row. Later chapters offer more specifics concerning rowing technique, including how to do it efficiently, what to do to complement it, and how you can fit it in with other forms of exercise and your daily life.

The essential point is to row every day. There is no required level of skill or effort. To the contrary, you should moderate your level of effort so that you row in your comfort zone and want to do it again. Here is the basic plan in four parts:

1. *Row every day;*
2. *When you miss a day, simply get back to it the next day and row every day again;*
3. *Over time, make it a point to miss fewer days.*

To begin, find a rowing machine and row at your own pace for up to ten minutes. Do not try to set any records or test yourself. After a few minutes, take a break, get up and move around, and be sure you are not overly winded. After the break, row again for a few minutes at a pace that is entirely comfortable for you.   Over a period of a month or more, at a pace that is comfortable for you, work up to a daily row of twenty to thirty minutes without stopping. While you can certainly do more if it is comfortable for you, avoid the most common error of overdoing it in the early weeks.

The fourth step is as important as the first three:

4. *Record what you have accomplished at the end of each workout.*

Start a journal or log. Record the date, time spent rowing, and how you felt. With these notes, you begin to create a record of success. Later, you can develop goals for yourself. Do not worry at the beginning about details or format as, over time, you will develop a sense of the information you want to track.

Here is a page of a sample log you can copy and use until you develop your own:

Log of Daily Rowing

(1) Cum. Exercise	(2) Cum. Miss	(3) Score	Day/ Date	What I Did/ Comments	Totals

Fig. 3
This sample page of a log contains six suggested columns. The most important column is the one for your comments. The final column on the right is a place you can insert totals if, for example, you are keeping track of the distance you row each day. The date simply identifies when this exercise occurred. The first three columns are places you can record whether you exercised or not each day and keep track (if you wish to) of how you are doing. More on that in chapter four.

Many exercise log formats focus on score, distance, and date. I suggest you make a point to include two things every time you record your workout:

- Record when you do not exercise as well as when you do. In other words, note when you miss and why.

- Record your observations. Do not limit yourself to the time and distance you rowed. Note how you felt. Did you row despite not wanting to? Are you fighting a cold? Did you feel especially energetic or tired? Did you experience a particular ache or pain, such as a blister or sore joint? How was your breathing? Did you feel you had plenty of wind as you worked hard, or did you feel like you got out of breath so easily that your muscles could not work at all? You can also note, for example, the stretches and other exercises you do, as well as how you feel the rest of the day. If you have selected three stretches to do after rowing, put that down. If you try a new core exercise, note that. (There is more information on stretching and core exercises in the next chapter.) If you feel your rowing has affected your sleep or diet, make a note of it.

To summarize, consider again the question whether a glass is half full or half empty, which I raised above in the context of different size and shape glasses. Consider a different perspective on that question: Are you emptying your glass or filling it? If you are inactive, not exercising, I submit you are emptying the glass that represents your energy and health. On the other hand, if you row daily, that healthful stimulation of your lungs and heart and the rest of your body is filling the glass. Get in a daily row; fill the glass. That you do it is more important than how much you do of it.

To review, row daily because the body reacts daily. The biggest challenge for most people is developing the habit or practice of exercising daily. Therefore, focus your energy on that challenge. Think ahead about the next day; how, when, and where will you be able to row? You may not do exactly as you plan, but odds are your attempting to plan will help you succeed more often. If trying to row at one time of day does not work, try another. If you cannot make it to a health club to row, look for other options. If your work or family schedule makes it hard to find time to exercise, consider how you can change the schedule. Consider who can help you with your schedule. If you love all three of those TV shows you watch each night, row while you watch. Pay attention to what works.

3.2 SELECTING A ROWING MACHINE

One of the greatest advantages of indoor rowing is that all you need is a rowing machine. Rowing machines are readily available directly from the manufacturer and are quite affordable compared to other exercise equipment. Also, you can often keep rowing while traveling because rowing machines are becoming widely available at hotel fitness centers and health clubs around the world. If I have to travel and will be staying in a hotel with a fitness center, for example, I ask the hotel whether it has rowing machines before reserving a room.

Here are several considerations for you as you decide where to row:

- The simplest solution may be to purchase your own rowing machine and use it at home. However, if you do not want to buy your own, there are many options in health clubs and YMCAs. Some hotels even allow local membership for the use of their (usually smaller) fitness facilities. Look around and you likely will find a health club that has rowing machines. If not, ask them to purchase one.

- When you consider where to row, take into account availability and your schedule. If you want to exercise at 6:00 AM and the rowing machines at the YWCA are always in use at that hour, you may want to row elsewhere. If you want to row at a different time each day, you may need a health club as a resource (for example, for use during your lunch hour) even if you purchase a machine for home use (for evenings and weekends). If you spend time at a second home, you may need to make arrangements there, as well.

- As you learn about rowing machines, you may find you have a personal preference for one brand or another. You may also decide that your choice is affected by what is available at health clubs and other locations so that you can consistently use the same brand of machine. On the other hand, you may prefer to buy a different machine for your home use than the one you use at the Y.

- If you decide to buy your own rowing machine, you can purchase a used machine or a new one. New is nice and simple; all you have to do is make one call or order on the Web. You receive your new machine a few days later and, in less than an hour, you have put it together. On the other hand, a used rowing machine is cheaper and can work well, too. If a used machine has been well-maintained, it should last for years. Or, with a little effort and parts from the manufacturer, you can take an old machine that is not in good shape and make it like new.

Fig. 4
Rowing machines in a health club. Although it is still rare for YMCAs, YWCAs, and health clubs to offer as many rowing machines as treadmills and stationary bicycles, they are increasingly available.

If you live in a community with one or more rowing clubs, you may want to ask if they allow someone who is not a rower to use their indoor rowing machines. If they do, you may find the rowers there very supportive, a benefit even if you have no desire to row on the water. Since some new indoor rowers may feel self-conscious around competitive rowers, that solution may not be for everyone. In addition, many communities simply do not have the water resources to support an outdoor rowing team and few clubs have begun based solely on indoor rowing.

When you look at the possible purchase of a rowing machine, consider reliability, durability, price, ease of use, storage, the monitor on the machine, and manufacturer support. You may also have your own criteria.

I offer information here on three well-known manufacturers of rowing machines, the Concept2, the WaterRower and the RowPerfect. Each company has something to offer, and each sells directly to the consumer. You can contact them through their Web sites or by telephone and order a machine today.

I should note in fairness that I am most familiar with the Concept2 products. Concept2 is the most widely used brand. I bought one of the company's first models for my personal use nearly thirty years ago. I have seen them in use at many college boathouses, rowing clubs, and rowing competitions. We bought and used them for the high school team I coached. It is the machine I normally use still, today. And it is the machine I have seen almost universally at the Y, at clubs, and in hotel fitness centers in places like Chicago, New York, Seattle, Florence, and London. Concept2's basic model is also the least expensive offering of the three main manufacturers.

Here is a little background on these three manufacturers of indoor rowing machines. You will want to review their Web sites for yourself and call or e-mail them to have your questions answered so you can make a decision for yourself.

RowPerfect: The Australian-made RowPerfect rowing machine was developed for competitive rowers. The manufacturer says it provides the experience that is most like rowing on the water. You will find that the RowPerfect folks provide links to a great deal of information about rowing at the bottom of their home page. See www.RowPerfect.com. You can click on "ordering and shipping" in the series of links at the bottom of the page to find a sales contact in your country. The RowPerfect machine is less likely to be of interest to the beginning indoor rower, who may not be concerned with its unique feature involving body position and motion. Perhaps because of its higher price, the RowPerfect machine is more likely to compete for the business of the competitive rower who is using the machine to supplement rowing on the water.

Fig. 5

The RowPerfect machine is marketed as allowing the rower to mimic more precisely the actual motion of rowing in a racing shell. Photograph courtesy of RowPerfect.

WaterRower: A second well-known rowing machine is made by WaterRower and was developed in Rhode Island. The original model comes with a wooden frame. The other main distinguishing feature of this manufacturer's rowing machines is that they use water enclosed in a horizontal wheel instead of air in a vertical wheel to create resistance. Some people say they prefer the sound and feel of the water. You can stand the WaterRower upright for storage. For more information, see the company's Web site at www.WaterRower.com. You can click on "how to buy" and "ordering direct" and your region to see prices and ordering information. I rowed a long piece recently on a WaterRower. It felt good. The seat was soft and comfortable. However, I also noted that there was more water in the wheel than I would have used (and therefore more resistance), which I could not readily change. And it seemed that the tracks were flat rather than slightly downhill toward the wheel.

Fig. 6
The WaterRower folks came out with two unique features, a wooden structure and an inertial wheel moving through water instead of air. Photograph courtesy of WaterRower.

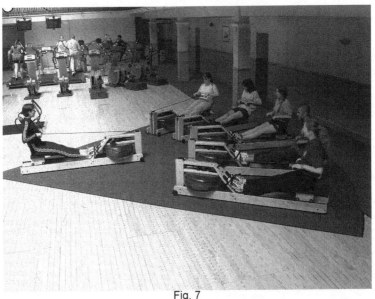

Fig. 7
Here are WaterRower machines set up in a health club for a rowing class.
Photograph courtesy of WaterRower.

Concept2: The Concept2 indoor rowing machine is made in Vermont. You can purchase your own health club–quality machine for under $1,000 directly from the manufacturer. The Concept2 machine is now in its fourth and fifth iterations, called the Model D and Model E.

To learn more about the Concept2 rowing machines, go to www. Concept2.com. You can explore the Web site to learn more about the machines and to order. Or you can call them directly and order over the phone.

Concept2's support and web site are both considered exceptional. One satisfied user, the CEO of a major cooperative corporation in the United States, agreed to let me share his experience:

> "I am sixty-three years young . . . and have been erging [using an indoor rowing machine] since February 2006. Up until 1993 I was a racquetball addict – playing five to six times a week. Unfortunately, severe hip pain (culminating in a hip replacement operation in 2000) ended my racquetball.

> "In the years after I stopped playing racquetball I tried many activities (health clubs, etc.) to keep in shape. The only thing that really stuck was road biking. With everything else, work and family time commitments along with interest level got in the way. The biggest problem with road biking was its weather and seasonal limitations. As a result, over the years I got more and more out of shape and gradually put on the pounds.

> "In December 2005 a number of factors combined to make me decide I had to really get serious about exercise again. These factors were being tired of being overweight, aches and pains from minor activities and my cholesterol level. I did a fair amount of research to find what I deemed the "perfect" exercise. My criteria were low impact, total body (I did not want to buy a gym), efficient (a good workout in a relatively short time), year round, and something I enjoyed and would stick with. Indoor rowing was the exercise that fit this bill perfectly. I knew I enjoyed doing it because I had rowed as a warm-up exercise for racquetball. . . .

> "To me, the equipment is only half the story with Concept2. I have never dealt with another company that gives the 'after sale' support that Concept2 does. The challenges, prizes, clubs, logs, advice, etc., [accessible via the Concept2 Web site] show an unsurpassed dedication to helping their customers strive to make the best use of their purchase. This is a very impressive company that

really knows the meaning of customer service. I am a big advocate of the company and unabashedly spread that word around."

For many users, the fact that the Concept2 machines are in such wide use makes it appealing since you can row at home, the Y, or many other places and be using the same machine. That allows you to keep a consistent record of your exercise. For example, I use a Concept2 Model C at home and their Model D at the health club. In addition, the low price for the Model D makes it very popular. You will also see that parts are available from the manufacturer for the repair and upgrade of older models. Thus, if you wish to buy a used, older machine, you can fix it yourself.

Fig. 8
It takes only a few seconds to split the Concept2
rowing machine into two parts and stand them up
for storage.

Other Rowing Machines: A number of other exercise machines have been sold and marketed as rowing machines. Do a search on the Web and you will find other machines. Some models have shock absorber-type resistance attached to handles that move in an arc. These and others used to appear more frequently in health clubs. However, they tend to be selected less often by health clubs these days and are not regularly used by rowing teams or rowing clubs.

A new addition to the offerings of rowing machines is designed by Oar-Tec of Australia. The machine appears to be an attempt to make indoor rowing more closely resemble rowing with an oar in a boat. It offers the option of rowing using different handles to simulate the motion of either sweep rowing or sculling. (More information is available on these terms in the Appendix.) The possibility of doing indoor training using the same motion of the arms as in a boat has great appeal for some rowers, but may be irrelevant for beginning indoor rowers. I have seen comments from rowers about wanting to buy this machine as soon as it is available. The downside is that the price is several times as high as the price of the other machines.

Fig. 9
Here is the sculling set-up of the Oar-Tec machine in use.
Photograph courtesy of Oar-Tec.

Fig. 10
This is the sweep version of the Oar-Tec machine. Photograph courtesy of Oar-Tec.

3.3   Start to Row: The Basic Motion

Many people are surprised to find, when they sit down on a rowing machine for the first time, that it feels foreign to them. This may be because the exercise of rowing, unlike rowing a rowboat, involves the legs.

Rowing uses the whole body working together on a sliding seat. You do not sit on a stationary bench as you would in a row boat, where you brace your legs and row with your arms and back. Instead, your seat moves and your feet are "tied in" or attached to a non-moving platform, the foot stretcher of the rowing machine. As you row, your seat slides toward your feet on the *recovery* in preparation for you to push or drive your seat away from your feet with your legs on the *drive*. While rowing uses the core, the back, and the upper body muscles, the legs are the main power source.

The central role of the legs in rowing is, for the beginner, not just a matter of learning to use them at all, but of learning to use them for their quickness and their power. Another challenge is coordinating how and when you use your arms, back, and legs so that they work efficiently together. Many of the tips in chapter five are intended to help you learn to coordinate your use of the different parts of the body. A coordinated stroke is more efficient, allows you to relax the smaller muscles, and empowers you to get more out of the larger, stronger muscles. That in turn does more for your heart and lungs.

Rowing is a smooth, continuous motion. There is not a beginning or end; there is no position between strokes, no place where you stop moving completely. You can begin from any position. One stroke simply means one complete cycle of motion.

In order to discuss the motions of the body and how to coordinate them while rowing, we divide the stroke into parts. See the body positions in the pictures below representing different points in the stroke. However, keep in mind that the goal is fluid, continuous motion and that the parts run together.

Rowing coaches and fitness trainers will break the stroke down into catch, drive, finish (or release), and recovery in order to discuss this cyclic motion, and into even finer points to discuss technique. We can begin more simply by dividing the stroke into two parts, the recovery and the drive.

- *The Recovery Phase of the Stroke:* When you sit with the legs straight and the handle drawn in to your body at the finish (see the figure below) and then start to move the hands and handle away from the body, you are beginning what is called the recovery. On the recovery, think of the handle drawing you forward, so you move the arms out first to straighten them. Then, following the handle, begin to swing the upper body forward. Only once the hands are past the still-straight knees will you begin to raise the knees and roll the seat forward on the track or slide. (There is more information about rowing and rowing terms in the Appendices.) At the end of this recovery motion you will be in what is called the catch position in the figure below. The catch position is essentially a posture at the end of the recovery and the beginning of the drive rather than a separate part of the stroke.

- *The Drive Phase of the Stroke:* On the drive (which begins when your body is all the way forward and your legs compressed, and you start to straighten or "drive" the legs down), let your arms relax and merely act like chains connecting your body to the handle (that is, let them stay straight at first rather than attempting to bring them to the body). Press the knees down and begin to swing your shoulders back, then bring your arms in to the body as you finish, leaning back just past vertical. The drive and finish positions below illustrate this process. As you hold on to the handle with your hands throughout the drive, keep them relaxed; they should not become a source of tension in the arms or shoulders. Once you reach the finish position, you have the handle against your body, your legs are straight, and you are leaning back slightly. You are now ready to start the hands/handle moving away from the body, as described in the previous paragraph on the recovery.

Fig. 11

This figure shows body positions at certain points in the stroke, courtesy of Concept2. Note that in the first and last pictures labeled "catch" the rower has just moved forward, from left to right in the image, and is ready to move back again. Note also that, in the "recovery" picture, the knees had remained flat (legs straight) until the hands passed above the knees. After that, the knees begin to bend and rise as the body moves forward as shown in the picture.

Two other general issues with new rowers are that they find it uncomfortable (1) to be moving continuously and (2) to have both hands in use all the time. If you are more comfortable at first taking breaks, do so. For example, after rowing a few minutes, get off the machine, walk around, stretch for a moment, get a drink of water, do whatever makes you comfortable. Then get back on and resume rowing. Over time, this sense of strangeness or discomfort will disappear as your body gets used to continuous, whole-body motion using both hands.

Another general question some have is how far forward to go during the recovery as you approach the catch. A simple rule of thumb is to slide forward on the recovery until your shins are vertical. You should not go past that point and should not allow the seat to strike your heels. On the other hand, many people are too stiff or overweight to get that far forward. Do not let that worry you, either. Simply go as far forward as you can comfortably reach without letting the upper body slump over. Your ability to attain your full reach will improve over time.

Yet another concern for beginners is how hard to push themselves. The simple answer is "not too hard." Some experience the opposite problem; they feel like there is no pressure to row against. Do not try to adjust your machine to create more resistance. Instead, obtain resistance by the speed with which you push the legs down at the beginning of the drive. As you drive the legs harder, you create resistance against the air or water in the wheel.

There are as many issues and questions as there are people. Review the manufacturer's instructional DVD. Talk to other rowers, a coach, or a trainer. Most importantly, stick with it, use moderation, and give it time.

3.4   Rowing as Dynamic Stretching

Picture yourself lying on the floor on your back and stretching your legs by drawing your knees toward your chest. You are stretching out the hamstrings (the muscle group on the back of the leg between the knee and the hip) and other muscles in the leg and lower back. This stretching motion is repeated (albeit from a sitting position) with each stroke as you row. As you slide forward on the recovery to prepare to drive with the legs, you stretch out the muscles you are about to use.

Fig. 12

Compare this hamstring stretch, pulling the knee toward the chest while lying on the back, to the position of the body at the catch as shown above.

When you start to row, sit up comfortably, arms out in front of you holding the handle, and begin to move your hands easily toward your feet, keeping the handle at the same height as you go forward, as though it were moving across a tabletop. Roll the body forward only as far as you can without strain. Feel the leg muscles stretch out as you slide the seat forward.

For comparison, those who have lifted weights consider the weight lifting exercise called the clean to be similar to the rowing motion. The main difference, of course, is that the clean is done standing up and holding a weight bar in front of you. Note that you should lift weights only after instruction and with supervision. Unlike indoor rowing, where you are sitting down and have only as much resistance as you create by pulling, lifting weights on a bar can create a precarious position.

Fig. 13

In performing a clean, the weight lifter lowers the bar slowly and under control toward the floor until, without pausing, she drives the legs to lift the bar up to shoulder height. When rowing, your body movement during the recovery phase of the stroke is very similar to lowering the weight while doing a clean. Weight trainers learn early that lowering the weight and the body slowly and under control makes the exercise more effective. The slow stretching of the leg muscles on the way down prepares them for a powerful drive on the way up. The same applies to the recovery during the rowing stroke.

If your muscles are tight or you are full of girth, you may only roll the seat forward a slight amount on the recovery. That is fine; move the distance that is comfortable for you. If you are fit and flexible, your hands may extend well beyond your feet as you move forward during the recovery. Play with the adjustable setting of the foot stretcher to see whether you are more comfortable rowing with your feet higher or lower in the stretcher.

When you reach the point where the shins are vertical (or as far as you can go toward that goal), drive the legs (straighten them out forcefully), bringing the knees back down so the legs are straight or flat. Using the comparison of the clean again, in lifting the weight you would stand up, straightening your legs. During that effort, the back and upper body would stay close to vertical so that the leg effort moves the bar.

In rowing, you stay seated and, as you drive the legs, move the upper body just past vertical so you are leaning back slightly as the knees straighten. Then, after the hands move out to the knees again, the same gradual stretching of the legs and back occurs as you move forward once again and prepare to drive with the legs and pull with the arms.

Because this motion extends certain muscles well beyond normal daily use for most people, you should treat your early rowing as stretching and follow the two most basic rules of stretching: (1) Go slow; (2) No pain. And do stretch *after* you row to help improve your flexibility. That topic is discussed in more detail in section 4.4.

3.5   Rowing Entertainment

A common objection to rowing indoors is the perception that it is boring. As a beginner, you may find yourself wanting to stop without knowing why simply because it seems tedious. When you are starting to row, find ways to make your rowing more interesting so it is easier to continue.

One type of entertainment is playing music. Some people like rousing music that gets their hearts pumping, from Sousa marches to the Planets to the Who. Some prefer something softer or more random, just a background soundtrack to serve as a distraction. In the beginning, find and use what works for you to keep you on the rowing machine. Later, you can consider whether you feel you get more out of the experience using one type of music or entertainment over another.

Another type of entertainment is to watch television while you row. You can turn up the volume to listen or watch with the sound down. One marathon rower likes to watch back-to-back movies while rowing. (It is a simple matter to get off the machine briefly to change movies without upsetting the working of the monitor.) Others prefer to watch the news each day while rowing, accomplishing two things at once. There are also videos of rowing you can obtain that may inspire or interest you.

A third way to entertain yourself is to row with mirrors in front or to the side so that you can periodically check your technique in the mirror. We tend to feel that we are moving efficiently when we engage in a physical activity. The truth is that, for most of us, when we first begin to do something new, our bodies often move in ways that are less efficient or even awkward. We tend not to feel that; seeing it can be a useful way to help improve technique. If you do not have mirrors but can set up a video camera, that may provide a similar opportunity. Tape a few minutes; then get off the machine to observe. With what you see, row and tape again to see if you can make a difference.

Rowing in front of a television or to music may be beneficial because it helps you continue your rowing. An even better way to entertain is to use your attention to improve your rowing while making the time pass. Here are three basic ways to vary your rowing that will give you a focus for your attention and can help you make your workout more effective. Doing each for as little as a couple of minutes is a useful beginning. Or you can try one for an entire workout. You will find more on these and other ideas in chapter five:

- *Vary the Intensity:* Think of your rows as one of two basic types, long and steady or short bursts of greater effort with rest periods of relatively easier rowing in between. One model for varying how hard you pull is to base it on how you feel rather than by counting strokes or following the clock. When you feel your rowing is very comfortable, begin to pull harder until you become more winded (so that you want to ease off). Then put less energy into your rowing, as by driving the legs down slower or more easily. Once you feel your breath has come back to you and you feel more energetic again, increase the level of effort a second time. Continue to alternate how hard you drive the legs based on how you feel.

- *Vary the Stroke Rating:* Your goal at first should to be to row slowly and steadily in order to increase the length of your workout and establish a baseline for your fitness and muscle tone. A variation you may want to try is to change the stroke rating. The stroke rate or rating is the number of strokes you row each minute ("spm"). Your rowing machine monitor will show on the display what your stroke rating is. Most people at first tend to row at around twenty spm using long strokes, or to use rapid, short strokes at well over thirty spm. Try to aim for a middle ground, approximately twenty-four to twenty-six spm. You can row one minute (or row for a number of strokes, such as twenty or thirty strokes at a time) at a slightly higher or a lower stroke rating before returning to that middle rating. Repeat, perhaps with a different variation.

- *Work on Ratio:* A third variation you can focus on is your ratio, the relative amount of time you take on the recovery compared to the drive. You should spend relatively longer on the recovery (rolling forward toward the monitor into a compressed position) even though it is easy. For good ratio, you should take relatively less time on the drive (driving the legs down firmly). During a longer row, focus occasionally on your ratio for ten strokes.

With these basic variables in mind, your goal should be to row continuously for increasingly longer times. If you started with two five- or ten-minute pieces with a rest in between, gradually extend the two or add a third. Continue that approach until you are rowing thirty to forty minutes or more total. Then increase the length of the pieces and shorten your breaks over a period of days or weeks until you can row that entire time without stopping.

Record what you try for variety and what you accomplish with it in terms of interest, improvement, or both. Compare your results over time. For example, include whether or not you are repeating an earlier workout and how it feels.

3.6   Start with Your Present Fitness

When you begin to row, your approach may vary depending on how fit you are to start:

Out of Shape: Some of us have long adapted our bodies to be out of shape. If you are in that situation, exercise cautiously and deliberately. As you begin:

- See your doctor for an examination and for approval to exercise. Your doctor may be able to refer you to a physical therapist, trainer, or coach who can work with you specifically on the issue of starting in a manner that is based on your present condition. Then you can work your way to independence.

- Start slowly and easily. Focus on time rather than distance or speed.

- Take more breaks during your daily row for a longer period of days or weeks as you gradually build up your stamina.

- Think about and plan on a longer trial period so that your expectation for results is not overly optimistic or based on too short a period of acclimatization.

Remember that the body's potential is there. But if it is stored away more deeply, it can take more time to blossom. Note that this caution may apply even if you seem generally fit and do things like gardening regularly. Many activities that are healthy for you do not stimulate the whole body and result in deeper breathing over a period of time every day. If you have not been doing regular aerobic exercise, take your time. Be patient. Keep at it.

Somewhat in Shape: If you have been playing ball or doing other exercise regularly, you should use your first several rowing workouts to get a sense of pace. Gauge your strength and wind and do not expect too much! Only after observing how your body responds to the demands of rowing does it make sense to engage in a series of planned workouts.

Sometimes we use the term *second wind* to refer to the sense of power and energy that may come several minutes into aerobic exercise. Once the bodily systems have adjusted to the demand of the workout, the lungs and muscles start to deliver and you feel more energized rather than fatigued as you exercise. Do not expect that experience to occur in your early workouts.

Also, watch for feeling extremely winded less than a minute into a workout you have started too hard. You may feel during the first few strokes that you can row hard forever and therefore begin by pushing harder than you should. The simple fact is that rowing very hard the first strokes is a good way to reach a point of gasping for breath.

All too often, many of us who already exercise approach something new like the proverbial weekend warrior. And many of us who work out daily do a lot of standing around. Weight lifting is great for strength but rowing places a different demand on your heart and lungs. It takes time to develop stamina, even for the very strong. Be patient. Keep at it.

Very Fit: Even the very fit athlete with exceptional endurance should start rowing attentively. There are two reasons for this. First, with very few exceptions, those who feel they are very fit (and who probably are by most people's standards) still may be relatively out of shape for the full-body workout rowing provides. If you start strong and feel challenged, that should not be a source of discouragement. Rather, it confirms that you are working effectively to use the maximum muscle mass. Do not doom yourself to failure or disappointment by assuming it will be easy. Do not give up if your rowing performance does not initially meet your expectations. Just ease off slightly to a pace you can maintain and keep track of your results.

Second, most mature adults who are already very fit have become fit for one particular reason or function. Whether you have run marathons, have played ball, or have had some other specific activity of choice, you likely have developed a high degree of fitness adapted specially for that pursuit. Be ready to take time to allow your body to adapt to rowing.

Pay attention to your strengths and weaknesses. Log them. Develop a good cross-training program to complement your rows. Work on all of it over time and compare your results.

4

Rowing and Other Exercise

○ ○

"I took up cross-country skiing at the age of fifty-six. I had drifted into skiing haphazardly, buying my second-hand equipment at an auction. . . . I went out on the snow and began fooling around. Whatever was possible to do wrong, I did wrong. . . . But I never got hurt and I had great fun."

Complete Cross-Country Skiing and Ski Touring
—William J. Lederer

"[P]eople question why we undertake these [three-to-five-month-long wilderness rowing] trips at all. They might as well ask us why we breathe or eat. Our journeys are food for our spirits, clean air for our souls. We don't care if they are firsts or farthests; we don't seek sponsors. They are neither a vacation nor an escape; they are a way of life."

Rowing to Latitude: Journeys Along the Arctic's Edge
—Jill Fredston

"The Alexander Principle states that there are certain ways of using your body which are better than certain other ways; that when you reject these better ways of using your body, your functioning will begin to suffer. . . . The Alexander Principle says that use affects functioning."

The Alexander Technique
—Wilfred Barlow

"Athletes learn their skills through their kinaesthetic sensations. . . . Speaking generally, all athletes are best left unaware of the exact nature of their movements and need only sufficient detail to correct faults, satisfy curiosity and inspire confidence."

The Mechanics of Athletics
—Geoffrey Dyson

4.1   ROWING: A FOUNDATION

Rowing can provide a foundation for any exercise program. If you have a favorite sport or activity, use rowing to support it. If not, start with rowing. In either case, evaluate collectively all the exercise you do. Select the exercises you want to use. Keep track of what you do. One reason to combine rowing with other exercises is to enhance your fitness. Another reason is simply for your satisfaction and enjoyment. Playing a game you enjoy, such as racquetball, basketball, tennis, or soccer, can support your daily rowing (and vice-versa) by giving you the benefit of variety. If including other activities in your routine helps you achieve daily exercise that includes rowing, you are better off than if you exclude them and fail.

4.2   KEEP SCORE OF YOUR PROGRESS

Keep score of how you are doing. You can keep track of your fitness by timing a piece you row for a set distance, by seeing how far you can row in a pre-determined time, and so on. Here, the point is a different sort of keeping score, namely to grade whether you are getting to it every day, rather than assessing how fast or strong you are. I have suggested that you keep a log of your daily rowing. Part of that log is a record of whether you exercise each day. Let's consider scoring, generating a number to represent your success at rowing (or otherwise getting exercise) every day.

Some folks, such as those who have taught themselves to count every calorie they consume, may wish to keep score of everything. They may wish to record every change in stroke rating, every sit-up they do, every minute they spend playing racquetball. If it works for you, do it.

If not, start by scoring yourself more simply based on whether you have done your rowing on a given day. How might you grade or score your daily exercise?

Here are five examples. Consider them and use what works for you. Begin with a more forgiving approach that recognizes every effort you make. Later, as you make progress, use one of the more demanding scoring methods to reward yourself for your accomplishments. Similarly, if you start by walking four days a week and rowing three, eventually give yourself a better score for the days you row based on the higher overall intensity of the exercise. But to start, keep it simple and count whatever matters to you.

- *No Calculation:* The first and easiest way to score is simply to exercise and mark it down as accomplished on your log. But if you do not row or otherwise exercise every day, you may need a more sophisticated approach to take into account the days you miss.

- *Total Days:* The second way to grade your rowing is to count the days you row or do other exercise and add them up each week and each month. Compare your score over a period of months. As you become more consistent, your numbers will go up. If you want to value rowing more than something else that you like to do but which gives you less value, count the other activity as a fraction each time you do it. See if you can increase your score each month.

- *Consecutive Days:* A third and more demanding way to score is to keep track of the number of consecutive days you row. (If you decide in advance to count the days you play ball, include them. If you are doing something else simply to play hooky, be tough on yourself and do not count it.) If you miss a day, start over at zero. See how high a number of consecutive days you can reach each month and compare that over time. Decide for yourself whether to apply this process strictly, in effect voiding your high number if you skip, or to apply it more liberally by retaining your record number of days exercised during the month even if you then skip one or more days.

- *Subtraction:* A fourth way to grade yourself is to add up days rowed each month and subtract the total number of days you skip. This score gives you a "daily" value because it takes into account the negative effect of the days you miss. It is similar to using the point spread at the end of a game to evaluate the outcome. How much did one team (days rowed) beat the other (days missed) by?

- *Division:* A fifth way to score is to divide the days rowed by days missed. If you prefer ratios or decimals to simple whole numbers, you may prefer this to the fourth method. You will see dramatic improvement as you approach a perfect record of rowing every day. On the other hand, since you cannot divide by zero, once you reach that perfect record, you will need to change to a different method of scoring (such as the first or third).

In all of these cases, the larger your resulting score, the better. Each method just gives you a different take on what you are achieving. Pick one that appeals to you and consider changing the way you grade yourself over time. Do not pick the most unforgiving method, such as suggestion three, to manage your progress in the beginning.

Consider some examples of the scores you would achieve as a result of these methods. Suppose in a month of thirty-one days, you rowed sixteen days and missed fifteen.

- If you use the first method, you will have filled in your log with an entry for every day, noting the days you missed, but will not apply or calculate a number for your totals.

- Your score under method two is sixteen, the total number of days you rowed that month, without regard to how many days were consecutive.

- Under the strict version of method three, your score would depend on when you last missed a day; it might be zero. Alternatively, under the looser or more liberal approach of method three, you could keep track of the highest total you achieved during the month, even if you missed a day after that. If you rowed every other day, your score would be one or zero. If you rowed the first sixteen days of the month, your score would be sixteen or zero. If you skipped the first two weeks and then rowed the final sixteen days of the month, your score would be sixteen.

- By subtraction (method four) your score will be one, the difference between the total days you rowed and the total you missed.

- By division (method five) it will be 16/15 or 1.07, the total number of days you rowed divided by the total days missed.

If, on the other hand, you rowed twenty-five days and missed only six, your score for the month using the fourth and fifth methods would be nineteen or 25/6 (4.17).

Determine which method feels right to you or develop your own. Probably the most important benefits you receive from keeping score will be the conclusions you draw from it and the satisfaction you feel as you improve. You may also find after a frustrating month that you understand your lack of progress better once you see that, despite your efforts to exercise regularly, your score indicates you are giving your body conflicting instructions. For a variation on the approach of the third method, see the notes after the sample log, below.

Examples of Record Keeping and Scoring
Daily Rowing Log

(1) Cum. Exercise	(2) Cum. Miss	(3) Score	Day/ Date	What I Did/ Comments	Totals
1	-	1	Mon, 4/23	Rowed 30 minutes in three pieces with 5 min. break, at 20-22 spm; felt weak; shoulder hurt; right forearm tight; blister on right heel; (could also add: where you rowed; who else rowed with you; how this compares to a prior workout; how what you did compares to what you planned to do when you started for the day; your stretches; your core work; cross-training; etc.)	(Time, distance)
2	-	2	Tues	(Insert description, taking as many lines as you need)	
-	1	-1	Weds		
1	-	0	Thurs		
2	-	1	Fri		
3	-	2	Sat		
-	1	-1	Sun		
1	-	0	Mon		
-	1	-1	Tues		
-	2	-2	Weds		
1	-	-1	Thurs		
2	-	0	Fri		
3	-	1	Sat		

Fig. 14
Explanation of One Way to Use the First Three Columns
(stricter version of method three):

(1) Column (1) is the number of consecutive days you have exercised and zeroes out as soon as you miss a day. Start over again at one the next day you exercise.

(2) Column (2) is the number of consecutive days you have missed (not exercised). Start over at one each time you miss a day after exercising and number consecutively until you exercise again.

(3) Column (3) is your score during your beginning weeks. Take your current (that day's) score for column (1) (remember, it zeros out as soon as you miss a day, so when you miss and until you exercise again, it is zero), and subtract your most recent score for column (2) (which does not zero out once you exercise again). The goal is to see how high a score you can achieve.

4.3   USE ROWING TO CROSS-TRAIN FOR OTHER ACTIVITIES

You may be interested in rowing primarily because of your dedication to another sport or exercise. Many people find they can successfully use rowing as a cross-training exercise to support their sport. If that is your desire, you may already have a log and scoring system you use. And you may want it to reflect primarily your progress in your cycling, basketball, running, or whatever activity you are pursuing.

One reason rowing provides beneficial cross-training is because its non-impact work does not strain joints that may already be stressed with your primary sport. In fact, rowing can actually strengthen and protect the joints that athletes depend on for other sports. For example, rowing strengthens the leg muscles that hold the knee in place.

Runners and cyclists have found rowing can be a great way to train indoors when the weather is bad. It also can make them stronger overall, improving leg power and stamina. It adds an element of arm strength without excessive muscle mass in the arms, while doing good for the key leg muscles.

Rowing uses the full mass of the thigh muscles, back as well as front (and sides), and links them with use of the back to develop great leg power. Using most of the body's muscle mass at the same time also creates a greater demand on the heart and lungs. Thus, rowing can offer athletes in other sports a way to improve their overall cardiovascular fitness.

Rowing can be a useful way to get safe exercise at any age. Since you row sitting down, there is significantly reduced risk of falling or incurring injury. The rowing machine is useful equally to the eighty-year-old looking for non-threatening, self-paced exercise to supplement his or her walking and the twenty-five-year-old professional athlete who wants more stamina. The monitor provides a mechanism to keep track of your progress either way.

Rowing also involves quickness that is useful in other sports and activities. To row harder on the rowing machine, you do not add weight or resistance. Instead, you learn to apply leg power more quickly. The quicker application of power is new to most beginners. Many try to heave the upper body into the stroke or tense up before they learn the secret of driving the legs more quickly.

Rowing enhances coordination among all the major muscle groups and joints. An attentive rower who achieves a well-coordinated stroke develops an increased ability to concentrate on what the body is doing and how the limbs are working together. Experiment with rowing two to three days per week to supplement your routine of running, cycling, basketball, other sports, and other forms of recreation.

4.4　CROSS-TRAIN FOR ROWING

There are two additional things I recommend you do every day with rowing: stretching and core exercises. Adding as little as a few minutes of each will be beneficial.

Some people will want to round out their rowing with some weight lifting or other exercises, too. Although rowing is one of the best all-around forms of exercise, it is not a perfect exercise in the sense of using and training all muscles and joints equally and for all purposes. This is especially true for the beginner who is already out of condition. Rowing provides a great base. Add other exercises in coordination with your daily row to gain the fitness you want.

Here are the two essentials:

- *Stretching:* Muscles need to be stretched out when you are done exercising and the muscles are still warm to enhance your overall flexibility. Otherwise, these tired muscles will tend to tighten up as they recover, making the next day's row harder rather than easier. When you stretch, do not force, but hold your maximum comfortable position for thirty seconds to two minutes and repeat each stretch. Stretching is important enough that the next section (4.5) is devoted to it.

- *Core Work:* The other key supplemental exercise is strengthening the core, the muscles of the lower back, sides, and abdomen. The muscles around the core of the body weaken and fall into disuse as we age. They need work. And they are critically important for your posture, your breath, and your power. Once you start to get your core into shape, you will find you enjoy it and that it helps you with all exercise. As with stretching, core work is so important that a section (4.6) is devoted to it.

Other great cross-training exercises for rowing include:

- *Cycling:* Some people who row competitively use biking as an alternative way of pushing their legs, lungs, and heart without the whole-body demands of rowing. Cycling can provide a day off from rowing or a lighter second workout on a given day. Other aerobic activities can also be useful, including running, swimming, and the use of indoor aerobic equipment.

- *Weight Lifting:* Serious competitive rowers lift weights, at least during part of the year. Often, they will include weight exercises that strengthen complementary muscles as well as strengthening the ones they need most for rowing. That keeps the body balanced, helps avoid injury, and, some believe, enhances your ability to become a stronger rower overall. You do not have to approach weight lifting with a goal of lifting the maximum possible weight to get real benefit from using weights. A moderate program of lifting weights three times per week under supervision can give you more power to bring to your rowing.

- *Specific Areas of the Body:* You may further develop some areas of the body that are used regularly in rowing, such as the lower back and ankles, by using other exercises. If you feel rowing is not helping enough to strengthen a set of muscles you want to develop for other purposes, supplement your rowing. Working on a particular part of the body is usually based on personal preference. Working with a personal trainer can help focus this supplemental effort.

Another basis for cross-training, perhaps the most important one, is your enjoyment. If you enjoy kayaking, canoeing, swimming, downhill skiing, walking, or other activities, include them in your routine. If you love tennis, basketball, or soccer, do not give it up to row. Supplement your rowing by engaging in another enjoyable activity in addition to rowing.

4.5 Stretch Daily after Exercise

The most obvious and necessary complementary "exercise" to add to your daily rowing is stretching. Even a few short minutes each day after you row can make a difference.

Some people like to stretch before they exercise. That is a form of warming up, preparing the muscles for activity. That is not what we are discussing here. Stretching before exercise to warm up may be useful, but may also be unnecessary if the exercise you are doing does not involve strain or you start out slowly.

Stretching after your exercise while your muscles are warm can help your muscles avoid tightening from the exercise. It can help limit the stiffness you might otherwise feel. Over time, it can help you become more flexible.

Start by selecting three or four stretching exercises to do each day after you row. Once you get used to doing those, you can modify what you do or add more if you wish. Do not let the fact that there are many possible stretches interfere with your doing something every day. One day, if you feel you must take a day off from rowing, one of the best substitutes you can use is an hour of stretching and core work.

When you stretch after exercise, do not strain or force. Rather, stretch to your maximum comfortable position without bouncing. Hold that position for thirty seconds to two minutes. Repeat each stretch a second time.

These six pictures depict just a few stretches out of many more you can do:

Fig. 15
This picture and the next show toe-touching stretches of the legs and back. The stretch of each leg separately, feet separated, is especially helpful because you will feel the muscles on the inside of the thigh tightening up when you row. As with all stretches, reach out to your comfortable limit. When you repeat the stretch the second time, you may be able to reach slightly farther. Hold the position you can reach to allow the muscles to relax in the stretched position.

Fig 16
You can also stretch out by reaching to both feet together.

Fig. 17
The hamstring stretch shown here should be repeated separately for each leg, and then with both legs together. It is most effective if you keep your lower back flat on the floor while drawing the knee toward your chest, rather than lifting the butt and bending the back while you stretch.

Fig. 18
This stretch is based on the hamstring stretch but is actually working other muscles in the hip of the leg with the ankle up. Place one ankle against the thigh near the knee of the other leg. Pull on the knee/thigh of the second leg in order to draw the ankle toward the head, stretching that leg and hip. Hold as noted above and repeat. Then do the other side.

Fig. 19
This photo shows another way you can stretch the hamstrings and back.

Fig. 20
Stretching the quads along the front of the leg is also important. As your leg strength increases, these muscles will tighten and need more stretching. After stretching one leg, switch legs. Keep the foot you are holding behind the other leg rather than to the side and only draw the ankle up to a comfortable position.

Increased flexibility offers many benefits. Keep it simple to avoid creating too great a demand on your time. Add a small number of basic stretches to your daily routine to improve your range of motion. Stretch the muscles that are sore or that you can feel you are using as you row. Occasionally, look for other stretches to add to your routine or to use for variety.

One test you can give yourself of your overall flexibility is to lower yourself slowly from a standing position to a squatting position. Keep your heels flat on the floor. How far down can you lower your body without losing balance?

4.6 DAILY CORE EXERCISES

The most important supplemental work most of us can do along with stretching is strengthening our core, commonly thought of as the stomach area, including the muscles of the lower back, sides and abdomen. These muscles weaken from bad posture, lack of use, and as our girth expands. The core muscles need daily work, and need it increasingly as we age.

Having a fit set of muscles in your body's core will help you row more comfortably and more effectively. With better posture on the rowing machine, you will sit higher and have greater leverage for pulling. You will also enhance your ability to breathe deeply because you will hold your body up in a way that frees the diaphragm to move easily without your gut feeling compressed or crimped.

Expect to be very sore the first few days you do core exercises if you have not been keeping these muscles in shape. The soreness will pass and you will find yourself handling the core work much more easily after the first few days. To minimize that soreness, start slowly and with few repetitions.

As you did with the stretches, start your core work by selecting only three or four to do each day. Plan to spend just a few minutes each day. Later, you can consider adding more to enhance your exercise. Also, like stretching, core work can be learned and expanded through work with trainers, in classes, and by exploring the many resources that describe core exercises. But, most importantly, keep it simple and short in the beginning so it is easy to include it.

Begin core work by trying one or more of these exercises or a simpler version based on them. Repeat a small number of times, such as ten, or hold the position initially for a short period, like ten seconds. You can increase repetitions or duration later.

Fig. 21
This photograph illustrates one type of sit-up. Sit-ups from lying flat on your back to the position where arms and legs are parallel to each other at forty-five degrees to the floor are one of many types of sit-ups and crunches you can do for your abdominal muscles. If you find these difficult, begin with a simpler and more easily completed type of sit-up or abdominal crunch that works for you.

Fig. 22
In this "Superman" position, you work the muscles of the back by holding up the arms and legs. Do not strain to lift the legs high. Get the benefit simply by using your back muscles to hold the legs up slightly.

Fig. 23
One variation on the prior position is to lift one arm and opposite leg to a higher position. Then switch which arm and leg you hold higher for dynamic back strengthening.
Beginners may want to let the opposite arm and leg rest on or press against the floor
when not raised instead of holding all four limbs up at once.

Fig. 24
Another way to do the opposite arm and leg core work is from a kneeling position.
This position is especially useful in that you can hold the outstretched arm and leg
parallel to the floor instead of trying to lift them higher than your body. This works
the back muscles while allowing you to keep the back straight. Tighten the stomach
muscles while you work the back.

Fig. 25
In the plank pose, hold the body in a stiff position while resting on your toes and forearms on the floor.

Fig. 26
Do the same on each side to work more core muscles.

Fig. 27
You can repeat the same exercise face up.

There are many other useful exercises for core fitness, including work on balancing balls and using a roller.

4.7 FIVE BEGINNERS AND HOW THEY STARTED

There are as many reasons to begin and ways to start rowing as there are people. Consider the stories of five hypothetical beginning rowers:

Karen, age 67, is a retired school teacher. Her husband passed away three years ago after a two-year battle with cancer. She lives alone in the home where they raised their two children. One of the kids returned after college to raise her family in the town where Karen lives. Karen and her husband used to have the grandchildren over every Friday night when they were little. Now that the grand-kids are 13 and 16, they usually have other plans besides spending Friday night with their grandmother. Karen learned about rowing from a neighbor whose daughter rowed in college. When the YWCA where she has taken aerobics and Pilates classes bought some rowing machines, she and her neighbor decided to try rowing. Her friend soon quit, saying she would just be a rowing mom instead of becoming a rower, but Karen is determined to stick with it. She decided not to spend the money on her own rowing machine or to look for a personal trainer. She is hoping that the Y will offer rowing classes some day.

Karen decided that she would row at the same time every day. She began deliberately with short periods of five to ten minutes on the rowing machine, getting a drink of water during her short breaks. The first week she starting rowing, she went on-line to find advice about indoor rowing and to learn more about possible workouts. After increasing the length of her continuous rowing each day, she began to schedule in four stretches and two core exercises at the end of her row. She began a log her second day and usually records several lines of information about what she did and how she felt. After the first three months, when she had a better idea what she was comfortable doing, she plotted out goals for the next month. Now, she includes those targets in her log like a lesson plan, followed by her description of how she did. She is working on a two-tier scoring system that assigns credit for stretches and core work apart from her rowing score. She is not interested in setting goals for how fast she rows.

Joe, age 72, is a semi-retired emeritus professor at the university. His wife remains busy with her career in real estate. Joe has never competed on a team, but has always exercised, going back to intramural sports in college. He does some running, but no longer competes in the half-marathons he used to run each spring. He enjoys bicycling on the growing network of trails on the old railroad rights-of-way in his area. Joe heard about rowing over the years from students he taught who were on the university crew. He occasionally would sit down on a rowing machine at the university fitness center, but did not start taking it seriously until a friend told him about an on-line group that rows together. Since then, he has begun to use the rowing machine at the fitness center more often and stays in touch with other rowers. He also has started to check out the information available on-line about records and scores for various distances and times by age group. Other than getting some tips on technique from some students on the rowing team, Joe simply began on his own.

Joe decided he would try to row three days a week to start. He did not want to give up his running and cycling, but figured he would give rowing equal footing for a while. He does not schedule his rowing, just as he has not previously scheduled runs or rides (unless he was going to run or bike with someone else). But having decided he will exercise every day, he usually gets it in. Sometimes he will do it first thing when he knows he has a busy schedule all day. Sometimes he fits it in after dinner. He keeps a diary on what he is doing for exercise, just as he has always done, but does not include details. After rowing regularly at the fitness center for several months, Joe ordered a rowing machine for home use so he can row when the center is not open. He is looking into indoor rowing events for the future.

Ellen, age 89, and her husband of over sixty years moved a few years ago to be closer to one of their children. They travel abroad two or three times a year and spend a couple of months in Sarasota each winter. They talk about considering assisted living options for the future, but have not made a decision yet. Ellen is a walker and has risen early to walk with friends for years. She learned about rowing by chance when they were visiting friends in Boston one October. When one of her walking friends suggested they take an indoor rowing class at the downtown health club, she initially resisted. When she found it was pleasant to do, and that it left her only mildly sore and feeling good, she decided to continue with the classes.

Ellen has continued to attend rowing classes three days each week when she is in town. When she and her husband traveled to London last fall, she found a hotel with rowing machines in its fitness center. She began to keep track of her walks and rows, as well as stretching and core exercises, in a personal log. She took another fitness class to learn more core exercises, and is considering trying a weight lifting class. She sometimes skips the stretching. She does not plan her workouts or keep track of distances she rows. Instead, she goes to the classes and follows the instruction there. When she traveled, she got some workouts from her class leader and did them on her own. She has told her husband she wants her own rowing machine for home for her ninetieth birthday.

Pete, age 63, is at the height of his career with a downtown corporation. He commutes by car and train from the suburbs. He divorced years ago without children and has never re-married. He usually works or reads the paper on the train, then does more work at home each evening. The closest he came to sports when he was younger was playing clarinet in the marching band in college. His physician told him about rowing after several years of discussing his progressively worsening weight, cholesterol, and blood pressure readings in his annual physicals. When talk alone did not lead to a change, his doctor referred him to a physical therapist (PT) with a rowing background. After meeting with the PT, Pete agreed to try a limited plan to do some indoor rowing and to return to discuss it with him. In a follow-up session, Pete started asking enough questions that the PT suggested that Pete video-tape his rowing one day and bring the tape to the next session with him.

After rowing for several months on the physical therapist's instruction, Pete ordered a rowing machine for home and starting using the athletic club facilities at his club near work. In spite of beginning slowly and having direction from the PT, he stopped and started for weeks. He was very sore initially. He thought a couple of times that he was hurting himself. He kept with it, but after three months was still considering quitting. After seeing his doctor for a follow-up physical and showing little improvement, the doc ordered him to take it more seriously. He began to keep a log and hired a personal trainer the PT recommended. A year later, he was alternating rows at home in the early morning with rowing at the club other days. His log showed he was rowing for at least forty-five minutes a day six to seven days a week. He goes back in for his annual physical next month and is looking forward to his doctor's reaction.

Cynthia, age 42, is an executive with an advertising company. She lives a ten minute walk from work in a high-rise condo. She is an avid tennis player. She belongs to a downtown tennis club and competes in tournaments when her schedule allows. She had heard when she turned forty that the forties are the decade when most people's fitness begins to decline more rapidly. She decided to find a way to resist that and took up weight lifting. The trainer who taught her how to use free weights safely suggested she add some aerobic work to her routine. She did some research and started using the rowing machine at the club. She soon found that most people working at the club could not help her with her rowing technique. After looking for books on rowing and going on-line, where she found some helpful information, she learned that a couple of the other club members using the rowing machines had rowed in college and were willing to give her some tips.

Cynthia started rowing twice a week to cross-train for her tennis. With what she learned from the Web and her rows, as well as suggestions from the other indoor rowers, she began to keep track of how far she could row in twenty, thirty, and forty-five minute segments or pieces. She added to her workout schedule so she could row four times each week. She decided to keep a log with a record of how she felt playing tennis as well as rowing. She also added stretching for both rowing and tennis. After a period of higher than normal work demands that kept her at the office into the evening, she decided to order a rowing machine for home so she would have more control over getting her row in even when the tennis club was closed.

5

A Dozen Pointers for Progress and Satisfaction

o o o o o o o o o o o o o o o o o o o o o o o o o o o o o

"He not busy being born is busy dying."

"It's Alright, Ma (I'm Only Bleeding)"
Bringing It All Back Home
—Bob Dylan

"I was so much older then; I'm younger than that now."

"My Back Pages"
Another Side of Bob Dylan
—Bob Dylan

"My bewildered brain toils in vain
Through the darkness on the pathways of life.
Each invisible prayer is like a cloud in the air.
Tomorrow keeps turning around.
We live and we die, we know not why,
But I'll be with you when the deal goes down.
We eat and we drink, we feel and we think.
Far down the street we stray."

"When the Deal Goes Down"
Modern Times
—Bob Dylan

5.1   Introduction: Technique, Coordination, and Power

The sections of this chapter offer a dozen suggestions to help you improve your technique and get more out of your rowing. These are tools you can apply on your own to improve how you use your body on the rowing machine. Try alternating what you focus on every ten or twenty strokes. Or simply re-focus on a particular technique point when you realize your mind has wandered.

There are additional benefits to focusing your attention on technique while you row. Your rowing will be more comfortable if done correctly. You will also increase your awareness of what your body is doing and what is happening to it. While the back and forth motion looks easy when done correctly, there are as many ways to get it wrong or to do it inefficiently as there are body parts in motion.

One key to making your rowing motion graceful is learning to work the stronger muscles harder while relaxing the smaller ones. Do not engage in unnecessary motion. Coordinate efficiently among muscle groups. Balance the effort of the drive and the relaxation of the recovery.

As you work on your technique, you will find your rowing becomes smoother, more effortless in appearance, and more powerful. You will row harder and get a better workout, while to an observer you appear not to be working as hard as when you first started and your technique was rougher.

5.2   The First Lesson: Relaxed Hands

The ability of the body to work continuously over time is phenomenal. But you must allow the muscles to relax as well as to contract. Suppose you row twenty minutes at twenty-five strokes per minute. You will take 500 strokes during that time. If the muscles you use remain tense, they will tire quickly. If you over-use the smaller muscles, they will limit the more powerful work of the larger muscles.

Most importantly in rowing, if you attempt to control the handle by gripping it firmly in your hands instead of holding it easily in a relaxed manner, you will tire the small muscles of the forearms long before the rest of your body gets a workout. Instead, let the arms, wrists, and hands relax as you row. Learn to "control" the handle effortlessly rather than with effort. While this may sound simple, it is natural for the smaller muscles to tighten automatically as they become fatigued and as we work the larger muscles harder. Conscious attention to how you use your hands will help you modify this automatic response over time.

Hold the handle as lightly as you can. Imagine someone coming along beside you and pulling the handle out of your hands as you row. They should to be able to do that because the handle is so loosely held in your fingers. There should be pressure of the fingers against the handle as you pull, but there should not be pressure around the handle from gripping it.

Let the oar handle rest in the last two knuckles of the fingers, like you hold the handle of a heavy suitcase walking through the airport. (Remember the old days when there were suitcases without wheels?) You do not grip a suitcase in your palm or curl your wrists to hold it up. Rather, you let it hang in the ends of the fingers with the thumb lightly touching the other side for balance. That is all you need to do to hold on to the handle to row.

Fig. 28
Overcome the normal desire to control the handle by gripping it. That approach results in unnecessary tension and arching of the wrist, as here. The effect of that is wasted energy and tight forearms that interfere with efficient use of the larger, stronger muscles of the body.

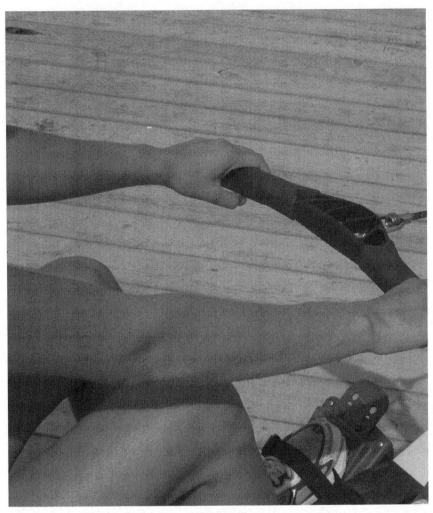

Fig. 29
By consciously holding the handle lightly in the last knuckles of the fingers, you have all the control you need, remain relaxed, and allow the wrists to be flat. With this technique, you are more effective with less effort.

Part of relaxing the hands is letting the wrists lie flat as you pull on the handle. Again, think of the example of holding a heavy suitcase or imagine doing a pull-up. You would not wrap your hand around the handle or pull-up bar so far that the wrist is bent. Instead, you let the back of the hand flow straight into the forearm with the wrist flat. The hand and arm are designed to hold with great strength, but not if you work against them by bending the wrist.

5.3　ROW WITH RELAXED SHOULDERS

Many beginning rowers tend to lift their shoulders up toward their ears. As they work hard and their muscles tire, the smaller muscles in the shoulders and around the neck tighten up. The lifting of the shoulders is an unconscious, unintended result of working the small muscles harder than you should or need to.

Fig. 30
Be aware when beginning that your shoulders may tend to tighten and "scrunch up" toward the ears as the smaller muscles in and around the shoulders tire.

Fig. 31
Consciously relax and allow the shoulders to stay level in a lower, unstrained position.

It will help you relax the arms and focus on the legs if you can relax the shoulders and let them stay down and level. Ultimately, you want to use the small muscles in the arms and shoulders less than the larger muscles in the legs. Learning to let them relax is an important step in development.

Think of the shoulders as being level with one another, in the position you would feel them when you are standing and you take a deep breath to the point that your chest expands, shoulders down and back. Feel the arms like chains simply connecting the shoulder and back to the handle as the legs begin to drive.

Try to find a place to row, at least some of the time, where there are mirrors that allow you to see yourself while you row. Seeing mistakes and unintended inefficient postures is a great aid to correcting them.

5.4 LEG SYMMETRY: USE BOTH LEGS FULLY AND EVENLY

We naturally expect and imagine when we are working hard that we are using our bodies in an efficient and balanced way. That is not necessarily so and is especially likely to be incorrect when learning a new activity.

Focus consciously from time to time on using both legs equally and you may discover that your knees are not straightening together or going down evenly. You may also notice when you focus on using both legs evenly that you have more power than you had been using before. A common mistake for beginners is to let the legs "follow" rather than lead. Do not use the legs to maintain pressure for what is primarily an upper body rowing motion. Instead, accelerate the legs with a forceful drive as the arms serve the secondary function of connecting the handle to the body.

One knee should not go down less than the other or after the other. You will also notice after some early long rows that the inner side of the thigh becomes tight or sore. What you are discovering is that the leg from the knee to the hip is surrounded by bundles of muscle that you had not been using. You will find that you can and will use all of those muscles. Give them time to strengthen.

Think "drive both legs fully and evenly."

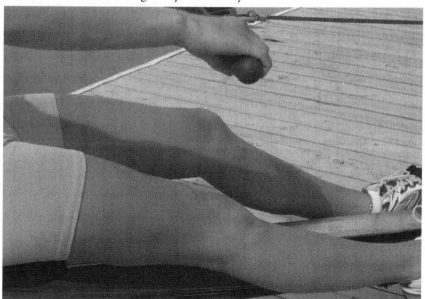

Fig. 32

While a difference as distinct as is shown here is unusual, it is not unusual for one leg to be stronger than the other or for a beginner to emphasize the use of one leg at the expense of the other. A similar effect may also result if your upper body is twisted or leaning, or if you use your arms unevenly. Pay attention to the even application of power.

5.5   POSTURE: MAKE ROOM FOR THE LUNGS

Believe it or not, having adequate breath or wind while rowing starts with your backside. Many of us first sit down on a seat to row with poor posture and place our backsides down on the front of the seat instead of sitting tall on the middle of the seat. In the wrong position, the lower back may be curved out rather than arched or straight, the abdominal muscles relaxed rather than firm, and the upper body slumped over. That position interferes with your ability to breathe freely.

Fig. 33
Good posture is essential for good breathing not only so that the chest can expand outward but also because the diaphragm must be able to move downward to fill the lowest portions of the lungs. It cannot do so if the gut is compressed because the upper body is hunched over. The problem of sitting on your backside, as here, rather than upright on your sit bones may be a sign you have tight hamstrings and need to work on your flexibility.

To improve your posture for rowing, you cannot simply sit up straighter. Rather, you must:

- shift your weight on the seat so that
  - your sit bones are pointing down into the seat and
  - you are sitting on the middle of the seat rather than on its front edge;

- use your abdominal muscles to hold your upper body in a relaxed but upright posture; and

- swing your body from the hips, stretching and using the hamstrings rather than simply curving and un-curving the middle and upper back.

Fig. 34

The starting point for better rowing posture is how you sit. Sit up comfortably straight, but not ram-rod straight. Then you can adjust your posture to keep your back either straight or rounded, as you prefer. You can adjust your reach by bending from the hips rather than curving the upper back and compressing the gut.

Your sit bones are the two pointy lower ends of the hip bones which, when you sit with good posture, form a solid foundation for the base of your spine as they press directly against the seat, with the hip bones vertical and in line with the spine. You will see on some rowing seats that they are not flat but have either holes or contours designed to provide you a place to position your sit bones comfortably. (There are also seat pads you can buy for rowing seats. Some seat pads have the same formation with holes for the sit bones.) Then you can sit up, not slump, swing at the hips, and breathe more freely.

Use your core muscles to hold your upper body erect but relaxed. To reach forward, swing at the hips, keeping your core strong rather than collapsing downward with the upper body. Rowing in front of a mirror can be a good way to help you see this issue and measure your improvement.

5.6   Combining the Body with the Arms: The Lats

As you learn to let the hands, arms, and shoulders relax while you drive the legs, you will develop the ability to work the larger muscles of the legs harder. In between and linking the arms and legs is the back.

There are many small muscles in the back—as well as throughout the core of the body—that help with your posture and support one another in the application of power. You can feel for them. You can work them and feel the soreness from doing core exercises.

While the back as a whole obviously is an important link in the chain of power (and many of us think of the central lower back as the key point of strength or weakness), become aware of the lats, or *latissimus dorsi*, the muscles on the outside of the shoulder blades behind and beneath the shoulders. The lats are among the most visible back muscles (you can see them flex if you look at yourself sideways in a mirror and cough) because they run from the shoulder blades down to the waist. They form a key link from the arms and shoulders to the whole of the back and then the legs. You can see them in illustrated anatomy books or by looking at a picture of the back on Michelangelo's *David*.

Let the lats do the work you may have initially tried to do with the shoulders and upper arms. Feel them while rowing as your legs work, your shoulders relax, and you "hang" on the handle as if getting ready to do a pull-up. Pay attention to them toning up over time from your rowing. At some point, see whether you are "hanging" on the handle correctly by seeing if you can lift your weight off the seat while driving the legs.

Paying attention to the lats can offer an added advantage of supporting your effort to relax the shoulders. As you are more aware of the links through the lats from arms to lower back, you will realize you do not need to rely on and therefore tense up the shoulder muscles. As you relax the hands and shoulders, you will find it easier to work the legs harder, to breathe deeper, and to get more benefit from each day's row.

5.7   COORDINATION OF BACK AND LEGS

Two of the most common errors in basic technique happen when a beginner uses the body either before or after the legs instead of in synchrony with them. As the legs finish the drive, the body should reach its full layback (only a few degrees, not laying back even close to 45 degrees), as illustrated in the picture of the finish. The arms and hands should pull the handle in to the body at the same time.

If you are dramatically early in applying power with the back, you will notice that your knees are not starting down but stay bent as the shoulders swing away from the handle at the catch. If, on the other hand, your back moves late, you will find the legs going down and straightening quickly and early so that you need to swing the back most of the way after the legs are straight. Both of these sequential approaches to combining back and legs are less efficient, less powerful ways to use the body. And shooting the slide (as it is called when you use the legs first) is an almost sure sign of weak hamstrings. Pay attention to how you couple the legs and back.

Fig. 35

As you row, open the back simultaneously with pressing down your legs. Shooting your slide, when exaggerated as shown here, looks like you lean over more as the legs start to push, making it look like your seat is shooting out under you on the slide. Maintain good posture as noted in the pictures showing the parts of the stroke, and apply the legs and back together throughout the drive.

The motion of swinging the body from its forward position at the catch to leaning back at the finish should occur at the same time the legs are driving down in one smooth motion. The back ideally should swing as if pivoting from the hips and should begin to do so at the same time that the legs begin to drive, at the instant of the catch. When the back swing couples smoothly with the leg drive, you get maximum power.

Many beginners will find that it is hard to coordinate the back and legs, or even to tell whether they are succeeding, because their legs are tight or their stroke is short. Rowing over time with stretching will help extend the length of the stroke, especially as the hamstrings lengthen out. Using mirrors, video, and a coach or observer will help you see how well you are combining the parts of your body.

5.8   Long and Easy for Fitness

Think back to the first principle: Our bodies adapt to daily healthy demands. If ten minutes is good for you as a stimulus to tell your body to upgrade your cardio-vascular system (to counterbalance twenty-three hours and fifty minutes of telling your body to rest), think what sixty minutes of rowing can do. During an extended period of exercise, your body can adjust more to the enhanced pace you give it while rowing.

Here are two rules of thumb: (1) Rowing twenty minutes a day will create a noticeable effect; and (2) Rowing forty-five minutes or more each day will yield significantly more benefit than shorter workouts.

Rule of reason: Spending more time is not overdoing it as long as the pace is right for you. Build up gradually to a longer row so you are prepared for it in terms of your strength, flexibility, and muscle nutrition. If you are rowing for a longer period than usual and begin to feel extremely tired, it may be that you are reaching the limit of the energy stored in your muscles. That storage grows over time with your exercise. Do not be discouraged by your fatigue. It is a good sign. Eat and rest well and try again the next day. Over time, you will find your stamina for longer rows will increase.

Another rule of reason: Since the actual exercise is a small part of the time it takes to exercise, make the most of it. For many people, the time spent getting to and from a gym, changing clothes, and showering is greater than the exercise time itself. Find a way to add those extra minutes to the exercise instead of the travel and preparation. For some, this is the best reason to have their own rowing machine at home.

Once you are doing longer pieces, you may find you pick up the pace after beginning slowly. On the other hand, you may find that you ease off as a long piece proceeds in terms of your pace or distance rowed per minute.

This can happen even while you may remain right on target in terms of heart rate or how deeply you are breathing. If your breath is deep, you are doing yourself some good.

Two ways to build up to doing a longer piece on the rowing machine are: (1) to do shorter pieces with breaks in between during the same workout, and (2) to do more than one workout per day instead of trying to do it all at once at first. Try either or both if you are stuck in a routine of doing a short row each day that does not seem to improve.

- In using multiple shorter pieces, vary the length of the shorter pieces before you put them together into a longer piece.

- If you take breaks for a drink of water, put a water bottle next to the rowing machine and take quick drinks without getting up to walk to a water fountain. Then gradually wean yourself from those.

- Try a much longer row than you are used to, but with less leg pressure and at a lower stroke rate at first. Once you know you can do a longer piece at an easy pace, it is easier to ratchet up the pace slightly to what is right for you. At that point, put it all together and try to maintain a pace that is a challenge for you for the whole duration of a longer row.

Within reason, the more time you spend at the body's design level (breathing more deeply), the sooner it will adjust to that level.

5.9 Use Short Intense Intervals to "Up the Ante"

You are on your own on the rowing machine. You do not have to coordinate with any other person. The pace varies with your motion; it is not pre-set on the machine. One technique you can use to improve your fitness (as well as for variety) is to adjust how hard you pull.

NB: Even though we call it pulling, the primary force is that of pushing, of driving the legs. Do not let the use of the term *pulling* mislead you into emphasizing your use of the arms. When you "pull harder," you should focus on pressing the legs down faster.

You can vary the power you apply casually based on how you feel from time to time during your row. There is a short discussion of that approach in section 3.5. Or you can row portions harder according to the clock or the monitor and then rest by rowing more easily in between those portions or intervals. As your fitness improves and you have built up your daily rowing time to a long, steady row, try some "interval" work occasionally. For example, if you are going to row for thirty minutes total, instead of doing it at a steady pace, you can warm up and then row harder for four intervals of five minutes with two minutes of easier or more restful rowing in between.

Incorporating occasional interval work into your routine will improve your strength and help you raise your level of fitness. You will find over time that by including some interval work you will increase your ability to maintain a strong pace on the longer, steady-state pieces, too. This is also a great way to test how relaxed your hands are and how coordinated your use of the parts of your body has become. Working harder will tend to bring out weaknesses, if you have any. It is natural to tense up the smaller muscles as we work the larger muscles harder. See whether you can remain relaxed and row smoothly even as you row harder.

To benefit from interval work, you do not have to undertake a competitive training program. You can proceed at your own pace and try different intervals as they suit you.

Here are three examples of ways to incorporate interval work:

- After a thorough warm-up (perhaps five to ten minutes rowing), row ten strokes harder than you usually would row. Then row easily as long as it takes to catch your breath. After you have recovered and are breathing easily again, take ten harder strokes again. Repeat the rest, once again until your breathing is not heavy. Continue taking ten harder strokes followed by an easy, un-timed recovery for the total time of your row (such as thirty minutes). If you want to have a measurement, keep count to see how many harder ten-stroke drives (or "pieces") you do during that total time rowing. Over a period of weeks or months, compare the length of your rest periods and the number of ten-stroke pieces you can do in the same total time. Gradually shortening rest periods and increasing the number of ten-stroke pieces you can do in that set time will confirm your improving fitness. Eventually, if you want to vary this exercise, you can lengthen the number of harder strokes to twenty or thirty at a time.

- After a warm-up, row *pyramids* as follows: ten strokes harder (or "on"), followed by ten easier strokes ("off"), twenty on/twenty off, thirty on/ thirty off, and so on. If you are ambitious, you can build up to forty or fifty or more harder strokes before you reduce the number by ten each time until you return to ten on/ten off. Once you get back to ten on/ten off, start going up the pyramid again and back down repeatedly until you complete the time you set to row (such as thirty minutes). (Alternatively, row steady state for part of your row but do pyramids for a break from the pace you usually follow.) A different, harder way to do a pyramid is to take only ten easier strokes between the harder pieces no matter the number of strokes that are harder or "on." So, you might row ten on/ten off, twenty on/ten off, and so on. Try that after you have become comfortable with the more modest, balanced pyramid.

- After a thorough warm-up of five to ten minutes rowing, do several short pieces in which you row harder, followed by rests (rest by rowing lightly rather than stopping) in between to catch your breath. The harder pieces can be for time (for one minute each or two minutes each or five minutes each, for example) or for distance (such as for 500 meters each or 1,000 meters each). Decide in advance how many pieces to do (and consider how much harder to pull, with the goal of becoming more winded but not overdoing it) and what length rest you will take between pieces. For example, you could do:

  - six 500 meter pieces rowing harder with two or three minutes' rest between them;

  - two minutes rowing harder followed by two minutes rest, repeated for a total of eight pieces;

  - five minutes on/three minutes off and repeat four times;

  - One minute on/one or two minutes off for twenty or thirty minutes.

The possibilities are almost endless. Experiment to see what you enjoy and what challenges you. The point of all these types of interval work is simple. You can row harder during each interval than you would if you tried to pull hard the whole time.

It may seem backwards to take breaks. In fact, you will find that your overall pace for thirty minutes is slower than you can maintain steady state because of how much you ease off while resting. But the benefit from the extra effort you put into the shorter, harder pieces will pay off by increasing your power and fitness. It is like lifting weights, where you work hard and then rest and repeat. However, with interval training you are using the resistance of the rowing machine instead of lifting weights. That allows you to do this effective, power-building exercise using all of the muscles together in the risk-free position of sitting down. And it allows you to do the harder work at your own pace without having to select weights or change them.

One question many beginners ask is whether to set the damper on the Concept2 rowing machine up (higher on the wheel, toward the number ten setting, rather than lower on the wheel, toward the number two or three setting) so that you feel more resistance. (Similarly, WaterRower users have to decide how much water to put in the wheel for resistance.) Read what the manufacturer says about that. Until you do, I suggest you keep the C2 damper at three (and not over-fill the WaterRower wheel) and use leg speed and power to vary your intensity.

5.10   Vary the Stroke Rating

Another way you can vary the pace during a thirty or forty-five minute row is to modify the stroke rate or rating, the number of strokes you take per minute ("strokes per minute" or "spm"). Obviously, when you do interval work as just described, you may find it causing a change in your stroke rating. That is fine. However, you can also change the number of strokes you take per minute for variety without consciously trying to modify how hard you pull.

Modifying your stroke rating also causes you to pay attention to what you are doing in a different way. To try it, change your stroke rating every minute or two minutes (or count strokes, if you like). For example:

- Row the first two minutes at twenty spm, then go up by two spm each two minutes until you are rowing at thirty spm for two minutes. At that point you will have rowed six two-minute pieces or twelve minutes total. Then bring your stroke rating back down by two spm each two minutes. You will find out something new about your power and your wind.

- Another way to vary the stroke rating is to row every other minute or segment (the first, the third, the fifth, etc.) at the same low stroke rating, such as eighteen to twenty spm. During the alternating segments (the second, the fourth, etc.) row at a higher stroke rating. Your higher rating can vary with how you feel, be the same higher rating each time, or follow a pattern you set.

- A third technique you can use is to vary the stroke rating and power together. Start with a comfortable amount of power at a stroke rating that feels easy to you. Note on the monitor what your pace is (your pace per 500 meters, for example, or the number of calories or watts your work reflects). Then gradually take the stroke rating *down* while trying to maintain the same pace on the monitor. You will find this forces you to push the legs harder during the drive, while at the same time giving you more rest on the recovery.

These techniques can be used with timed pieces, by distance, or by counting strokes. Try different ways of measuring. Use what appeals to you.

In theory, when you vary the stroke rating, you should use consistent pressure or leg power in all the different ratings unless you are trying to vary it as in the third example. You may notice significant differences in how it feels to drive the legs hard at different stroke ratings.

5.11   WORK ON RATIO

Good rowing has good ratio, the relationship between the duration of the recovery and the drive. Some say it ideally should be a ratio of two to one, that you should spend twice as much time on the recovery as you do on the drive. Working on intervals and your stroke rating, as in the two preceding sections, can affect ratio. You can also work on ratio separately.

A good ratio comes from combining a strong drive and a slow, controlled recovery. Even in the beginning when you are not pulling hard on the drive, make the recovery slow and relaxed to feel your ratio.

- The Drive: A quick drive, a strong drive, is good for the legs. While it is hard to do in the sense that a quicker drive takes more power and will tire you faster, it will feel more natural as you become acclimated to it. Many beginning rowers are not accustomed to using their legs and have to work consciously at learning to press the legs down affirmatively rather than using them reactively for the arms to pull against.

- The Recovery: If the recovery is slow and relaxed, you are more likely to begin the next drive composed and ready to work. Your leg muscles in particular will be better prepared for the drive if you continuously but gradually ease forward to the catch, the point when the legs start to push. If you rush forward into the next drive, you risk moving like a bumper car bouncing back and forth. This is ineffective and will quickly lead to fatigue without a great deal of benefit.

Pay attention to your ratio. If you have to reduce your stroke rating to achieve a good ratio of slow recovery to fast drive, go ahead and do it to get that two-to-one feel.

5.12   VARY THE SLIDE, THE DISTANCE YOU DRIVE THE LEGS

You can create an opportunity to learn more about coordinating your legs and back by varying the amount of slide you use. To work on the slide, select an interval like ten strokes or a minute. Change the use of the slide at the end of each interval. For example, start your row by beginning with no slide (using the arms and back only) and then add the use of the slide a bit at a time. Alternatively, at some point during your row, reduce your use of the slide every few strokes from full slide to half slide to quarter slide and then no slide; then, reverse the sequence by using quarter, half, and then full slide.

Full slide is the normal stroke. You reach out to the standard catch position described earlier.

At *half slide*, you move the knees up less than you would for full slide and the seat should go only about half the distance you usually travel down the slide toward the catch. Check it visually, feel it, then do it for a minute or whatever interval you have selected. Despite the reduced use of the legs, the use of the body should be nearly the same as at full slide.

Fig. 36

If the knees start up as the hands come out on the recovery, the hands have to be raised as if they are going over a barrel, instead of staying at the same height at all times as they should. In addition, the body does not get into position early, as it should, when the knees start up early. Although you can lift the handle to miss your knees while rowing on a machine, you will benefit from leaving the legs straight at first while the hands come out on the recovery.

At *one-quarter slide,* the hands come out and the body leans forward, but the knees barely lift up. The seat moves at most a few inches down the slide (you may find that your back can swing forward and the knees begin to bend with very little movement of the seat). At that point, the legs should press the seat back in the other direction. This is a good drill to use to teach yourself to let the handle lead the hands into the recovery and to start to swing the back toward the feet before beginning to raise the knees at all.

Fig. 37
Instead of lifting the hands over a barrel, keep the knees straight at the end of the drive until the handle is out to the knees and the body has become upright, then start to raise the knees and move the slide as the body is swinging forward.

At *no slide*, you are using only the arms, perhaps with a slight body movement. Unless you are extremely flexible, you will find you cannot move your body forward much at all with the legs straight. That is fine (and is one reason quarter slide feels much more comfortable than no slide). In fact, one version of no slide is to keep the body completely upright with no motion at all so that it is strictly an arms-only exercise.

Do some of each of these. Continue each one for a few strokes or minute at a relaxed pace. Repeat them. Take your time. It is a great way to focus on what your body is doing during the stroke and to become more attuned to how it moves.

After you have worked on and gotten used to varying the slide, think about your leg pressure as you increase the slide. Keep the recovery slow, taking a longer time on the recovery as you increase the slide. Yet press the legs down firmly on the drive as you use them for the increasingly long slide. You will find yourself rowing with more relaxation and a better ratio.

5.13   Finish Strong

At the finish of the drive, feel the strength in your core as the abdominal muscles hold the upper body high in the seat. A common error is to let the body collapse forward or sink down at the finish of the drive as the hands come in. The back and shoulders should move past vertical and provide a solid platform for the arms throughout the finish. The elbows should pull past the ribs. The hands and handle should come in and up to the body, not dropping down to the lap on the way in. Do not reduce arm pressure or the pulling motion as the drive ends, but keep it strong. Continue to push the balls of the feet against the stretcher until the handle touches the body and, without a pause, begins away.

One type of weak finish is to stop pulling before the arms get to the body. Pull the handle all the way in until it touches the body. Do not let the hands coast in to the body with no pressure.

Most people will find that they have automatically adopted a motion that is far less effective, more akin to simply bouncing back and forth, stopping at each end (catch and release or finish), with little attention to the transitions. You may find that paying attention to a strong and continuous finish helps you have a longer drive and feel more relaxed on the recovery.

6

Troubleshooting: Identify Obstacles to Overcome Them

o o o o o o o o o o o o o o o o o o o o o o o o o o o o o o

"I had left camp with eight dogs and a lightly loaded sled just after midnight. They were my 'problem' dogs. In all teams there are good dogs, some not-so-good dogs, and then there are 'problem' dogs . . . . They require extra effort, the problem dogs—more time to understand, time to know, time to learn how they think and act and work.

"So, once every four days or so I would harness the problem dogs and head up a mountain and try to learn from them and about them."

Winterdance: The Fine Madness of Running the Iditarod

—Gary Paulsen

6.1 INTRODUCTION TO TROUBLESHOOTING

Everyone at some time has a day (or longer) when for one reason or another they feel like quitting. This chapter looks at some examples of feelings, thoughts, and troubles that may intrude. You will want to work through them rather than letting them block your progress. Whether these obstacles are blisters, muscle aches, or moods, their affect on you can be important. Rather than trying to ignore them, recognize them as "problem dogs" (to use Mr. Paulsen's term). You may learn from them; you can get past them.

Some coaches would simply advise, "Tough it out!" in response to a complaint or problem. However, sometimes identifying and addressing a specific concern dissolves a problem and makes progress easier. Trying to "tough it out" may feel burdensome or feed the problem, especially when you are working on your own.

I assume you have no pressure on you to row, and are doing it for your personal well-being. You have to overcome the inertia that is part of human nature. Sometimes, personal goals or benefits seem to pale in comparison to hurdles. Even though an obstacle may not be large, it can dominate your attention. Working to overcome unnecessary hurdles is smart management of your time and energy.

These examples are by no means an exhaustive list. If you come up with a different issue, consider your situation and see whether you can solve it. Contact your local coach or fellow rowers for suggestions. Contact an independent trainer who can respond to your concern. Sometimes the act of looking for a solution is the key to overcoming the obstacle.

6.2   Dealing with Reasons to Quit

Sometimes when you do not feel like rowing, you will have a specific reason in mind. You may find yourself thinking of any number of excuses, such as one of the following:

- I just can't get started.

- I should prepare for that meeting instead.

- It is too hard to fit into my schedule.

- I started but can't stick with it after a few days.

- I did great for a month, but cannot keep doing this.

- I am not losing weight.

- My muscles are not getting toned up as much as I wanted.

- This is not as easy as I expected.

- This is too easy; it can't be doing me any good.

Identify the thought that is distracting you, your reason to skip or quit. If you have a legitimate problem with rowing on a given day and acknowledge it, that may make it easier to get back to it the next day. On the other hand, if you simply feel like skipping that day, decide to start slowly or to do a short row instead. Give yourself permission to stop early. You may often find once you start that it feels good and you want to keep going.

If you are tempted to give up on your daily exercise generally, remind yourself why rowing daily will work for you. Re-focus on your long-term health and energy.

Above all, remind yourself that you must be patient; significant change happens slowly. Continuing on whatever basis or frequency you can manage maintains not only the possibility but the inevitability of improvement over time; stopping takes away that opportunity.

Consider what you can do that would be different and yet still keep a period of exercise in your daily routine. If you alternate days of rowing with running or walking and that keeps you rowing, it has been helpful. If you are spurred on by rowing at the Y instead of at home, it may be worth the effort to go there to row. If you have tried the ideas on giving yourself variety and something to concentrate on and need something else, ask a coach or personal trainer for more ideas. Read a magazine or book on rowing. Even if you create continuity with distraction or less than perfect exercise, the fact that you keep going is positive. In fact, it is the only essential part of the whole program. You do not succeed by going for the hardest or best workout on a given day if that causes you to quit out of frustration.

Keep in mind that your body does not need your thoughts or emotions to buy in to the process for it to do some good. Your body simply needs you to stimulate it. Get on the rowing machine even though you do not want to, even if you must put the rowing machine in front of a television.

In short, acknowledge that you have an issue. Consider the issue. Keep going.

Don't hold on to the issue or belabor it. Solve it if you can. Find a way around it if you can. But do not stop for it.

As time passes, if there is a continuing issue, such as with scheduling, you will find a solution.

6.3 FEELING BOTHERED

Sometimes we experience an obstacle to continuing which is more a feeling than a rational reason to stop. It may be harder to pin down. It may be non-specific. It may even seem more troubling because you are not certain what is troubling you.

Part of the solution is to look for what is bothering you. When you do, you may find one of these "emotional" obstacles:

- I feel like I am becoming *addicted* to doing this every day.

- I feel *bored* after the first five to ten minutes.

- I am *afraid* I am not doing it correctly.

- I feel like I *will never get good* at this.

- I feel *lonely* doing this on a machine by myself.

- I feel *angry* when I exercise.

- This is *not as much fun* as basketball (tennis, etc.).

- I do *not feel like I am making any progress* rowing.

- I do not feel progress with my *health*.

- I am *unhappy* with a lack of progress with my weight.

The worst trap you can fall into is to assume your feeling bothered is not important. The second is to consider it too important, to decide you need to stop in order to resolve it. Pay attention to it and acknowledge it. Even note it in your log. If it troubles you, it is important. But do not stop for it. Do not let it control you. Keep going. Observe it and see how it varies over time. Eventually you will get past it.

You certainly can look for ways to address a feeling of dissatisfaction once you realize what it is. If, for example, you feel especially bored, you can try some distractions while rowing like listening to music or watching television. Put on a DVD and watch as you row. If that keeps you going when you feel like skipping your row, it has been helpful even if you do not breathe as deeply that day. Take note of what works and try different approaches. Over time, pay attention to what is most effective for you.

Keep in mind that a feeling of dissatisfaction or discomfort may just be inertia talking. It may be a normal reaction to your attempting to modify your habits. There is a great deal of literature on the power of the mind to affect what we do and how we feel. The point here is simply to be aware of the possibility that a negative feeling comes from an unconscious resistance to changing old habits.

In any case, stick with it. What bothers you will either crystallize into something you can address or it will melt away with time and progress.

6.4   PHYSICAL DISCOMFORT

There are numerous aches and pains that can intrude and cause you to consider stopping or taking time off. They do not have to be serious health issues to seem like major problems to you at the time. Sometimes the smallest discomfort can seem like a good reason to quit or take a day off.

Here is a list of some of the physical aches and pains that may tempt you to stop early or skip a day of rowing:

- I have blisters on my hands.

- I have blisters on one of my heels.

- I have sore shins.

- I have sore or tight forearms.

- I have sore or tight shoulders.

- My wrists hurt.

- My butt hurts from sitting so long.

- Part of the body is much more tired than the rest.

- My arms are tired, my legs never are.

- I am too winded.

- I never get winded enough.

- I get winded a little, but I don't like it.

- I sweat and I do not like it.

- I sweat too much and drip on the floor.

- I never break a sweat (and the list could go on).

These and other objections are best dealt with by finding a way to treat the problem while still getting in your daily row. You can clean, tape, and treat blisters. You can adjust how you use your arms and hands to minimize discomfort. (In fact, the discomfort may be a sign of poor technique and could actually help you improve. Review the twelve tips. Row in front of a mirror. See a coach.) You can buy a seat pad.

You can use discomfort with feeling winded or with other parts of your body to help you focus your attention on what is happening with your body. Note it in your log. And whatever the issue, you can continue to maintain progress by getting the next row in even if you have to alter the type of workout you have been doing.

6.5   Technique and Equipment Concerns

The information that is available on technique and equipment may not make complete sense to you as you begin. Give yourself time. Review it after you have rowed for awhile.

A great deal of information is available from manufacturers through their web sites about their equipment. As you row, over time you will develop an interest in the information they have on many topics that will help you row better as well as answer questions about your rowing machine.

As with physical and emotional concerns, use the concern as a springboard to learn more but keep your focus on your daily exercise. Once you have rowed for a period of time, you may want to learn more about parts of the equipment that you ignored when you started. Use the monitor in different ways to record your workout or to gain additional information about your rowing. You may want to experiment with adjusting the resistance of the wheel. You can try different foot heights by adjusting the stretcher. By considering changes in how you use the equipment and how you feel, you can learn more about yourself and enjoy some variety. Entertain yourself by learning more when you feel ready to do so.

You can also raise technique questions with friends, other local rowers, other rowers on-line, or with a coach (whether physically present or through email). The technique ideas in the last chapter are only a few of many you can learn about and use. But while you do that, keep going. Do not let a desire to know more interfere with your progress.

6.6   Dealing with Family, Friends, Co-Workers, and Other Non-Rowers

Parents, spouses, children, and other non-rowers will not understand at first when you say that you have to row, much less when you explain that you want to row every day. Saying that you cannot join them for lunch (or cannot attend some event, will miss the game, or will be running late) because you have to fit in your row that day will lead to blank stares from folks who otherwise could be supportive and understanding. "But you just did it yesterday," they will say.

If you were not already thought of as an athlete, you may find some well-meaning family members commenting negatively on how you are not one and should not try to become one at your age. It may just slip out before they realize what they are saying. In fact, they may even comment about how you do not seem to be that much more fit than when you started three months ago, as if to ask why you are bothering.

Be patient with them. You know you are in training to modify your daily routine more than to achieve a given state of fitness in a set period of time. You know that we are all naturally capable of being more fit than the norm in modern society. Those offering discouraging comments may have unintentionally but effectively "retired." You know it will take time, lots of time. But you may not want to try to explain that to them. They probably have not thought about how the body adapts automatically to what they do (and what they do not do) each day, much less put that fact to work for them.

Do not try to convince them. When they are ready, they may ask for more information. Then they can understand it easily. Do not try to turn them from the downhill slope they are on by yourself. You need your energy for yourself. And if you are feeling altruistic, just keep in mind that a good example is the best teacher. Think of your daily row as similar to what you are instructed to do with the oxygen bag in an airplane in the event of an emergency: Take care of yourself first before assisting others.

Stick with your program. This is not an addiction, a need that has to be filled out of compulsion. It is not unhealthy. It is what is best for your body, something you do consciously to stimulate your body to improve.

They do not understand how the routine works. You do. Use it to your benefit and be patient but persistent with your progress. It is your daily effort that counts for you. Don't let others' doubts or good intentions interfere with your rowing each day.

And when anyone in your family or circle of friends or co-workers begins to recognize or acknowledge what you are doing, accept their support. Nurture the support as it nurtures you.

Rowing is an activity for all ages. When your grandchildren finally realize what you are doing and ask if they can try, consider letting them use your rowing machine when they visit.

7

Rowing and Daily Life

o o o o o o o o o o o o o o o o o o o o o o o o o o o o o o o

"Be not afraid of growing slowly; be afraid only of standing still."

—Chinese Proverb

"I'm very pleased with each advancing year. It stems back to when I was forty. I was a bit upset about reaching that milestone, but an older friend consoled me. 'Don't complain about growing old - many, many people do not have that privilege.'"

—Chief Justice Earl Warren

"Nobody grows old merely by living a number of years. We grow old by deserting our ideals. Years may wrinkle the skin, but to give up enthusiasm wrinkles the soul."

—Samuel Ullman

"All afternoon he sat at the base of the statue, moving along with the old men whenever the shadows shifted, and watched what was going on in the plaza . . . . Nelio couldn't make out everything they said; . . . . But from the contemptuous comments of the old men, Nelio understood that the women . . . were arguing about everything that was of little consequence. The old men then began arguing with each other over this, about what could be considered of value in life."

Chronicler of the Winds
—Henning Mankell

"For me, though, the slice of meat loaf and the baked potato were plenty. What is it? Medical? The more you do, the less you need? I don't get it."

Smithy Ide, after beginning his journey in
The Memory of Running
—Ron McLarty

7.1   REST

Rest comes in many forms. You will find as you incorporate rowing into your daily routine that you become more attuned to how and when you rest. Many people find that they sleep more soundly at night if they have exercised during the day. Pay attention to how you feel and what forms of rest you take each day. Be open to modifying your patterns.

Moderate daily rowing itself provides a form of rest from the stress and physically monotonous routine of work and daily life. Exercise provides a mental break from the pressures of being at your desk all day. Even if you think about work while rowing, it can still serve as a form of decompression. In addition, the physiological changes that occur internally as your breath deepens and your pulse quickens during exercise stabilize a body that is under stress.

Rest can also occur when you exercise more easily or differently. You can protect some muscles while using others, protect some joints by using them less. As you pay attention to your body while you exercise, you will develop sensitivity to what your body is telling you it needs. As an example, I had developed soreness in my right forearm that seemed to get worse when I rowed. I knew it could not be caused by the rowing alone, as I had rowed for years without this problem. When I considered how I was holding the handle, I realized I had started to grip it, especially with my ring finger and little finger on that hand. I changed how I held the handle. I focused again on a relaxed approach and emphasized using the first and second fingers to hook around the handle. That seemingly minor change helped.

Sleep is a key time for the body to rebuild for the coming day of activity. If you do not get adequate sleep, your body will not make as much progress the next day as it could. As a result, you will not progress as much over time. In addition, a lack of sleep will reduce your energy level compared to the benefit you could gain with adequate rest. Moderate exercise will not cause you to have to sleep longer. But if you have been short-changing your sleep, you will now have an incentive to take better care of that part of your day.

Normally, the only time it will make sense to take a day off will be when you need to do so to get the rest you need before your next workout. This status, if it occurs, will depend on how hard you are working and what your goals are. It does not make sense to skip exercise to "rest" because you missed needed sleep. Lack of exercise does not make up for needed sleep. If you are bothered by a particular ache or pain, modify your program temporarily to baby that part of your body. If you are considering taking a day off, try to fit in a shorter or easier workout instead.

The above points on sleep and days off apply as well to routines in which you are working out more than once per day or using rowing as cross-training. The point is simple. As you push yourself harder, use good judgment about rest just as you would use common sense to get enough fluids, manage the length and intensity of your workouts, and eat well.

7.2 DRINK

Drink water to stay properly hydrated all day long.

One benefit of rowing and perspiring is that it gets your bodily fluids circulating in more ways than merely increasing the flow of blood. Add water; you will lose some as you row.

How much water should you drink and when? While my suggestion is that you should listen to your body, the common wisdom is that most people are used to drinking far too little water. As an experiment, keep track for a couple of days. Do not count coffee, soft drinks, sport drinks, or anything with sugar or chemicals or color in it. Simply add up how many glasses of plain water you drink each day. You may be surprised at how low your intake is (and at how refreshing plain water is).

A second question is when to drink water. The answer is all day long. As long as you are properly hydrated generally during the day, you will not be harmed by thirst during an hour-long workout indoors on a rowing machine. Thus, do not worry about needing to stop to drink during a moderate workout. If you are working out in hotter weather, out in the sun, or for a longer or more intense workout, consider having water available and taking the time to drink it in moderate quantities during your workout.

Use your judgment about sugared drinks and sport drinks that claim to restore lost components. There are drinks you can buy or mix that provide chemicals the body uses. Some even offer a balance of carbohydrates and protein to help maintain stamina during your workout or promote recovery afterwards. You do not need any of these specialty drinks simply to do moderate daily rowing. If you decide to expand your routine into training for competition, you will find many resources that provide information on nutritional resources.

Some advise never to drink alcohol in any form. Others laud it as civilized, as a food of choice for the athlete, or as healthy in moderation. You will want to engage in activity that supports your daily rowing routine and avoid anything that interferes with it. If drinking in the evening causes you to sleep in and you want to do your row first thing in the morning, be aware of that outcome. Decide what to do about it. Keep in mind that alcohol tends to rob the body of water, so you may find you need more water if you have a drink. You may also find if you drink too much alcohol (or caffeine) that a good row helps clear out your system and leaves you feeling better.

Pay attention and learn from your body as part of your rowing routine. Anything that undermines your accomplishment of adaptation based on daily stimulus is a negative. Part of the process of incorporating rowing into your daily routine is to be attentive to the rest of your routine so that it supports you.

Keep in mind that the body is approximately seventy percent water. It is full of systems that involve filtering and balancing chemicals, all of which depend on concentrations of those chemicals in water. Those concentrations can be affected by your having too much or too little water in your body. Rowing each day will help you pay attention to balancing your water intake based on how you feel.

7.3 FOOD

Although what you eat may not seem central to daily rowing, you will find that it becomes important to you. What you eat can affect how you feel. You need food to supply the nutrition your body needs. As you row more, you will pay more attention to getting good nutrition. You will tend to eat less of the foods or snacks that do not enhance how you feel.

Eat what makes you feel good over time. Pay attention to what gives you energy, not just at one moment but throughout the day. Use your experience paying attention to how you feel when you work out to guide what you eat. Instead of thinking about cutting out food to reduce intake, think about what you should add or replace in your body to help you recover and to prepare for your next row.

Pay attention to how you feel when you row depending on when you ate as well as what you ate. Notice that despite feeling hungry when you start to row you may feel less hungry afterwards and more satisfied with smaller portions.

Many people take vitamins and other over-the-counter supplements. Unless your diet includes those food pyramid-recommended quantities of fruits and vegetables, you may want or need to take a daily vitamin. On the other hand, as you row you may find yourself eating more fruits and vegetables because you then feel better and have more energy.

With rowing daily, you will increasingly want to take care of yourself, including watching what you eat, to support your rowing. Do not look to food intake or supplements to do your work for you. Instead, focus on the basic nutritional quality of everything you eat.

7.4   SELF-APPRAISAL

Periodically review what you have been doing and how you feel about it. How has your body responded over time? What conclusions can you draw from that to help you adjust your routine? Here are three suggestions for a self-appraisal.

First, assess what you feel is a normal level of effort for your body. Consider your comfort zone while exercising. If you enjoy the exercise and look forward to doing it the next day, rather than feeling put off by the effort you have to expend, you are probably within your comfort zone. If you are breathing deeply but not feeling uncomfortably out of breath while rowing, you are probably fine. The issue is balancing the desire to improve your fitness against trying too hard. What are the upper and lower limits of your comfort zone? Consider whether your comfort zone is different now than it was six months or two years ago.

The second task is to consider what you have learned about your limits as compared to your norm. I have suggested you not push yourself but rather exercise moderately. However, it is OK to push yourself occasionally when it feels good. If you feel you are never trying hard, explore different approaches using the ideas in chapter five. Or, if at some point you feel you have tried too hard, instead of skipping a day to rest, row the next day but purposely make it an easier row. Have your longer or shorter (or harder or easier) rows taught you something about your ability to do more than your average performance? Have you learned anything about getting value out of a relatively easy exercise?

A third task is to consider goals. Setting a goal can help guide you toward improvement by linking your action today to the longer term. Having a goal does not require you to be dissatisfied with where you are or to push your limits. A goal can be something modest you seek to achieve over a long period of time. A goal can be general, like enhancing your wind and energy. Or your goal can be specific, like wanting to row a certain distance in a set time or planning to exercise a certain number of days in a row.

As a few examples, you can set a goal based on:

- Scoring your daily rowing for a month, as discussed earlier, and improving that score several months later;

- Rowing a far longer time or distance on a one-time basis than you normally row;

- Attending an indoor rowing event, without regard to your score or result (You do not have to aim to win or place at an event to enjoy attending it.);

- Achieving a particular score or place at an indoor rowing event (These events are usually divided into categories of competitors based on age. Look it up before you go. Set a reasonable goal.); or

- Achieving a better time or distance for a particular piece a month or a year from now compared to how you do today.

The list of possible goals is long. Most important is that you set your own goal based on what is reasonable for you and what appeals to you.

In sum, periodically review your progress and your perspective on daily rowing. Your response to each of the three points (comfort zone, limits versus norm, and goals) can and will change over time. You may feel your level of effort is right for you at one time, only to feel months later that your exercise has become either stale (too easy or not changing) or too hard. You also may set a goal you would like to meet at a selected date, only to find that you reach it earlier or need more time to achieve it. Perhaps the greatest benefit of having a goal is gaining the incentive it gives you to show up each day.

On all of these points, you may find that you want to learn more about what others do. Talk with other folks you see rowing at the Y or health club where you row. Contact your local rowing club if there is one. Go on-line and check the many lists of scores and training tips. Introduce the rowing machine to your children and grandchildren and see what you learn from them.

7.5   Learning that Change Takes Time

The concept is simple: Just as Rome was built gradually, one stone at a time, the body can become dramatically fitter and healthier over time. The human body is constantly rebuilding itself. Rowing each day is simply a tool that applies automatic adaptation to your benefit.

Change over time is a challenging concept for most of us, and an even more challenging experience. The inherent problem is that the changes occur later and come gradually, while the effort must come today. It is a formidable challenge to make your rowing happen daily. I submit that once you are convinced that you will reap the benefits eventually, you will find it easier to act daily. Look for ways to make it easier. Develop support that reminds you of the long term objective rather than the immediate challenge.

Something as simple as keeping a record in your log can be a tool to see the change more clearly. Consider how you record what you do. Is it helping you? Modify it to include information you feel is important for you.

It can also help to know another rower, whether more experienced than you or someone who starts with you. He or she does not have to row with you physically for you to compare notes and learn from one another. One of the nice things about rowing is that you will become part of the growing community of rowers, indoors and out. You will be pleasantly surprised at the scope of this diverse community and the support it offers you.

Take the long view regarding how you treat your body. Think not only about what you expect from it on a given day, but also what you expect it to be able to achieve in the next month and year. Pay attention to your accomplishments, which at first means patting yourself on the back simply for the fact that you rowed that day. Later, your accomplishments come with making progress toward goals you have set.

Be persistent because you know that it takes time. You are not in this to make a change in a day, a week, or a month. You are establishing a routine of daily behavior with the goal of continuing it.

Think cellular: Rowing each day affects your body on the cellular level. Apart from the changes you can see or feel on a gross physical level, you can take encouragement from knowing that many positive changes are occurring that you cannot see.

Do not overdo it in an attempt to get a quick benefit. Exercise within your comfort zone. Look for deeper breathing but not gasping. When you breathe a little more deeply today and continue every day, your breathing will be even deeper six months from now.

Give yourself time to succeed. If you start out intending to row every day, but only do it twice each week, accept that start. If you stop at that point, you have failed. But if you continue and, over time, start to get your row in three times a week, you are succeeding. You can increase to four days a week later.

Just as you cannot go out and achieve a peak performance by sheer will when your body is not prepared to perform at that level, the opposite is equally true. Your body can develop the ability to perform far beyond your present level when you incrementally stimulate it day by day over a period of time. Work toward a consistent, moderate program and see where it takes you. It is not only OK to take time to get there; the only way to get there is to take the time.

Be persistent in your efforts and patient with the process.

7.6 ROWING YEAR ROUND: THE FIVE BEGINNERS CONTINUE

Once you settle in to the routine of daily rowing, you will find as the seasons pass that there are a number of steps you can take to maintain your program and increase your enjoyment of it. Here are some ideas for longer-term maintenance:

- Look for new types of goals to set for each season. For example, select a goal for a long row one season and a goal for a shorter, more intense row in another season.

- Take lessons or attend group sessions. Your local health club may offer group rowing sessions. You can find online groups to participate with.

- Record your progress in different ways. Look back at your progress rowing daily. Try using different methods of scoring your "attendance." Look for on-line record keeping options at rowing machine manufacturer Web sites.

- Compare your progress to that of others. You can do this in person with other rowers in your community. And you can compare notes with other rowers through virtual rowing clubs and masters rower listservs.

- Find other rowers. Just as rowers use groups and lists to ask for help with equipment and rowing questions, you can use them to look for rowers with a similar background or concern.

- Join a rowing club (indoors or out). Traditional rowing clubs are focused on rowing outdoors on a lake or river. You will increasingly find opportunities to join an indoor rowing club. Check on-line and ask around.

- Row outdoors on your rowing machine. Because the newer rowing machines are so easy to move, you can move yours to a deck, balcony, or driveway during good weather to row and then store it inside.

- Take up outdoor rowing with sweep rowers in the warm season. Most rowing clubs offer lessons. A benefit of learning to row sweep (see the Appendix for a glossary and information about rowing) is that you row with other people.

- Take up sculling in the summer by taking lessons at your local rowing club. (Sculling is defined in the Appendix.) A benefit of sculling is that you can row on your own.

- Attend a rowing camp. There is information about finding rowing camps in the Appendix. While some rowing camps are geared for experienced rowers, others pride themselves on teaching rowing to novices. With initial coaching in the relaxed atmosphere of a camp, you may be able to return home, obtain your club's certification for boat use, and begin rowing outdoors right away.

- Incorporate seasonal cross-training, such as cross-country skiing in the winter and cycling in the summer. Include what appeals to you and works for you.

These types of actions can enhance your rowing experience and the progress you make with it. That makes it easier to stick with your routine and, thus, helps you continue to improve.

Here are some additional notes about the five hypothetical beginning rowers introduced in chapter four:

During her second year of indoor rowing, Karen asked about outdoor rowing classes at the local rowing club. She took a series of evening classes learning to row in an eight-oared shell with other adults. The lessons ended with a graduation party in which each rower was invited to join a group of adults who met regularly to row together. She tried that a few times, but they always rowed very early in the morning or during the evening. She preferred to row during the day. She kept up her indoor rowing. The next winter, she went with some rowing friends to see an indoor rowing competition. Karen volunteered to help at the event and watched the racers compete in the indoor rowing machines, but did not compete herself. She was pleased at how many people she saw who were her age and older. That Spring, she signed up for sculling lessons at the local rowing club so she could learn how to row by herself. Several weeks later, she was certified to take out the club's Peinerts, Alden Stars and other recreational boats whenever she wanted. Now, she keeps track in her log of when she rows indoors and when she rows on the lake. She has also started a list of the birds, jumping fish, deer and other wildlife she sees while rowing outdoors. Every Monday, weather permitting, she meets two other friends to row together in singles. Karen has offered to watch the grand-kids evenings for a few weeks so her daughter can take rowing lessons, too.

Joe developed a very sore lower back after raking the yard about a year after starting to row. At first, he blamed the rowing and stopped doing it. But he missed the exercise and wanted to start again, so he contacted the team coach. With his advice, Joe started doing core exercises more seriously. He had felt he was in good shape. He had always done certain calisthenics. He did not think he needed more. But when he spent extra time on more abdomen and back work and added some stretches for his legs and hips, he found the ache in his back went away. During the second winter he rowed, Joe decided to enter one of the indoor rowing events. He purposely did not set a goal for himself, but for several weeks before the event, he found himself pushing harder when he rowed. He kept track of his times for different distances. Although he liked long steady rows best, he added some short hard interval work to get ready for the race. He was pleased to set a personal record during the event. He also learned from the university coach that he could row out of the boathouse during the summer if he wanted to row outdoors.

As soon as she got her own rowing machine, Ellen started rowing every day. After a week, she felt a pain in one of her knees and became very worried. Her rowing instructor advised her to skip class for a couple of weeks. She called one of her rowing friends and joined an on-line group of older rowers who exchanged advice about rowing-related topics. With their guidance, she reduced the length of her rows and added some strengthening and stretching exercises for her legs. When she did a longer row a week later, her knee still hurt, although not as much as before. After two more weeks, she found the pain was gone. When she turned ninety-two, she convinced her husband to try the rowing machine for the first time. He did not agree to join her rowing class, but did take a couple of lessons from Ellen. Now, he sometimes uses her machine while watching the news.

Pete impressed his doctor during his next physical. Both blood pressure and cholesterol were reduced and his resting pulse had changed for the better. Pete's weight was still higher than ideal, but by less than ten pounds, far better than before. Pete started to apply his business planning skills to his rowing and mapped out a set of targets for the next year. He also learned about some training techniques and wrote down a schedule for what he would work on each week. He found he liked having a three-week rotation that started with long, easy rows and gradually worked down to shorter, more-intense rows by the third week. He continued to see the personal trainer once a month. He asked for technique drills and used those every other day for the first ten minutes on the rowing machine. He found he had no interest in competing in any event or learning to row outdoors. But he did start to review rowing results for different age groups on-line. He is thinking of trying to row a marathon distance while watching the Superbowl next winter.

Cynthia worked on her rowing technique to tailor it to help her tennis. Some days, she would use the machine mostly for arm exercises. Other days, she would focus on using her legs. At least once a week, she would try to push so she got and stayed winded for a long row to help her stamina. After a few months of rowing, she found her right elbow became very sore, much like the tennis elbow she sometimes suffered from in the past. It bothered her when she played tennis, so she cut out the rowing for a while. Checking on the manufacturer's web site, she made contact with a rowing coach who would work with her personally. She got and followed advice on how to strengthen and heal the elbow. After a month, she was back on the rowing machine and felt great. Working with the rowing coach got Cynthia thinking about trying to compete in rowing. She signed up to keep working with the coach and set a goal of doing an indoor event the following winter. She also decided to go to a summer rowing camp. Although she did not plan to start rowing outdoors regularly, she thought it would be good for her technique.

7.7   CONCLUSION: ROW TODAY

The two biggest obstacles to success are not getting started and not continuing. There are often reasons we give ourselves, reasons that seem good at the time, for not starting something, for quitting it, or for simply letting it fall away from our routines. Sometimes those reasons are good ones. But too often we fail to begin, decide to quit, or let a good thing go simply because the activity is something we have not done before and the rewards are distant.

Success can be simple. When you realize that the mere fact of participating each day is the most important measure of success, you can more easily find ways to fit your daily row into your schedule. And that, in turn, will confer long-term benefits.

To recap, here are some reminders and suggestions for making it work for you:

- Send your body a signal, gently but firmly, by rowing today. And then make the decision to do it again tomorrow.

- When you miss a day, simply return to it the next day. Record your missed exercise in your log each time, as well as the days when you do exercise.

- Pay attention to your breathing as you row. Are you breathing more deeply than you normally do during the day? Are you challenged but comfortable? When you are breathing more deeply, what does the rowing machine monitor tell you about how much work you are accomplishing?

- When you feel a need for variety, vary your rowing or use another form of exercise to cross-train. Count that exercise, too, recording it in your log.

- Over time, evaluate for yourself which exercises do you the most good.

- Include a short period of stretching and core exercises at the end of your exercise each day. Both will help your overall fitness and comfort. Stretching when your muscles are still warm at the end of exercise helps increase your flexibility.

- As the months go by, consider how you are doing in terms of a score for your daily rowing. You can use suggestions offered in this book or apply your own method of scoring.

- As the months pass, pay attention to how you feel. You will find you have more wind, the ability to keep from gasping for breath while performing daily activities. You will experience other benefits, too, such as muscle growth and strength gain, weight loss, better sleep, and better attention to your diet.

- If you decide you want to become more competitive, you can learn more by checking scores for various distances, by attending indoor rowing events, by talking with other rowers, and by engaging the help of a coach or personal trainer.

- You will have aches, pains, objections, and complaints. Instead of trying to ignore them, look for them. Acknowledge them as part of your routine. Keep going in spite of them. Compare over time what they are and how they become resolved.

Get whatever help you need. If you have concerns about your health or your ability to use any specific part of your body safely, see your doctor. Look for support; welcome it and use it.

Start at your own pace today . . . and keep rowing, every day!

Fig. 38
Sunset over the bay. Take a deep breath!

APPENDICES

"The General Rule of Gear: . . . There is one black-letter rule that you should know and act upon as you get older: . . . [You] are out there . . . [so you] deserve the best equipment that money can buy. . . . it's not that easy just to get out of bed in the morning and train, six days a week. So, if you're doing it, you deserve decent gear."

> *Younger Next Year, A Guide to Living Like 50 Until You're 80 and Beyond*
>
> —Chris Crowley & Henry S. Lodge, M.D.

"Of the times in my life I must count as wasted, squandered, spent aimlessly, I knew our river days would never be among them because, ephemeral as they too were, the river had done what it could to make them memorable enough to carry forward to the end. I floated along contentedly. Brevity does not make life meaningless, but forgetting does. Of the gifts of the rivers, none was greater than their making our time upon them indelible . . . ."

> *River-Horse, The Logbook of a Boat Across America*
>
> —William Least Heat-Moon

[Having accepted a tow from a motor boat, as he pulled closer with the tow rope to accept an offered beer, the author capsized in the tow boat's wake:] "Jack de Crow lay completely upside down in the water, her yellow hull wallowing half submerged like a strange luminous turtle. On the broad bosom of the river floated various bits of debris – my parrot cushion, my pith helmet, my small rucksack that contained all my writing equipment, wallet and so forth. The oars were making a spirited bid for freedom some way down the river . . . ."

> *The Unlikely Voyage of Jack de Crow, A Mirror Odyssey from North Wales to the Black Sea*
>
> —A.J. Mackinnon

Appendix One

ROWING AND OTHER SELF-POWERED BOATING

Rowers sometimes refer to their sport as the one you do sitting down and going backwards. Here is a little more explanation about the sport (and recreational activity) of rowing.

You do in fact exercise sitting down when you row. You sit on a sliding seat (a seat with wheels) and use your whole body as you push with your legs, pull with your arms, and couple the work of the whole body by coordinating the legs and the back. As in an old-fashioned row boat, the rower sits facing the stern or back of the boat. So far, this all applies to indoor rowing, too, except that to row indoors you sit on the seat of a machine instead of in a boat. Here are some basic ways to explain rowing and differentiate it from other activities.

Rowing is just one of many activities you can engage in on the water in a boat you power yourself:

- Canoe: You sit or kneel facing the bow; use one paddle with a blade at one end; power the canoe with arms and upper body; steer with the paddle; usually involves one or two people in the canoe paddling together, possibly with a passenger in the middle.

- Kayak: You sit facing the bow; use one paddle with a blade at each end; power the kayak primarily with arms and upper body; hold the body's position in the kayak with legs and feet; steer with the paddle (or some have a tiller); usually one or two people.

- Dragon boat: The rowers face the bow; use one paddle per person as you would in a canoe; one person steers; usually, many paddlers work together.

- Rowboat: You sit facing the stern; use two oars; power with arms and upper body; steer with the oars; usually one person rows, perhaps with one or more passengers.

- Rowing boat or shell: You sit facing the stern; use one oar (for sweep rowing) or two oars or sculls (for sculling); sit on a sliding seat and power the boat with legs, back, upper body, and arms; steer with the oars or some-times, in certain boats containing more than one rower, a person called a coxswain steers with a tiller; usually one, two, four, or eight rowers.

In sum, rowing is distinguishable from kayaking, canoeing, rowing a rowboat, and other similar activities that may involve water and paddles or oars because you use the whole body when you row. Indoor rowing is very much like outdoor rowing in that you use the same full-body motion to do it.

Rowing can be either sweep rowing or sculling. Sweep rowing and sculling differ from one another in two basic ways. One difference is in the oars used. In sculling, each rower has two oars (or "sculls"), each about nine feet long.

Fig. 39
A sculler can pace herself and enjoy the beauty of the river on her own.

In sweep rowing, each rower has one oar that is about twelve feet long.

Fig. 40
Here is a four-with-coxswain landing at the dock. The coxswain sits in the bow or front of this four and gives her commands from there.

Fig. 41
This picture of four women wet-launching their boat (i.e., wading into the water instead
of using a dock) provides another perspective on the size of the oars and the boat.

A second difference between sweep rowing and sculling is in the configurations of people in the boat, which can include the rowers/scullers and the coxswain (who faces forward and steers the boat). Scullers usually row in one of three types of boat or shell:

- A single or single scull or 1x (one person);

- A double or double scull or 2x (two rowers or scullers); and

- A quad or quadruple scull or 4x (four rowers or scullers).

Normally, scullers do not use coxswains or even have a seat in the boat for someone to sit in and steer. An occasional exception is that a quad may sometimes include a coxswain. Some clubs rig an eight for sculling and train scullers in a coxed octuplet.

Fig. 42
A quad has four rowers (known as scullers) in the boat, with two oars or sculls per person.
Here are scullers on the river with their coach in a double, a single, and a quad.

Sweep boats normally come in one of three configurations of rowers:

- A pair with coxswain (2+) or pair without coxswain (2-), also called a straight pair (two rowers);

- A four with coxswain (4+) or four without coxswain (4-), also called a straight four (four rowers); and

- An eight or eight-oared shell, always with a coxswain (eight rowers).

There are many additional ways to distinguish among different forms of rowing or approaches to rowing, including:

- The type of boat used: Recreational boats tend to be shorter, wider, and heavier, as well as easier to balance. Racing shells are built to minimize the weight of the shell and with a hull shape designed for speed.

- The material the boat is built from: Older boats were made of wood; most new shells are made of plastics and modern composite compounds.

- Levels of competition: Rowing is done around the world by people of all ages from approximately ten years old through adulthood into the eighties and nineties. Beginners of any age can compete in novice categories. Some competitions are limited to specific schools or teams. These range from races between two high schools to Olympic events among national teams. Many other rowing competitions are open to anyone who wishes to enter. These include many rowing regattas in the summer and fall. Such regattas usually include events or score results by age, with different events and/or handicaps for rowers of different ages.

- Seasons: In the winter, most rowing competition is on indoor rowing machines. The spring is the primary outdoor racing season for youth and college rowing teams. In the summer, rowing clubs and individual rowers compete, usually in short races of 1,000 or 2,000 meters. This is also the time when national rowing teams compete around the world. In the fall, many clubs hold head races, often named the "Head of the . . ." (insert the name of the river where the competition takes place). Head races are usually three miles long or a similar distance that works at the particular venue. Some clubs that sponsor head races also run longer distance races, up to marathon length. Competitors in head races often include everyone from novices and youth teams to college and national team boats, as well as older rowers, usually referred to as masters rowers. Masters categories usually begin at about age twenty-three to twenty-seven and include all ages above that. There is no age limit for rowing.

Of course, there are other forms of rowing and human-powered boating around the world. Some examples include punting in England, boating on the Amazon, and the work of gondoliers in Venice, Italy. You can see gondoliers training on the Grand Canal in Venice in wider boats designed for two, four, or more rowers.

Like outdoor rowers, indoor rowers also row sitting down on a sliding seat with the feet fixed and the hands pulling on a handle. In the case of the indoor rower, the handle is attached by a chain or belt to an inertial wheel instead of being attached to the water via an oar. Indoor rowers may not feel like they are facing backwards because they are not moving anywhere and they are facing the wheel and monitor on their machines. (With any luck, they are also facing a window, a mirror, or some other form of education or entertainment.) In short, indoor rowers differ from scullers and sweep rowers primarily because (a) they are on a stable machine instead of in a tippy boat, and (b) they are indoors instead of being outdoors on a lake or river. Indoor rowers are like any rower in the way they use the body and like scullers in that they can row alone.

For the sake of completeness, I should mention that there is another form of indoor rowing, rowing in tanks. Ever since someone thought to put a pool of water under an oar next to a sliding seat with rigging to hold the oar, there has been indoor rowing with oars. Rowing in tanks has become far more sophisticated than it used to be, with many newer tanks having motors that move the water past the rower. The moving water helps the rower get the feel of handling an oar in the water from a moving boat. Tanks are still relatively uncommon and are used almost exclusively for training members of competitive rowing teams. As a result, they are not likely to be available for the non-rower to use as an alternative to rowing on an indoor rowing machine.

Appendix Two

GLOSSARY OF SELECTED TERMS

Following are some selected rowing terms to get you started. Many distinctive terms are used in the sport of rowing. However, for your indoor rowing it is not critical for you to know port from starboard or the terms used by a coxswain (the person who steers the boat) or that are part of competitive rowing.

Some General Terms

Ergometer (or erg): Literally, a machine that measures work. A term used for rowing machines because they can be used to measure work. ("I rowed twenty minutes on my erg today.") For example, on the Concept2 rowing machine, you can use the monitor to measure the work you do in meters, watts, or calories.

Muscle mass: The amount of muscle you have or are using. If you use all of your muscles at once, you are using your full muscle mass. If you exercise, the mass of your muscles tends to increase.

Rowing machine: A machine you can sit on and use to approximate the rowing motion.

Stroke: One complete cycle of the rowing motion. ("I rowed twenty-four strokes per minute during my workout.")

Stroke rate or rating (or simply rate or rating): The number of strokes rowed per minute. ("I warmed up at twenty strokes per minute [spm] and then did pieces at different ratings, from twenty-four spm to thirty-four spm.")

Wind: Amount of breath you have to perform a task; may also indicate ability to keep breathing comfortably while working harder than usual.

Parts of the Stroke (See pictures at Figure 11 in section 3.3)

Drive: The part of the stroke during which the legs are pushing or driving down and you are pulling the handle toward the body.

Recovery: The other part of the stroke, when you are moving your hands and the handle away from the body and the seat toward your feet to recover and prepare for the next drive.

Catch: The transition from the recovery to the drive; the point when your legs, having compressed as if you are squatting from a standing position, begin to straighten or drive, causing the handle to catch the resistance of the flywheel.

Finish or Release: The transition from the drive to the recovery; the point when your hands and the handle have pulled firmly into the body and begin to move away and the arms begin to reach away from the body while the legs remain straight at the knee.

Ratio: The amount of time spent on the recovery compared to the amount of time spent on the drive. Some say the ideal ratio is two to one (twice as much time spent on the recovery as on the drive).

Parts of the Rowing Machine

Handle: Wood or plastic piece (attached to the chain or other material which connects it to the flywheel), which you hold and pull while rowing.

Flywheel or Wheel: The mechanism which you cause to move against resistance (air or water) by pulling on the handle, and which may be adjustable, contained within a round cage or structure.

Foot stretcher or Stretcher: The part of the rowing machine where you strap your feet to the machine.

Monitor: The small box with a read-out in front of you as you row, and which may record information for your log such as distance, pace, stroke rating, and time rowed.

Seat: The small padded platform on wheels on which you sit, and which moves back and forth while you row.

Slide or Track: The part of the rowing machine on which the seat rolls or slides back and forth during the drive and the recovery.

General Terms Concerning Groups of Rowers

Crew: A rowing team (the term "crew team" is redundant, though often heard); the sport of rowing ("She went out for crew in college and rowed on the lightweight women's crew.").

Juniors: Youth rowers and crews, generally age eighteen or younger; may include members of a scholastic crew (all from same school) or from many schools rowing together as a junior crew.

Masters: Generally, any rower over the age of twenty-seven (although some now use a younger age, such as 23). The term is based on age and does not imply (or require) expertise. Use of the term can vary from club to club and event to event. Masters' races may provide for handicapped scoring based on age or may include different events by age (or both).

Novice: Usually anyone of any age in his or her first year of rowing.

Open: An open event is open to any rower of any age, size, or background (although still usually divided by gender). As a result, the open event is usually the top level of competition, often involving rowers in college or in their twenties.

Some Other Basic Rowing Terms

Blade: The portion of the oar at the opposite end from the handle that goes in and out of the water and is used to apply pressure against the water to move the boat.

Coxswain: Pronounced "cox'n" or shortened to "cox," the person who steers a racing shell, usually a four or an eight. Preferably small and light. Also, has other critical responsibilities, starting with the safety of the boat and crew (since she or he is the only one facing in the direction the boat is moving). May also coach the crew or otherwise remind the rowers about matters of technique and teamwork.

Double: A sculling boat with two rowers or scullers.

Eight: A sweep boat with eight rowers and a coxswain. Usually approximately sixty feet long and weighs around two hundred pounds.

Four: A sweep boat or shell with four rowers, with or without a coxswain.

Handle: The portion of an oar or rowing machine where the rower places his or her hands.

Head race: Races traditionally held in the fall, usually longer (standard is three miles) than other racing (which is usually two thousand meters or shorter), and usually involving racing against the clock after starting one at a time in single file.

Oar: The tool, comparable to a paddle, that a rower or sculler uses to move the boat through the water.

Pair: A sweep boat with two rowers, with or without a coxswain.

Quad: A sculling boat or shell for four rowers or scullers.

Rower: Someone who rows or sculls.

Scull: The oar(s) used by a sculler. To row.

Sculler: Someone who sculls, who rows with two oars/sculls each and can row/scull in a single, double or quad.

Sculling: Rowing with two oars (or sculls, approximately nine feet long each) per rower in a single, double or quad.

Shell: A boat used in rowing, called a shell because of the lightweight construction; made of a very thin "shell" of wood or composite material over a minimal frame.

Single: A shell made for the use of one sculler.

Sprint race: Traditional racing among high schools, colleges, and international teams (and masters), normally two thousand meters long or shorter, with six or fewer teams lined up next to one another to start, starting together on the command of a starter, and racing in lanes down a straight, buoyed course to the finish line.

Sweep rowing: Rowing with one oar (approximately twelve feet long) per rower in a pair, four, or eight.

Numerous other resources provide information concerning terminology about rowing. For example, the United States Rowing organization has information about terms and about the sport of rowing that you can access at www.usrowing.org

Appendix Three

THE RECENT DEVELOPMENT OF INDOOR ROWING

With the recent development of the high quality, inexpensive indoor rowing machine, the experience of rowing is now available to almost everyone. Yet, while it is easy to learn and readily accessible, rowing still seems foreign to most people.

There are a number of historical reasons why many people do not think of rowing as their sport or recreation of choice. One factor is that rowing outdoors takes place in out-of-the-way places, on rivers and lakes. Too often, we consider rivers obstacles (or places to sit and fish) rather than places to exercise. Rivers have historically been hidden behind industrial plants in many cities. Many communities are now working to reclaim access to rivers for recreational use.

Another reason rowing has a reputation as not being an activity for everyone is that the sport of competitive rowing has had the aura of being an upper-class, exclusive activity. In the United States, at least, rowing is viewed as historically British, and what is more upper class and exclusive than things British? In fact, until thirty to forty years ago, rowing was primarily an activity of New England prep school boys and Ivy League college men, with relatively few other centers of rowing (*e.g.,* at the universities of California, Washington, and Wisconsin) being viewed as exceptions. Competitive women's rowing was virtually unheard of and sometimes actively discouraged.

Unfortunately, in the old days, gaining familiarity with the sport did not immediately lead to a better understanding of its accessibility to all. For one thing, someone learning about rowing would discover that it was quite expensive to purchase eights and fours, the forty- to sixty-foot long rowing shells used for most competitive rowing. Gathering enough rowers to fill an eight-oared shell was also a challenge. In short, there were serious logistical obstacles to starting a rowing team or club.

Familiarity with the sport of rowing also tended to undermine the allure of the sport as an activity for everyone for another basic reason—it was tough! In competitive rowing, the standard race demands an all-out effort for approximately six to eight minutes, a challenging mix of aerobic and anaerobic work that requires months of long, intense training. While the highly accomplished rower makes it look effortless, racing in the sport of rowing is a grueling, muscle-burning, lung-busting activity.

Other challenges faced the beginning rower in the past, as well. As an outdoor activity, it depended on the weather and water conditions. While a rower in serious training would not hesitate to row in snow or rain, a beginner understandably could be discouraged by either and, with no good indoor rowing alternative, would tend to give up and leave the sport. Another obstacle to learning outdoor rowing is the technique challenge of learning to deal with balance and timing. Without good coaching to explain how to maintain balance and handle the nine- to twelve-foot long oars, novices can be discouraged by the seeming impossibility of staying upright and balanced in a narrow rowing shell.

One simple but fundamental development changed all of this. When low-cost, dependable indoor rowing machines were developed in the 1970s, they made the sport accessible to all for the first time.

The growth in the use of indoor rowing machines or ergs (short for "ergometer"–a machine designed to measure work) did not initially affect the non-rower as much as it enlarged the training opportunities for competitive rowers. Among competitors, there was an explosive increase in the use of rowing machines by rowing teams and clubs. The new ergs made it possible for a coach to train and test a whole team of rowers efficiently and repeatedly. The team could afford many machines. They were engineered for reliability so the coach could compare scores. This new capability enhanced college and national team coaches' ability to train their rowers based on the developing understanding that training year round in a well-designed program could dramatically enhance performance in this endurance-based competitive activity.

While the first phase of the rowing machine revolution may have flowered among competitive teams, over time health clubs have bought more of the machines. Some clubs are now offering fitness classes using rowing machines. Many individuals purchase their own machines for personal use at home. With this extension to the general public, the indoor rowing revolution is now well under way.

The use of indoor rowing continues to grow. Some of the reasons relate back to the historical problems noted above and how they have been solved:

- Indoor rowing can be done anywhere. You do not need a river, a lake, a calm day, or a particular type of fitness center.

- It can be done any time. There is no need to row at 5:00 AM to avoid conflicts with other users of a river or to fit in the time needed to get to a remotely located boathouse before or after work.

- There is no challenge of balance or oar-handling technique complicating the process of rowing indoors. It involves simple, straight-forward coordination of the body.

- It is inexpensive. A new erg that can last you a lifetime is available for less than $1,000 delivered. Or access to one can be gained for the price of health club dues.

- It can be done alone as well as in groups. You do not need to be part of a club or group of dedicated rowers to enjoy its health benefits.

Perhaps most importantly for the non-rower, it can be done at your own pace! You do not have to be in good physical condition, much less competitive rowing condition, to benefit from a daily row. Nor do you have to attempt to keep up with others in better shape in order to enjoy and benefit from indoor rowing. To the contrary, the same monitor on the erg that enables international-caliber athletes to keep track of their work at competitive paces works equally well for all of the rest of us as we work at whatever pace is right for our present level of conditioning. You can just as easily stroll (or paddle, as rowers would say) recreationally on an indoor rowing machine as sprint or train for competition.

Another gap has been the absence of a book on starting to row for the non-rower, those who do not know the sport and who are not trying to become competitive rowers. Most writing on rowing has tended to take the perspective of the competitor and has been geared to those who already know something about the sport. A story about a person whose goal is to win an international competition is inspiring, but it may not offer the most useful model or information for the average non-rower. This book is intended to fill some of that gap.

Appendix Four

SELECTED REFERENCES
Cited Technical Works

I have purposely avoided filling the book with technical information about physiology and medicine for three reasons:

- I want you to experience your rowing, not think about rowing in the abstract. Do it; pay attention to what you experience. That is a better way to benefit from it than to study explanations.

- I want this book to be simple and usable.

- There is too much information available to include or even represent it in a basic guide like this. The book would become an encyclopedia.

I have included information from two texts simply to illustrate that there is more information available. Those two works, which are cited in chapter two, are:

Know Your Body, The Atlas of Anatomy, Introduced by Emmet B. Keeffe, MD (1999, Ulysses Press)
Physiology of Sport and Exercise, Jack H. Wilmore and David L. Costill (1994, Human Kinetics)

If you wish to learn more, try your local library, book store, or the Internet. At the library, if you ask a reference librarian for directions to books on physiology, exercise, anatomy, and the body, you will find many resources. On the Internet, you can use many combinations of search words, such as "lungs and breath," "muscles and exercise," "heart and blood vessels," "cells," and many more.

Sources of Quotations at the Beginning of each Chapter

Where the quotation is one I have taken from a book, additional information is supplied here:

Wilfred Barlow, *The Alexander Technique*, Alfred A. Knopf, New York (1973), at 3-7

Norman Cousins, *Anatomy of an Illness As Seen by the Patient*, W.W. Norton & Company, New York (1979), at 132

Chris Crowley & Henry S. Lodge, M.D., *Younger Next Year: A Guide to Living Like 50 Until You're 80 and Beyond*, Workman Publishing, New York (2004), at 139

Geoffrey Dyson, *The Mechanics of Athletics, Sixth Edition*, Hodder and Stoughton, London (1973), at 9

Jill Fredston, *Rowing to Latitude: Journeys Along the Arctic's Edge*, North Point Press, New York (2001), at xi

William Least Heat-Moon, *River-Horse: The Logbook of a Boat Across America*, Penguin Books, New York (1999), at 450-51

William J. Lederer, *Complete Cross-Country Skiing and Ski Touring, Revised Edition*, W. W. Norton & Company, New York (1972), at 7

A.J. Mackinnon, *The Unlikely Voyage of Jack de Crow: A Mirror Odyssey from North Wales to the Black Sea*, Seafarer Books/Sheridan House, Dobbs Ferry (2002), at 135

Henning Mankell, *Chronicler of the Winds*, Vintage, London (2007), at 95

Ron McLarty, *The Memory of Running*, Penguin Books, New York (2006), at 132

Gary Paulsen, *Winterdance: The Fine Madness of Running the Iditarod*, Harcourt Brace & Company , New York (1994), (Prelude, p.1)

J.R.R. Tolkien, *The Hobbit*, Ballantine Books, New York (1975), at 35-39

Scott Turow, *Ordinary Heroes*, Farrar, Straus and Giroux, New York (2005), at 108

Web Site to Offer Feedback on This Book

Go to www.sarahprimerowing.com

Resources on Rowing

There are many resources for the rower. As a beginner on a rowing machine, you do not need them. You may find that much of the information included at rowing Web sites, which is of interest to an outdoor rower with experience, is simply distracting to you. Often, these sites tend to focus on competitive rowing teams and highly experienced rowers and their issues. (Also, with the amount of information accessible to you through the Web sites of the three rowing machine manufacturers described in section 3.2, you may not want more, at first.)

However, in case you would like more information, a short list of Web sites where you can begin to find information on rowing clothing and other rowing topics is set forth below. There are many more sites which are easy to find on the Web, including sites for college and club rowing teams.

Selected General Rowing Web Sites:

• www.row2k.com A general information Web site on rowing with almost everything, from classifieds for used equipment to race schedule information to articles about rowing and links to other rowing sites.

• www.RowingNews.com This magazine covers United States rowing, with an emphasis on collegiate and international competition on the water but with an occasional article on using indoor rowing machines. One complaint about the articles is that they are not always thorough or complete. I sometimes find the magazine's glitzy appearance makes it hard to follow. (Perhaps my age is showing.) As a beginner, you will note that the Rowing News articles assume familiarity with rowing. One helpful feature is the advertisements, which will lead you to rowing camps, boat manufacturers, and more.

• www.regattacentral.com Based in Ohio, this company handles the logistics for many rowing regattas around the country and, thus, also serves as a source of information about regattas and race results. You can, for example, explore the information about rowing regattas to see more about categories of events.

• www.crash-b.org This is the Web site for the "mother of all indoor rowing competitions," still staged each February in Boston. This site is not dedicated to explaining rowing to the uninitiated, but does provide lots of information about and photographs of categories of indoor rowing competition, including some records of past races.

- http://top100.8oar.com/top100/ "Top 100 Rowing Sites" Check this out for yourself. You will find that one of its strengths is that it contains an interesting mixture of international sites and Web sites for a variety of rowing organizations, from boat manufacturers to local clubs.

Clothing and Gear:

Many companies that make general sportswear also make shorts and other clothing you can wear to row in. Note that there is not any single, critical item you must wear to row. Most clothing made specially for rowing is either tight fitting or suited for inclement weather, neither of which is critical for you as you begin indoor rowing. It is important not to have such large, baggy shorts that the fabric catches in the wheels under the seat as you row.

A few of the companies that offer clothing for rowing are listed below to start you off. Many more can be found on the Web.

- www.jlracing.com Rowing gear and links, founded by national team oarswoman.

- www.sewsporty.com California purveyor of rowing clothing and gear to teams and individuals.

- www.regattasport.com Canadian source for clothing, gear, gifts, and more for rowers and other athletes.

- www.rowbust.com Australian company with clothing and other items for the rower and other athletes.

- www.powerhouseclothing.co.uk Rowing clothing, safety vests, and other gear from Britain.

- www.crewlinefrance.com Rowing clothing and gear from France.

National and International Rowing Organizations:

If you would like to learn more about the sport of rowing from an organizational perspective, browse through the official sites of national teams and international rowing organizations. Here is a short list of examples, with one site that should help lead you to more:

- www.worldrowing.com The official web site of FISA, the international rowing federation.

- www.oara-rowing.org UK governing body for rowing.

- www.rowingcanada.org/ The National Sports Organization for the sport of rowing in Canada.

- www.usrowing.org United States national rowing body.

- www.rudern.de/ German rowing site.

- http://users.ox.ac.uk/~quarrell/assocs.html List of national rowing federations.

Club, College, and Youth Rowing:

These days, most rowing organizations have Web sites or at least Web pages devoted to their rowing teams or clubs. For college or university teams, do a general search with a search engine or go to the college's Web site and search for varsity teams and clubs. Rowing could be either an official team or a club sport. Some high school and youth rowing teams have their own Web sites, usually run by their parent booster organizations. Others have a page as part of a Web site for the rowing club that sponsors them. Often a search for a combination of words describing the body of water, the city or town, and the school or schools involved in the team will yield one or more hits.

Resources on Training Generally

The goal of this book is to explain why and how anyone can use daily rowing without any need to study or grapple with technical issues. If you would like more technical information on how to train and how to row, there is a wealth of technical guidance available in books and articles, on DVDs, and through many other resources. There are also many books and articles on specific topics like the physiology of training, use of the heart rate monitor, other measures of fitness, how fitness affects aging, and other aspects of how the body works. Check your local library, book store, or the Web. Look under running, triathlons, and other sports by name. You will rarely find books on rowing in book stores. There are many training books on rowing, but you will probably find them faster through companies that sell rowing gear and other items to competitive rowers, or through online book sellers.

If you would like the benefit of a coach or trainer to help you with your indoor rowing, ask at your local rowing club or the closest college or high school rowing team's boathouse. To find trainers for rowing try the Web sites of the rowing machine manufacturers for ideas. For example, the Web sites of makers of the three primary rowing machines discussed in the book offer information about training and, in some cases, links to trainers and their programs. Some trainers work with classes; some may work with individuals. Some even sell DVDs with training instructions, although these tend to be geared toward the experienced, on-the-water rower.

Finally, consider attending one of the many rowing camps around the country. Some of them accept campers who have never rowed and give them the basic training they will need to continue on their own. The oldest is Craftsbury Sculling Camp in Vermont (www.craftsbury.com). A number of the camps advertise in Rowing News and are listed at the row2k Web site, both mentioned above in this Appendix.

Some Books on Rowing—for Entertainment

Sometimes, reading about rowing can entertain, inspire, or encourage you to keep going, whether what you learn is about someone else's trials as they learned to row, rowing in the Arctic or across the Atlantic, tales of adventure, or stories about national and international rowing competition. Look for them at the rowing Web sites. Here is a selection of books on rowing that may interest you:

Anderson, Andy. *The Compleat Dr. Rowing*. Bend the Timber Press, Groton, Mass. (2001). A well-known coach and former coxswain educates and entertains with tall tales and lessons on rowing.

Boyne, Daniel J. *The Red Rose Crew: A True Story of Women, Winning, and the Water*. Hyperion, Groton, Mass. (2000). The story of the team training for the 1975 World Championships in the women's eight in preparation for the first Olympic women's rowing competition in 1976.

Brumham, Jennifer. *Oar-Some: The World's First Four-Man Crew Ever to Row Any Ocean*. Oar 4 Won, Dartmouth, Devon, England (2005). Story of four British rowers who trained to row across the Atlantic in an ocean-going double and completed the journey in thirty-six days in 2004.

Cuyler, Lew. *Ernestine Bayer, Mother of U.S. Women's Rowing.* BookSurge, Philadelphia (2006). Biography of seminal figure in the history of women's rowing in the United States.

Fredston, Jill. *Rowing to Latitude: Journeys along the Arctic's Edge.* North Point Press, New York (2001). Stories from rowing arctic coastlines and fjords as "a way of life."

Halberstam, David. *The Amateurs: The Passionate Quest of Four Young Men for Olympic Gold.* William Morrow, New York (1985). Pulitzer Prize-winning author uses the story of athletes training to earn a seat competing in the 1984 Olympics to tell the story of rowing competition.

Hall, Sara. *Drawn to the Rhythm: A Passionate Life Reclaimed.* W.W. Norton, New York (2002). After first learning to row in her forties, the author tells of the positive effect on her life as she went on to compete in the World Rowing Masters Regatta and numerous other events in her age group.

Kiesling, Stephen. *The Shell Game: Reflections on Rowing and the Pursuit of Excellence.* William Morrow, New York (1982). Rowing at Yale and on the national team in 1979.

Lambert, Craig. *Mind Over Water: Lessons on Life from the Art of Rowing.* Houghton Mifflin, Boston (1998). Former Harvard coxswain and sports writer muses on his "spiritual journey via boat."

Lewis, Brad Alan. *Assault on Lake Casitas.* Broad Street Books, Philadelphia (1990). A 1984 Olympic gold medalist in rowing tells the tale of training and competing for the opportunity to represent the United States.

Mallory, Peter. *An Out-of-Boat Experience . . . or God Is a Rower, and He Rows Like Me!* San Diego Writers' Monthly Press, San Diego (2000). ". . . one very opinionated man's journey in the sport of rowing . . ." with rowing stories and commentary on coordinating the use of the arms and the legs and the parabolic force curve.

Martin, Arthur E. *Life in the Slow Lane.* Peter E. Randall, Portsmouth, N.H. (1990). Biography of the developer of the Alden Ocean Shell, a popular open water boat.

Pinsent, Matthew. *A Lifetime in a Race*. Ebury Press, London (2004). Personal story of training for international rowing competition by winner of four consecutive Olympic gold medals and numerous world championships.

Redgrave, Steve. *A Golden Age, Steve Redgrave: The Autobiography, with Nick Townsend*. BBC Worldwide, London (2000). Biography of the winner of gold medals in rowing at five consecutive Olympic Games.

Ross, Rory with Tim Foster. *Four Men in a Boat: The Inside Story of the Sydney 2000 Coxless Four*. Weidenfeld & Nicolson, London (2004). The story of the Sydney Olympic gold medal straight (coxless) four from Great Britain.

Stone, Nathaniel. *On the Water: Discovering America in a Rowboat*. Broadway Books, New York (2002). Author's tales of rowing a skiff with sliding seat from New York City to Eastport, Maine, via the Erie Canal, the Mississippi, the Gulf of Mexico, and the Atlantic Coast in 1999 and 2000.

Stowe, William A. *All Together: The Formidable Journey to the Gold with the 1964 Olympic Crew*. iUniverse, New York (2005). Olympic gold medalist and respected rowing coach Bill Stowe tells the story of the crew he rowed with which won the gold medal in the eight-oared shell at the 1964 Tokyo Olympics.

Strauss, Barry. *Rowing Against the Current: On Learning to Scull at Forty*. Scribner, New York (1999). Cornell historian tells of the trials and satisfaction of learning to row.

Rowing Shells and Oars

Once you have developed a routine of daily rowing, and if you have the option of rowing on a lake or river, you may want to try rowing outdoors. Learn at a local club or attend a rowing camp. Here is some general background information about outdoor rowing equipment. It is not intended to be complete or to help you find a specific boat, so much as give you some background to start with.

In simple terms, there are two general types of rowing boat with a sliding seat: recreational boats and racing shells. Recreational boats tend to be shorter and wider and, thus, easier to balance and maneuver. Some are actually designed for open water rowing, although most are intended for rowing on protected water. Recreational boats tend to be heavier and are not intended for racing so much as to enable the rower to get out with less concern for balance or water conditions. Recreational boats are usually less expensive than racing shells. Some racing shell manufacturers sell boats that are shaped like a racing shell but are heavier. These versions of recreational shells offer the training challenges of rowing on a longer, narrower hull, but are less expensive than the lighter elite or racing shells.

Racing shells are longer and narrower than most recreational boats and, as a result, require more balance and finesse. You will want to become comfortable in a recreational shell before attempting to row in a racing shell. Most rowing clubs require proficiency in a recreational boat before allowing a novice rower into a racing shell. There are many manufacturers of racing shells around the world. Single racing shells tend to cost between $5,000 and $10,000 new and are also widely available for sale used.

If there is a rowing club in your area, contact organizers there about rowing lessons and boats that may be available for a beginner to use. There is a good chance they will have boats and oars you can use. They may offer lessons. If there is no rowing facility but you have access to water, consider getting your own boat.

One obvious benefit of rowing on the water is the opportunity it gives you to enjoy being outdoors as you exercise. And while you can set your rowing machine on the porch or deck and row in the sun, moving along a river can provide a different type of enjoyment and offer new challenges.

Appendix Five

FITTING EXERCISE INTO YOUR SCHEDULE

If you find, like many people, that the hardest part of exercising is fitting it into your schedule, consider using mediation techniques to solve that problem. Facilitative mediation is a process used to settle legal disputes, from personal matters like divorce and custody cases to business litigation. Mediation involves the use of techniques to help the parties resolve their differences.

Begin by recognizing that you are trying to resolve the tension between two competing forces, in this case the demands of a busy schedule and the desire to obtain the health benefits of exercise. Like litigators trying to negotiate an out-of-court settlement, you can use information about these competing demands, needs, and interests to resolve the problem. (You can even treat it as if it were a multi-party case, separately considering the perspectives of your inertia, lack of athletic history, fears, and any other problem that stands in the way of achieving your goal.)

One reason mediation works is that it is a process undertaken *with the intention of settling a dispute*. Adopt that perspective. Do not accept defeat or the inevitability of conflict. Start by acknowledging that resolution is not only possible, but is the goal you are committed to. This is not the same as deciding you will exercise no matter what the effect on your schedule. Mediation does not work by having one side overpower the other.

Another reason mediation succeeds is that *people work at it*. Differences rarely get settled by good will or good intentions alone. It takes time, preparation, and energy. Decide to dedicate all three to scheduling your exercise.

Keep two motivating factors in mind as you proceed: First, what is the worst alternative to resolving this? If you fail and, as a result, you do not exercise, you will miss the benefits exercise can confer on you in terms of well-being and health. Think about how that picture looks. Second, what positive reasons exist to get it resolved? Picture the benefits you want from exercise, such as weight loss, better sleep, more energy, and possibly including reduced blood pressure and other health benefits that matter to you. Consciously remind yourself of these motivating scenarios, both positive and negative.

Make an honest list identifying obstacles. What gets in the way of exercising? This list may contain many different types of obstacles. These may include fundamental concerns about work and family responsibilities. Not knowing how to proceed can seem daunting. The list should include all concerns you can identify, no matter how small or large, such as what clothing to wear, how you look, expense, and more.

Make a second list of opportunities to exercise. In other words, consider how and where you could row, walk, and engage in other forms of exercise each day. Write it down. This does not have to be a reasoned plan for each form of exercise. Start with a list of possibilities without burdening it with analysis.

Next, when you have the two lists (obstacles and opportunities), compare them. Look for ways to fit the exercise into your schedule and to resolve other concerns. This is a creative process, not definitive scheduling. Be realistic but not dogmatic on behalf of either side (schedule or exercise).

Now put on the hat of the mediator. Look for solutions to the obstacles and ways to tailor the exercise to fit. Be creative. Be open to solutions by steps rather than a total win by one side over the other (schedule or exercise). Nor do you want a forced, artificial compromise. Keep at it, insisting that solutions are possible. When looking at the obstacles, ask yourself how they can yield. When looking at preferred exercise, consider how it can accommodate schedule. Sometimes solutions come from unexpected sources. Keep an open mind.

With schedule in hand, plot out how you will fit exercise in each day, or as close to that goal as you can come. (Or, if you are engaging in this process mentally while commuting, for example, keep returning to the focus of working out a daily fit with your schedule.) What is most important is to find some progress and lock it in. You can build on that later. If you succeed in fitting in exercise every day from the start, your future challenges may be to deal with unforeseen obstacles or to expand the time you devote to exercise. If you find only two or three days a week you feel you can fit exercise into your schedule at first, come back to this process after a month and see if you can find one additional day per week.

Finally, as you mediate with yourself over this conflict, find a way to get help. Arrange to meet someone to exercise with you. Enlist a family member or friend to remind you and/or to praise you for each success. Talk with others about how they make it work. And remind yourself that each day you exercise is a success.

Made in the USA
Lexington, KY
26 December 2015